Christmas

Christmas

BY ELIZABETH BAIRD AND ANNA HOBBS

GRAMERCY BOOKS
NEW YORK

This 2006 edition is published by Gramercy Books, an imprint of Random House Value Publishing, a divison of Random House, Inc., New York, by arrangement with Madison Press Books.

Gramercy is a registered trademark and the colophon is a trademark of Random House, Inc.

Random House
New York • Toronto • London • Sydney • Auckland
www.randomhouse.com

Printed and bound in China

A catalog record for this title is available from the Library of Congress.

ISBN-13: 978-0-517-22879-1
ISBN-10: 0-517-22879-3

10 9 8 7 6 5 4 3 2 1

Produced by Madison Press Books
1000 Yonge Street, Suite 200, Toronto, Ontario, Canada M4W 2K2
www.madisonpressbooks.com

Contents

Make This the Merriest Christmas Ever!

CHRISTMAS — THAT MAGICAL TIME OF THE YEAR WHEN HEARTS WARM and homes glow. It's a spiritually beautiful time set aside for family and friends, for the joy that music and laughter, feasting and time-honored traditions bring.

For the writers and contributors who worked on this book, Christmas was a year-long event. Like preparation for the big day itself, we started early. First came the planning — then, choosing the most irresistible recipes and tucking away ideas for imaginative decorations and homemade gifts.

So our book begins well before the hustle and bustle of the holiday season, when there's more time to enjoy the creative experience. This is the time for filling festive tins and pretty jars with delicious gifts from the kitchen, for putting the finishing touches on handmade wreaths and ornaments, and for stocking the freezer with scrumptious main dishes and desserts for all the holiday gatherings ahead. This is also the perfect time to get little hands busy making one-of-a-kind creations for all the special people on their list.

Then, we take you on to the festive season itself. You'll find recipes and suggestions that will help you through the pre-Christmas scramble of open house, potluck and dinner parties — and set the mood for Christmas Eve and the big feast itself. Our memorable Christmas Dinner menu is both glorious for the guests *and* easy on the cook — with a fail-proof roast turkey, fabulous make-ahead vegetables and sensational desserts that will rekindle even the most satisfied appetites.

Once the 25th is over and it's time to relax, we offer festive breakfast

ideas, easy brunches and effort-less get-togethers with family and friends. And we haven't forgotten the leftovers! Read on for the best-ever turkey soups, casseroles, sandwiches — and more. Then, it's time to ring in the New Year with great nibbles and menus for the 31st.

Through it all, our goal has been to make the holiday celebration a pleasurable time. Our crafts are easy to make with materials that are close at hand. Our tested-till-perfect recipes will work beautifully every time — and that's especially important during the busiest entertaining season of the year.

We hope that within the pages of this book, you'll find everything you need to see you effortlessly through holiday planning and preparation — and to make this, and every Christmas after, your most memorable ever.

A very Merry Christmas from Elizabeth Baird, Anna Hobbs and all the contributors!

VISIONS OF SUGARPLUMS

❄

HOLIDAY BAKING FILLS THE AIR
WITH A DELICIOUS ANTICIPATION OF CHRISTMAS.

Light Orange Almond Fruitcake

❄

*Even people who claim they don't like fruitcake
won't be able to resist this delicious orange-accented one.*

3 cups	mixed candied fruit	750 mL
2 cups	golden raisins	500 mL
1-1/2 cups	halved candied cherries	375 mL
1-1/2 cups	coarsely chopped candied pineapple	375 mL
1-1/2 cups	finely chopped blanched almonds	375 mL
1 cup	candied citron peel	250 mL
2 cups	all-purpose flour	500 mL
2 tsp	baking powder	10 mL
1/2 tsp	salt	2 mL
1/2 cup	butter, softened	125 mL
1 cup	granulated sugar	250 mL
3	eggs	3
1 tbsp	coarsely grated orange rind	15 mL
1 tsp	almond extract	5 mL
1/2 cup	orange liqueur or orange juice	125 mL

Grease two 9- x 5-inch (2 L) loaf pans; line bases and sides with double thickness of brown paper. Grease paper. Set aside.

❄ In large bowl, combine mixed candied fruit, raisins, cherries, pineapple, almonds and citron peel; toss with 1/2 cup (125 mL) of the flour and set aside.

❄ Stir together remaining flour, baking powder and salt; set aside.

❄ In large bowl, beat butter with sugar until fluffy; beat in eggs, one at a time, orange rind and almond extract, beating well. Add flour mixture alternately with liqueur, making three additions of dry and two of liqueur and mixing just until flour is incorporated. Fold in fruit mixture. Scrape into prepared pans, smoothing tops.

❄ Set shallow baking dish half full of boiling water on bottom rack of oven. Bake cakes on center rack in 250°F (120°C) oven for 2-1/2 hours or until cake tester inserted into center comes out clean, covering loosely with foil if cakes begin to crack.

❄ Let cakes cool completely in pans on racks. *(Cakes can be wrapped well and stored for up to 1 month.)* Makes 2 cakes, about 90 small pieces.

CANDIED FRUIT

Not too many decades ago, making fruitcake or Christmas puddings meant hours of fiddly time-consuming chores — chopping whole candied lemons, oranges and citron, shelling nuts and seeding raisins. Now, prechopped candied peel, pineapple rings, already-seeded muscat or Lexia raisins and glossy glacé red and green cherries make these traditional desserts just as delicious and a whole lot easier.

❄ Choose these ingredients in bulk food stores or supermarkets, selecting moist tender peel with a fresh tart aroma, and clear cherries and raisins with a sweet winey fragrance.

❄ Mixed candied fruit includes orange and lemon peel, citron and cherries; mixed candied peel includes just orange, lemon and citron peel. Of late, expensive citron has been replaced by less expensive candied rutabaga.

Sherried Raisin Fruitcake

Moist dark fruitcakes usually need weeks to age, but this raisin-rich one slices cleanly without crumbling just three days after baking.

2 cups	dark seedless raisins (Thompson)	500 mL
1-1/2 cups	currants	375 mL
1 cup	seeded raisins (Lexia)	250 mL
2/3 cup	sherry	150 mL
1/2 cup	grated carrot	125 mL
1 tbsp	each grated lemon and orange rind	15 mL
2 cups	all-purpose flour	500 mL
1 tsp	baking powder	5 mL
1/2 tsp	each cinnamon, nutmeg, ginger and salt	2 mL
1 cup	butter, softened	250 mL
1 cup	packed brown sugar	250 mL
4	eggs	4
2 tbsp	fancy molasses	25 mL
1-1/2 tsp	vanilla	7 mL
3/4 cup	ground almonds	175 mL

*I*n large bowl, combine seedless raisins, currants, seeded raisins, sherry, carrot, and lemon and orange rinds; cover and let stand overnight. Toss with 1/4 cup (50 mL) of the flour.

᠅ Grease 8-inch (2 L) springform pan; line base and side with double thickness of brown paper. Grease paper. Set aside.

᠅ Stir together remaining flour, baking powder, cinnamon, nutmeg, ginger and salt; set aside.

᠅ In large bowl, beat butter with brown sugar until fluffy; beat in eggs, one at a time. Stir in molasses and vanilla; add almonds. Stir in flour mixture, one-third at a time; stir in fruit mixture. Scrape into prepared pan, smoothing top.

᠅ Set shallow baking dish half full of boiling water on bottom rack of oven. Bake cake on center rack in 250°F (120°C) oven for about 5 hours or until paring knife inserted into center comes out dry, covering loosely with foil if cake begins to crack.

᠅ Let cool in pan on rack until center is completely cool. Remove from pan; remove paper, wrap well and store for at least 3 days or for up to 1 month. Makes about 30 slices.

Extra-Fruity Dark Fruitcake

This cake, dense with fruit and nuts, is baked in a regular cake pan and cuts beautifully into six bars — perfect for gift giving.

3 cups	seeded raisins (Lexia)	750 mL
1-1/2 cups	dark seedless raisins (Thompson)	375 mL
1-1/4 cups	halved candied cherries	300 mL
1 cup	coarsely chopped candied pineapple	250 mL
3/4 cup	currants	175 mL
2/3 cup	chopped mixed candied peel	150 mL
1/3 cup	rum, brandy, sherry or fruit juice	75 mL
1-3/4 cups	all-purpose flour	425 mL
1/2 tsp	each cinnamon, salt and baking powder	2 mL
1/4 tsp	nutmeg	1 mL
1 cup	packed brown sugar	250 mL
1/2 cup	butter, softened	125 mL
1/2 cup	red currant jelly	125 mL
4	eggs	4
1 tsp	almond extract	5 mL
1-1/2 cups	pecan halves	375 mL

*I*n plastic container or bowl, combine seeded and seedless raisins, cherries, pineapple, currants, peel and rum; cover and let stand overnight or for up to 2 days, stirring occasionally.

᠅ Grease 13- x 9-inch (3.5 L) cake pan; line base and sides with double thickness of brown paper. Grease paper. Set aside.

᠅ Stir together flour, cinnamon, salt, baking powder and nutmeg; toss 1/2 cup (125 mL) with raisin mixture.

᠅ In large bowl, beat sugar, butter and jelly until fluffy; beat in eggs, one at a time, and almond extract. Stir in flour mixture; stir in raisin mixture and pecans. Scrape into prepared pan, tapping pan on counter to eliminate air pockets; smooth top. Cover pan loosely with foil, shiny side out.

᠅ Set shallow baking dish half full of boiling water on bottom rack of oven. Bake cake on center rack in 300°F (150°C) oven for 2 to 2-1/2 hours or until cake tester inserted into center comes out clean.

᠅ Let cool in pan on rack; remove from pan and remove paper. Cut crosswise into 6 bars. *(Bars can be wrapped in plastic wrap and stored in airtight container in cool, dry place for up to 1 year.)* Makes 6 small cakes, about 14 slices each.

FOR PERFECT FRUITCAKES EVERY TIME

PREPARING PANS

❧ Prepare pans before you start preparing batter.

❧ Bake fruitcakes in traditional round or square pans or in any pan that's at least 2 inches (5 cm) deep.

❧ Unless otherwise directed, line greased pans with heavy brown paper so edges don't get too brown or dry and cakes can be removed from pan easily; grease paper with shortening.

❧ Pour in batter to about 3/4 inch (2 cm) from top, smoothing and leveling batter.

BAKING

❧ Keep cake moist by placing pan of water on lowest rack in oven. Place cake on middle rack. Be sure heat can circulate around each pan.

❧ Test whether cake is ready by inserting cake tester into center of cake; it should come out clean but may be sticky with fruit.

❧ Prevent top of cake from getting too brown before it's done by placing foil loosely over top.

STORING

❧ Ripen a fruitcake by allowing it to mellow and let flavors develop. Ripening takes from three to eight weeks; the more fruit, the longer it takes. To speed ripening, mix fruit and nuts with spirit before baking and let soak overnight. After baking, make skewer holes in cake and pour in a small amount of heated brandy or other spirit.

❧ Wrap cooled cakes in cheesecloth moistened with brandy, sherry, rum or whisky. Wrap in waxed paper or plastic wrap, then foil.

❧ Place in airtight tin and store in refrigerator or in cool, dry place, moistening cheesecloth every two weeks if necessary.

❧ Freeze fruitcake after ripening for up to one year. Thaw in refrigerator for 24 hours before serving.

Chocolate Pecan Fruitcake

❧

Chocolate adds a luxurious new twist to this sensational holiday cake.

4-1/2 cups	mixed candied pineapple and cherries (about 2 lb/1 kg)	1.125 L
2 cups	coarsely chopped toasted pecans (see p. 30)	500 mL
4 oz	unsweetened chocolate, finely chopped	125 g
3 oz	semisweet chocolate, finely chopped	90 g
1 cup	golden raisins	250 mL
2 cups	all-purpose flour	500 mL
2 tsp	baking powder	10 mL
1/2 tsp	salt	2 mL
3/4 cup	unsalted butter	175 mL
1 cup	granulated sugar	250 mL
6	eggs	6
3/4 cup	brandy	175 mL
1 tsp	vanilla	5 mL

*I*n large bowl, toss together pineapple, cherries, pecans, unsweetened and semisweet chocolate and raisins; toss with half of the flour. Stir together remaining flour, baking powder and salt. Set aside.

❧ In large bowl, beat butter with sugar until light and fluffy; beat in eggs, one at a time, beating thoroughly. Beat in 1/4 cup (50 mL) of the brandy and vanilla. Gradually stir in dry ingredients until well blended. Stir in fruit mixture. Scrape into greased 13- x 9-inch (3.5 L) cake pan, tapping pan on counter to eliminate air pockets; smooth top.

❧ Bake in 300°F (150°C) oven for 1-1/2 hours or until cake tester inserted into center comes out clean. Let cool in pan on rack.

❧ Cut cake crosswise into 6 bars. Heat remaining brandy but do not boil. With skewer, make several holes through cake; pour in brandy.

❧ Moisten pieces of cheesecloth with brandy; wrap around individual bars. Wrap in waxed paper, then foil; store in airtight container in cool, dry place for at least 1 week or up to 2 months, checking occasionally and adding more brandy if cake begins to dry. Makes 6 small cakes, about 14 slices each.

> **Tip**: *It's easy to slice fruitcake if you refrigerate it a few hours before serving. Always slice with a very sharp knife and wipe the blade with a damp cloth between slices.*

Fruited Brazil Nut Loaves

With just enough batter to hold the big chunks of fruit and nuts together, this hurry-up Christmas cake is totally sliceable the day after it's made.

1-1/2 cups	dried figs	375 mL
1-1/2 cups	dried apricots	375 mL
1 cup	candied pineapple	250 mL
1/2 cup	candied cherries	125 mL
1/2 cup	chopped preserved ginger	125 mL
3 cups	whole shelled Brazil nuts	750 mL
1 cup	all-purpose flour	250 mL
1 cup	packed brown sugar	250 mL
1 tsp	baking powder	5 mL
4	eggs	4
1 tsp	vanilla	5 mL

Line two 8- x 4-inch (1.5 L) loaf pans with foil; grease well and set aside.

❧ Pour boiling water over figs and apricots; let stand for 5 minutes. Drain and chop into large pieces. Cut pineapple into chunks. Halve cherries.

❧ In large bowl, mix together figs, apricots, pineapple, cherries, ginger and Brazil nuts. Stir together flour, sugar and baking powder; add to fruit mixture and toss to mix.

❧ In separate bowl, beat eggs well; stir in vanilla. Add to fruit mixture and mix well; spoon into prepared pans. Bake in 350°F (180°C) oven for 1 hour or until cake tester inserted into center comes out clean.

❧ Let cool in pans on racks for 10 minutes; remove from pans and let cool completely on racks. (*Loaves can be wrapped well and refrigerated for up to 2 weeks.*) Makes 2 loaves.

Christmas Carrot Pudding with Apricots

※

*It's the addition of grated carrots and apples that makes
this pioneer pudding different from a traditional
plum pudding. The rest of the ingredients are
the same — spices, raisins, peel and cherries.
Serve it with Grand Marnier Sauce (recipe, p. 18).*

1 cup	seeded raisins (Lexia)	250 mL
3/4 cup	currants	175 mL
3/4 cup	quartered candied cherries	175 mL
1/2 cup	chopped mixed candied peel	125 mL
1/3 cup	chopped dried apricots	75 mL
1/4 cup	coarsely grated orange rind	50 mL
1-1/2 cups	all-purpose flour	375 mL
1 tsp	baking soda	5 mL
1 tsp	cinnamon	5 mL
1/2 tsp	salt	2 mL
1/2 tsp	nutmeg	2 mL
1/4 tsp	allspice	1 mL
1/2 cup	butter, softened	125 mL
1-1/4 cups	packed brown sugar	300 mL
1 cup	grated peeled carrots	250 mL
1 cup	grated peeled apples	250 mL
2 tbsp	orange liqueur or orange juice	25 mL

In bowl, toss together raisins, currants, cherries, candied peel, apricots and orange rind. Stir together flour, baking soda, cinnamon, salt, nutmeg and allspice; sprinkle about one-quarter over fruit mixture and toss lightly. Set aside.

※ In large bowl, beat butter with sugar until light and fluffy; stir in half of the remaining flour mixture. Stir in carrots and apples. Stir in orange liqueur, then remaining flour mixture. Stir in fruit mixture just until combined.

※ Line bottom of greased 6-cup (1.5 L) pudding bowl with circle of greased waxed paper. Pack batter in evenly.

※ Cover batter with circle of greased waxed paper. Make 1-inch (2.5 cm) pleat across middle of large piece of foil and place over bowl. Press sides down; trim edge, leaving 2-inch (5 cm) over-hang. Tie string securely around top of bowl; fold foil overhang up over string.

※ Place bowl on rack in large saucepan; pour in enough boiling water to come two-thirds up side of bowl. Cover and simmer over medium-low heat, adding water as needed to maintain level, for 2-1/2 to 3 hours or until cake tester inserted into center comes out clean.

※ Let stand for 10 minutes. Loosen edge with knife; turn out onto serving plate. Makes 10 to 12 servings.

> **Tip**: *Amounts of individual fruits and nuts in Christmas puddings and fruitcakes can be increased or decreased according to taste, as long as the total quantity is the same as what is called for in the recipe.*

RAISINS

Raisins are simply dried grapes. The most common, the plump oval **seedless** ones, come in shades of golden to dark brown. Look for them under the names of sultana or Thompson raisins and use them in puddings, cakes and cookies.

※ Muscat grapes, when **seeded** and dried, turn into flat, sticky raisins that are bursting with flavor and sweetness. Be sure to include them every time seeded or Lexia or muscat raisins are called for, especially to add character to Christmas cakes and puddings. Look for them in bulk food stores. Be prepared to pay a little more but they're worth every penny.

※ The third member of the family is the small dark **currant**, an essential ingredient in mincemeat and Christmas puddings.

※ Raisins or currants should be moist and pliable; if they're brittle and dry, cover them with boiling water and let soak for 10 minutes. Drain and pat dry before using.

Stir-Up Sunday

❧

Woven into the tapestry of a modern-day Christmas are customs from many lands, including the English tradition of Stir-Up Sunday. This was the popular name given by Church of England parishioners to the Sunday before Advent, from the opening words of that day's special prayer. Tradition was that by the Sunday before Advent, which usually falls near the end of November, puddings must be started, or "stirred up," if they were to be mellow and ready in time for the Christmas festivities.

❧ Everyone in the family, even the littlest, gave the pudding a stir, at the same time making a wish to bring good luck. Just in case a wish and a stir didn't do the trick, silver charms were poked into the mixture: coins for worldly fortune, a ring for marriage and a thimble for life's blessings.

❧ Christmas cakes, a later tradition, were also made just after Stir-Up Sunday because they, too, needed time to mellow, but they were never accorded such ceremony as the important pudding.

(left) Baked Cranberry Pudding and Syllabub Sauce (p. 18); Sherried Raisin Fruitcake (p. 12)

Baked Cranberry Pudding

❧

This pretty pudding is everything a Christmas dessert should be — neither too hard to make nor too rich to enjoy after holiday meals.

3/4 cup	granulated sugar	175 mL
3 tbsp	brandy	50 mL
4 tsp	grated orange rind	20 mL
1 tbsp	orange juice	15 mL
2 cups	cranberries	500 mL
1/2 cup	golden raisins	125 mL
1-1/4 cups	all-purpose flour	300 mL
2 tsp	baking powder	10 mL
1/2 tsp	nutmeg or mace	2 mL
1/2 tsp	salt	2 mL
1/2 cup	ground almonds	125 mL
1/3 cup	butter, softened	75 mL
2	eggs	2
1 tsp	vanilla	5 mL
1/4 cup	milk	50 mL
	Syllabub Sauce (recipe, this page)	

Glaze

1 tbsp	brandy	15 mL
1 tbsp	corn syrup	15 mL

*I*n bowl, combine 1/3 cup (75 mL) of the sugar, brandy, orange rind and juice; mix in cranberries and raisins. Let stand, stirring occasionally, for 2 hours.

❧ Grease 6-cup (1.5 L) deep ovenproof pudding bowl; sprinkle bottom with 1 tbsp (15 mL) of the remaining sugar. Set aside.

❧ In small bowl, stir together flour, baking powder, nutmeg and salt; stir in almonds. In separate bowl, beat butter with remaining sugar until fluffy; beat in eggs, one at a time, and vanilla. Stir flour mixture into butter mixture alternately with milk, making three additions of dry and two of liquid.

❧ Spoon 1/2 cup (125 mL) of the cranberry mixture into prepared pudding bowl; stir remaining cranberry mixture into batter and scrape into pudding bowl. Place on pie plate and bake in 350°F (180°C) oven for 60 to 75 minutes or until cake tester inserted into center comes out clean.

❧ Let cool in bowl on rack for 10 minutes. *(Pudding can be cooled completely, covered and refrigerated for up to 1 day.)* Run spatula around edge of pudding; unmold onto serving plate.

❧ GLAZE: Heat brandy and corn syrup; spoon over pudding. Serve with Syllabub Sauce. Makes 8 servings.

Syllabub Sauce

❧

Syllabubs have as noble a history as the Christmas pudding and serve splendidly as its sauce.

1/3 cup	granulated sugar	75 mL
2 tsp	finely grated orange rind	10 mL
3 tbsp	brandy or dry sherry	50 mL
2 tbsp	orange juice	25 mL
1 cup	whipping cream	250 mL

*I*n deep bowl, mash sugar with orange rind; stir in 2 tbsp (25 mL) of the brandy and orange juice. Refrigerate until chilled. Stir in whipping cream.

❧ Beat at medium speed just until mixture mounds slightly on spoon, being careful not to overbeat; fold in remaining brandy. Transfer to serving bowl; refrigerate for at least 4 hours or up to 1 day. Makes about 2-1/2 cups (625 mL).

Hot Spirited Sauce

❧

Butter and rum or brandy bring a warm glow to this old-fashioned sauce.

1 cup	packed brown sugar	250 mL
2 tbsp	cornstarch	25 mL
1/4 tsp	salt	1 mL
1-1/2 cups	water	375 mL
1/4 cup	dark rum or brandy	50 mL
2 tbsp	butter	25 mL
1/4 tsp	nutmeg	1 mL
1 tsp	vanilla	5 mL

*I*n heavy saucepan, stir together sugar, cornstarch and salt; stir in water and bring to boil, stirring constantly.

❧ Reduce heat to low and stir in rum, butter and nutmeg; simmer for 2 minutes. Stir in vanilla. Serve hot. Makes about 2 cups (500 mL).

VARIATION

❧ GRAND MARNIER SAUCE: Reduce sugar to 1/2 cup (125 mL). Substitute Grand Marnier or other orange liqueur for the rum. Omit nutmeg and vanilla.

Christmas Plum Pudding

Gloriously fragrant with sweet spices and rum-soaked fruit, this is the ultimate in traditional Christmas puddings. One bite, topped with luscious Orange Hard Sauce, is enough to recapture all the delicious memories of Christmas past.

1/2 cup	butter, softened	125 mL
3/4 cup	packed brown sugar	175 mL
2	eggs	2
1 tbsp	grated orange rind	15 mL
1 cup	all-purpose flour	250 mL
1 cup	fine stale (not dry) bread crumbs	250 mL
1 tsp	baking soda	5 mL
1/2 tsp	each salt, cinnamon and nutmeg	2 mL
1/4 tsp	each cloves and ginger	1 mL
1 cup	chopped mixed candied peel	250 mL
1 cup	seeded raisins (Lexia)	250 mL
3/4 cup	halved candied cherries	175 mL
1/2 cup	golden raisins	125 mL
1/2 cup	slivered almonds	125 mL
1/3 cup	rum, brandy or orange juice	75 mL
1/4 cup	rum or brandy (for flaming)	50 mL
	Orange Hard Sauce (recipe follows)	

*I*n large bowl, beat butter with sugar until fluffy. Beat in eggs, one at a time, beating well after each addition; add orange rind.

❧ In separate bowl, stir together flour, bread crumbs, baking soda, salt, cinnamon, nutmeg, cloves and ginger; stir in candied peel, seeded raisins, cherries, golden raisins and almonds.

❧ With wooden spoon, stir half of the dry ingredients into creamed mixture; stir in 1/3 cup (75 mL) rum, then remaining dry ingredients.

❧ Line bottom of greased 8-cup (2 L) pudding ring mold or 6-cup (1.5 L) pudding bowl with circle of greased waxed paper, pressing into any patterns of mold. Pack batter in evenly.

❧ Cover batter with circle of greased waxed paper; cover mold with lid. To cover bowl, make 1-inch (2.5 cm) pleat across middle of large piece of foil and place over bowl. Press sides down; trim edge, leaving 2-inch (5 cm) overhang. Tie string securely around top of bowl; fold foil overhang up over string.

❧ Place mold on rack in large saucepan; pour in enough boiling water to come two-thirds up side of mold.

❧ Cover and simmer over medium-low heat, adding water as needed to maintain level, for 1-1/2 to 2 hours for ring mold, 2-1/2 to 3 hours for pudding bowl, or until cake tester inserted into center comes out clean. Let stand for 5 minutes. Remove paper and unmold onto serving plate.

❧ In saucepan, warm 1/4 cup (50 mL) rum over medium-low heat just until heated through but not boiling. Remove from heat. Using long match, carefully ignite rum; pour over pudding. Serve with Orange Hard Sauce. Makes 10 to 12 servings.

Orange Hard Sauce

1/2 cup	butter, softened	125 mL
1-1/2 cups	sifted icing sugar	375 mL
3 tbsp	grated orange rind	50 mL
2 tbsp	orange juice	25 mL
1 tsp	lemon juice	5 mL

In bowl, beat butter with sugar until creamy; beat in orange rind and juice and lemon juice until fluffy. Roll into log shape or pipe into rosettes. Refrigerate until firm. Cut log into 1-inch (2.5 cm) thick slices. Makes 1-1/2 cups (375 mL).

REHEATING CHRISTMAS PUDDINGS

*S*teamed Christmas puddings are an ideal make-ahead dessert. Puddings can be made up to 2 months before Christmas and kept, well wrapped, in the freezer or cool, dry place.

❧ TO REHEAT IN MICROWAVE: Turn out pudding onto serving plate, cover with large microwaveable bowl and reheat at High for 5 to 10 minutes or until hot.

❧ TO RESTEAM ON STOVETOP: Set up a large saucepan with a rack on the bottom. Place foil-covered pudding in mold on rack; pour boiling water into pan to come about halfway up side of pudding mold. Cover the saucepan and bring the water to a boil. Reduce heat so water boils gently and resteam the pudding for 1 to 1-1/2 hours or until hot.

Chocolate Hazelnut Slices

*Either slice-and-bake these nutty cookies
or shape into crescents. Ground hazelnuts are
available at bulk food stores, or toast and
skin hazelnuts (see p. 30) and grind your own
in a food processor.*

1 cup	butter, softened	250 mL
1 cup	icing sugar	250 mL
1-1/2 cups	all-purpose flour	375 mL
1/3 cup	unsweetened cocoa powder	75 mL
1/2 cup	ground hazelnuts or almonds	125 mL

Garnish

6 oz	semisweet chocolate	175 g
3/4 cup	ground hazelnuts	175 mL

In bowl, beat butter with sugar until fluffy. Mix together flour, cocoa and nuts; stir into butter mixture until smooth dough forms.

❧ Gather dough into ball; divide in half. Place each half on sheet of waxed paper; using paper, shape dough into logs, each about 1 inch (2.5 cm) in diameter. Wrap paper around logs; chill until firm.

❧ Cut logs into 1/4-inch (5 mm) thick slices. Bake on ungreased baking sheets in 325°F (160°C) oven for 15 minutes or until set. Remove from baking sheets and let cool on racks. *(Cookies can be prepared to this point, covered and frozen for up to 1 month. Thaw before continuing.)*

❧ GARNISH: In bowl set over hot (not boiling) water, melt chocolate. Dip edges of cookies into chocolate, then into nuts. Let stand on rack until set. *(Cookies can be layered between waxed paper in airtight container and stored for up to 1 week.)* Makes about 5 dozen cookies.

VARIATION

❧ CHOCOLATE HAZELNUT CRESCENTS: Chill dough in bowl for 30 minutes. Form 1 tbsp (15 mL) dough each into crescents; chill on baking sheets for 30 minutes. Bake for about 30 minutes; dip ends in melted chocolate and sliced nuts. Makes about 36 crescents.

Glazed Nut Diamonds

*Absolutely decadent, these layered
shortbread, almond and honey caramel sweets
are definitely special-occasion!*

1-3/4 cups	all-purpose flour	425 mL
2 tbsp	granulated sugar	25 mL
1/2 tsp	baking powder	2 mL
1/2 cup	butter	125 mL
1	egg, lightly beaten	1
3 tbsp	sour cream	50 mL

Topping

3/4 cup	granulated sugar	175 mL
3/4 cup	packed brown sugar	175 mL
1/2 cup	butter	125 mL
1/2 cup	sour cream	125 mL
1/2 cup	liquid honey	125 mL
2 cups	sliced almonds	500 mL
1/3 cup	chopped candied cherries	75 mL

In bowl, combine flour, sugar and baking powder; cut in butter until crumbly. Stir in egg and sour cream just until mixture holds together.

❧ Pat into greased 15- x 10-inch (40 x 25 cm) jelly roll pan; bake in 375°F (190°C) oven for 10 minutes.

❧ TOPPING: In large saucepan, stir together granulated and brown sugars, butter, sour cream and honey over medium heat until boiling. Add almonds; boil until candy thermometer reaches soft-ball stage of 238°F (115°C), and when 1/2 tsp (2 mL) syrup dropped into very cold water forms soft ball that flattens on removal from water.

❧ Immediately remove from heat; pour over base. Sprinkle with cherries. Bake in 375°F (190°C) oven for 15 to 20 minutes or until caramel-colored and no longer runny.

❧ Let cool for 15 minutes; cut diagonally into diamond shapes. Let cool for 30 minutes longer; recut. *(Diamonds can be layered between waxed paper in airtight container and stored for up to 1 week or frozen for up to 3 months.)* Makes about 50 pieces.

In photo: (clockwise from top) Sugar and Spice Cookies (p. 62) in Christmas tree shapes and decorated with cocoa snowflakes (instructions, p. 62); Chocolate Orange Truffles and Brownie Miniatures (p. 28); Citrus Squares (p. 21); Glazed Nut Diamonds (this page); Sugar and Spice Cookies in bear, stocking and star shapes, painted with Royal Icing Paint (p. 60)

Citrus Squares

A tangy lemon topping teams up with a rich shortbread base in a hard-to-resist square. Vary the flavor with lime, tangerine or orange rind and juice, instead of lemon.

1 cup	all-purpose flour	250 mL
1/2 cup	butter	125 mL
1/4 cup	packed brown sugar	50 mL

Topping

1 cup	granulated sugar	250 mL
1 tsp	grated lemon rind	5 mL
3 tbsp	lemon juice	50 mL
2 tbsp	all-purpose flour	25 mL
1/2 tsp	baking powder	2 mL
2	eggs, lightly beaten	2

Garnish

	Icing sugar	
1 tsp	grated lemon rind	5 mL

In food processor or in bowl and using pastry blender, blend flour, butter and brown sugar until crumbly. Press into ungreased 9-inch (2.5 L) square cake pan. Bake in 350°F (180°C) oven for 15 minutes.

❧ TOPPING: Stir together sugar, lemon rind and juice, flour, baking powder and eggs; pour over baked base.

❧ Bake in 325°F (160°C) oven for 25 to 30 minutes or until lightly browned and firm to the touch. Let cool completely in pan on rack. (*Recipe can be prepared to this point, covered and refrigerated for up to 1 week or frozen for up to 3 months; thaw completely.*)

❧ GARNISH: Just before serving, cut into squares. Dust with icing sugar and sprinkle with lemon rind.
Makes 36 squares.

Simply the Best Shortbread

❦

These superb extra-tender cookies are runaway hits during annual Christmas bazaars and holiday parties.

1 cup	butter, softened	250 mL
3 tbsp	cornstarch	50 mL
1/4 cup	granulated sugar	50 mL
1-3/4 cups	all-purpose flour	425 mL

*I*n large bowl, beat butter until fluffy; gradually beat in cornstarch, then sugar. With wooden spoon, beat in flour, about 1/4 cup (50 mL) at a time.

❦ On lightly floured surface or pastry cloth, roll out dough to 1/4-inch (5 mm) thickness. Using floured fluted 2-inch (5 cm) round cookie cutter, cut out cookies. Place on waxed paper-lined trays; prick each cookie 3 times with fork. Freeze until firm. *(Shortbread can be prepared to this point, transferred to freezer bags and stored in freezer for up to 1 month.)*

❦ Place frozen rounds on baking sheet; bake in 275°F (140°C) oven for 40 to 50 minutes or until firm to the touch. Remove from baking sheet and let cool on racks. *(Shortbread can be stored in airtight containers for up to 2 weeks.)* Makes 24 cookies.

COOKIE DOUGH

*C*ream butter, sugar, eggs and flavorings with an electric mixer. Use low speed or wooden spoon to stir in dry ingredients. For tender cookies, fold in the last of the flour and don't overbeat.

❦ When rolling out dough, work in as little extra flour from the surface and rolling pin as possible.

❦ Use a pastry cloth and stockinette-covered rolling pin, or roll out between two sheets of waxed paper.

❦ Roll out only part of the dough at a time, keeping the rest refrigerated.

❦ If using cutters, flour and cut out as many cookies as possible in the first rolling, rerolling scraps only once for best results.

❦ Chilling cut-out cookies before baking them helps cookies keep their shape while baking and ensures tender results.

❦ Place unbaked cookies on cool baking sheets. Unless otherwise indicated, space about 1-1/2 inches (4 cm) apart to allow for spreading when baking; thin doughs spread more than thick.

Lemon Poppy Seed Shortbread

❦

Bake this crunchy shortbread as individual cookies or in a square pan.

1 cup	butter, softened	250 mL
1 cup	icing sugar	250 mL
2 tbsp	poppy seeds	25 mL
2 tbsp	grated lemon rind	25 mL
2 cups	all-purpose flour	500 mL
2 tbsp	granulated sugar	25 mL

*I*n bowl, beat butter with icing sugar until fluffy; stir in poppy seeds and lemon rind. Gradually blend in flour. Gather dough into ball; chill for 30 minutes if sticky.

❦ On lightly floured surface, roll out dough to 1/4-inch (5 mm) thickness; cut into 2-inch (5 cm) rounds and place on ungreased baking sheets. (Or, press dough into 9-inch/2.5 L square cake pan; prick surface all over with fork.) Sprinkle with granulated sugar.

❦ Bake in 300°F (150°C) oven for 20 to 25 minutes for cookies, or 35 minutes for square, or until set and very faintly browned. Let cookies cool on rack, or let large square cool in cake pan before cutting into bars. *(Shortbread can be stored in airtight containers for up to 5 days or frozen for up to 1 month.)* Makes about 40 cookies or 24 bars.

Chocolate Ginger Bars

❦

This sophisticated no-bake bar marries the wonderful taste of chocolate with ginger.

1/3 cup	butter	75 mL
8 oz	semisweet chocolate	250 g
3 tbsp	corn syrup	50 mL
1/2 lb	ginger cookies	250 g
2 tbsp	chopped crystallized ginger	25 mL
	Icing sugar	

*I*n saucepan, melt together butter, chocolate and corn syrup over low heat.

❦ In food processor, chop cookies to make 2 cups (500 mL) coarse crumbs; stir into chocolate mixture along with ginger.

❦ Spread in greased 8-inch (2 L) square cake pan; refrigerate for 2 hours. Cut into squares; dust with icing sugar. *(Bars can be layered between waxed paper in airtight container and refrigerated for up to 1 week or frozen for up to 2 months.)* Makes 20 bars.

Meringue Wreaths

Before baking, decorate these pretty wreaths with slivers of candied cherries, colored sugar, sprinkles, dragées, coarsely crushed candy cane or edible glitter.
These are excellent for guests on gluten-free diets.

2	egg whites	2
1 tsp	lemon juice	5 mL
1/4 tsp	cream of tartar	1 mL
2/3 cup	instant dissolving (fruit/berry) sugar	150 mL

*I*n small deep bowl, beat egg whites with lemon juice until foamy. Add cream of tartar. Gradually beat in sugar, about 1 tbsp (15 mL) at a time, beating well after each addition, until stiff shiny peaks form. (A small amount rubbed between fingers should not feel gritty — sugar should be dissolved.)

❧ Pipe small 1-1/2-inch (4 cm) rings onto parchment paper- or foil-lined baking sheets, or drop batter by teaspoonfuls (5 mL). Bake in 250°F (120°C) oven for 1-1/4 hours or until firm. Turn off oven; leave meringues in oven for 1 hour longer. *(Meringues can be layered between waxed paper in airtight container and stored for up to 2 weeks.)* Makes 24 wreaths.

Pecan Snowballs

These melt-in-your-mouth confections pack a toasted pecan punch with every bite.

2 cups	pecans, toasted (see p. 30)	500 mL
1 cup	butter, softened	250 mL
1-1/4 cups	icing sugar	300 mL
1-1/2 tsp	vanilla	7 mL
2 cups	all-purpose flour	500 mL
1/2 tsp	salt	2 mL

*C*hop nuts finely; set aside.

❧ In bowl, beat butter with 1/4 cup (50 mL) of the sugar until smooth; beat in vanilla. With wooden spoon, stir in flour, salt and nuts, using hands to finish mixing and form dough into ball. Wrap in plastic wrap; refrigerate for 30 minutes.

❧ Using hands, form dough into 1-inch (2.5 cm) balls; place 1 inch (2.5 cm) apart on ungreased baking sheets. Bake in 325°F (160°C) oven for 18 to 20 minutes or until lightly golden. Remove to racks and let cool for 5 minutes.

❧ Roll balls in remaining sugar; return to racks and let cool completely. Roll again in sugar. *(Snowballs can be layered between waxed paper in airtight container and stored for up to 1 week or frozen for up to 3 months.)* Makes about 40 cookies.

Meringue Wreaths

Sugarplums

Choose the most tender dried apricots for these delectable morsels. If possible, make sugarplums at least two days before packaging to let them set properly.

1/2 lb	dried apricots	250 g
1 tsp	grated tangerine or orange rind	5 mL
1/4 cup	tangerine or orange juice	50 mL
2 tbsp	liquid honey	25 mL
2 oz	crystallized ginger, coarsely chopped	50 g
1 cup	sifted icing sugar	250 mL
3/4 cup	flaked coconut	175 mL

Cut apricots into thin strips. In small heavy saucepan, combine apricots, tangerine rind and juice and honey; cover and bring to simmer. Reduce heat to low and cook, stirring frequently, for about 10 minutes or until apricots are very tender and shiny.

❧ Uncover and cook, stirring, for 3 to 4 minutes or until liquid is absorbed; let cool slightly. Transfer to food processor or blender and add ginger; purée until pastelike. Let cool.

❧ Place icing sugar and coconut in separate bowls. Drop teaspoonfuls (5 mL) apricot mixture into coconut. Using hands, shape into balls; roll in icing sugar.

❧ Place on tray lightly dusted with icing sugar. Cover loosely with waxed paper and let stand in cool, dry place for 2 days. Makes about 30 sugarplums.

A CHRISTMAS COOKIE EXCHANGE

Getting together with friends and exchanging cookies is a delicious way to say Merry Christmas! Our practical packaging tips make sure all the cookies stay crisp and crumb-free from one home to another.

❧ Avoid packaging crisp cookies with soft ones, or delicate-flavored cookies with strong-flavored ones.

❧ For cookies that freeze, choose airtight containers. Cookie tins are best. Coffee or cocoa tins or plastic containers make good substitutes.

❧ Line containers with paper towels for padding and layer cookies generously with waxed paper. Cover top of tin with plastic wrap before pressing on the lid.

❧ Package cookies in small plastic freezer bags. Tie with festive ribbons and label with personalized Christmas stickers.

❧ Carry your treasures home carefully — top side up!

Exchange cookies in a pretty package ready for gift giving include decorated Spritz Cookies (in center) and Sugarplums (top left and right)

Brandy Balls

Create an assortment of these easy no-bake goodies by rolling balls in different coatings — icing sugar, cocoa, coconut or very finely chopped nuts — or pressing a candied cherry or nut half into some of them.

3 oz	semisweet chocolate	90 g
1/2 cup	granulated sugar	125 mL
1/3 cup	brandy or rum	75 mL
1/4 cup	corn syrup	50 mL
2-1/2 cups	finely crushed vanilla wafers	625 mL
3/4 cup	finely chopped pecans or walnuts	175 mL
3/4 cup	mixed candied fruit or chopped crystallized ginger (optional)	175 mL
	Granulated sugar	

*I*n bowl set over pan of hot (not boiling) water, melt chocolate; stir in sugar, brandy and syrup. Stir in wafer crumbs, nuts, and fruit (if using); mix thoroughly.

⁂ Chill until firm enough to shape into 1-inch (2.5 cm) balls. Roll in sugar. Layer between waxed paper in airtight container and store in cool, dry place (not refrigerated) for a few days before serving. Makes about 50 balls.

Hazelnut Macaroons

If you're looking for a cookie without dairy products or chocolate, delight your guests with this fine one.

2 cups	flaked coconut	500 mL
2/3 cup	granulated sugar	150 mL
1/4 cup	all-purpose flour	50 mL
1/4 tsp	salt	1 mL
4	egg whites	4
1-1/2 cups	chopped hazelnuts	375 mL
1/4 cup	slivered candied cherries	50 mL
1 tsp	vanilla	5 mL

*I*n large bowl, stir together coconut, sugar, flour and salt. Whisk egg whites until foamy; stir into coconut mixture along with hazelnuts, cherries and vanilla.

⁂ Drop by tablespoonfuls (15 mL) onto lightly greased baking sheets. Bake in 325°F (160°C) oven for 20 to 25 minutes or until edges are golden brown. Remove macaroons to racks; let cool. Makes about 40 cookies.

Chocolate Chow Mein Clusters

These chewy treats are an addictive blend of chocolate, butterscotch, crunchy peanuts — and dry chow mein noodles!

1-1/2 cups	chocolate chips	375 mL
1 cup	butterscotch chips	250 mL
1/2 cup	butter	125 mL
1/4 cup	smooth peanut butter	50 mL
2 cups	dry chow mein noodles	500 mL
1 cup	salted peanuts	250 mL
	Candied cherry halves	

*I*n top of double boiler over hot (not boiling) water, melt chocolate and butterscotch chips, butter and peanut butter, stirring often.

⁂ In bowl, stir noodles with peanuts; pour in chocolate mixture and mix well.

⁂ Spoon into 1-inch (2.5 cm) mounds on waxed paper-lined baking sheets; garnish each with cherry half. Let stand for 30 minutes or refrigerate for 20 minutes or until firm. (*Clusters can be layered between waxed paper in airtight container and refrigerated for up to 1 week or frozen for up to 3 months. Let come to room temperature before serving.*) Makes about 50 clusters.

Spritz Cookies

Before baking, decorate these festive cookies with colored sugar, candies or chopped candied fruit.

1 cup	butter, softened	250 mL
1/2 cup	granulated sugar	125 mL
1	egg	1
1 tsp	vanilla	5 mL
2 cups	all-purpose flour	500 mL

*I*n large bowl, beat butter with sugar until fluffy; beat in egg and vanilla. Gradually stir in flour; mix well.

⁂ Fill cookie press with batches of dough; press out desired shapes onto chilled ungreased baking sheets. Decorate, if desired. Bake in 350°F (180°C) oven for 10 to 12 minutes or until very lightly browned. Remove cookies to racks; let cool. Makes about 40 cookies.

Walnut Phyllo Rounds

These golden phyllo spirals are a superlative Greek addition to Christmas baking.

1	pkg (1 lb/454 g) phyllo pastry	1
1 cup	butter, melted	250 mL

Filling

1-1/2 cups	walnut pieces	375 mL
1/2 cup	pistachios or slivered almonds	125 mL
1/4 cup	chopped candied orange peel	50 mL
1/4 cup	granulated sugar	50 mL
1 tbsp	orange blossom water (or 1 tsp/5 mL almond extract)	15 mL
1/2 tsp	each cinnamon and cloves	2 mL

Syrup

1	lemon	1
2 cups	granulated sugar	500 mL
1-1/2 cups	water	375 mL

FILLING: In food processor, combine walnuts, pistachios, candied peel, sugar, orange blossom water, cinnamon and cloves; chop finely.

❧ Place 1 sheet of phyllo on work surface, covering remaining phyllo with damp tea towel to prevent drying out. Brush sheet lightly with some of the butter. Top with another sheet of phyllo; brush with butter. Repeat with 1 more sheet of phyllo and butter. Sprinkle with about 1/3 cup (75 mL) of the nut mixture.

❧ Top with 3 more sheets of phyllo, brushing each with butter; sprinkle with 1/3 cup (75 mL) of the nut mixture. Repeat with 3 more sheets, then nuts, to make total of 9 sheets of phyllo.

❧ Brush long edges of phyllo with butter. Starting at long side, tightly roll up jelly roll-style. Brush all over with butter; trim edges. Cut into 3/4-inch (2 cm) thick slices; place on greased baking sheet. Repeat with remaining phyllo and filling to make second roll.

❧ Bake in 350°F (180°C) oven for 18 to 20 minutes or until crisp and golden, turning over halfway through. Let cool for 5 minutes on baking sheets. Remove to racks set on baking sheet.

❧ SYRUP: Meanwhile, using vegetable peeler, peel rind of lemon into thick strips. In saucepan, combine sugar, water and lemon rind; bring to boil. Reduce heat to medium-low and simmer for 25 to 30 minutes or until syrupy; strain.

❧ Spoon half of the hot syrup over phyllo rounds; let stand for 15 minutes. Spoon remaining syrup over top; let cool completely. (*Rounds can be layered between waxed paper in airtight container and stored for up to 3 days.*) Makes about 42 cookies.

Crunchy Biscotti

Long, crunchy and Italian, biscotti are double-baked to make them divine dunkers in a frothy cappuccino, creamy hot chocolate or steaming tea. Because biscotti keep so well, a pretty jar of them is a much-appreciated holiday gift.

1-3/4 cups	all-purpose flour	425 mL
2 tsp	baking powder	10 mL
3/4 cup	whole unblanched almonds	175 mL
2	eggs	2
3/4 cup	granulated sugar	175 mL
1/3 cup	butter, melted	75 mL
2 tsp	vanilla	10 mL
1/2 tsp	almond extract	2 mL
1-1/2 tsp	grated orange rind	7 mL
1	egg white, lightly beaten	1

In large bowl, combine flour and baking powder; stir in almonds. Whisk together eggs, sugar, butter, vanilla, almond extract and orange rind; stir into flour mixture until soft, sticky dough forms.

❧ Transfer dough to lightly floured work surface; with hands, form into smooth ball. Divide in half; roll each into 12-inch (30 cm) long log. Transfer to ungreased baking sheet.

❧ Brush tops with egg white; bake in 350°F (180°C) oven for 20 minutes. Remove from oven and let cool on sheet on rack for 5 minutes.

❧ Transfer each log to cutting board; with sharp knife, cut diagonally into 3/4-inch (2 cm) thick slices. Stand cookies upright on baking sheet; bake for 20 to 25 minutes longer or until golden. Remove biscotti to rack and let cool. (*Biscotti can be stored in airtight container for up to 2 weeks.*) Makes about 24 cookies.

Tips: To prevent crumbling when slicing the partially cooked log of dough, use a sharp chef's knife and cut with firm, decisive strokes.

❧

Standing the biscotti upright during the second baking ensures that they dry out evenly.

Crunchy Biscotti

Brownie Miniatures

These moist chocolaty brownies, baked in tiny paper cups, make delicious mouthfuls (see photo, p. 21). A simple topping of chocolate buttons, mint chocolate wafers or large chocolate chips doubles as icing.

1/3 cup	packed brown sugar	75 mL
1/4 cup	butter	50 mL
3 oz	semisweet chocolate	90 g
1/2 tsp	vanilla	2 mL
1	egg, lightly beaten	1
1/3 cup	all-purpose flour	75 mL
24	chocolate buttons	24

*I*n saucepan, melt sugar, butter and chocolate over low heat, stirring, until chocolate is just melted. Remove from heat and let cool for 1 minute. Blend in vanilla and egg; gently fold in flour just until blended.

❧ Spoon into tiny paper baking cups. Bake in 350°F (180°C) oven for 10 to 12 minutes or until set. Remove from oven; set chocolate button on top of each. Let cool. Makes about 24 miniatures.

Chocolate Truffles

Truffles have stolen our candy-loving hearts! Wonderful as gifts for special friends, these chocolate-and-cream-filled indulgences make a seductively simple dessert with a tiny cup of after-dinner espresso or coffee.

Ganache Filling

1 cup	whipping cream	250 mL
1/2 lb	semisweet or bittersweet chocolate, chopped	250 g
2 tbsp	chocolate liqueur (or 1 tsp/5 mL vanilla)	25 mL
	Icing sugar	

Coating

3/4 lb	semisweet or bittersweet chocolate, chopped	375 g
1 cup	unsweetened cocoa powder	250 mL

*G*ANACHE FILLING: In small saucepan, heat cream just until bubbles form around edge of pan; remove from heat. Stir in chocolate until smooth; stir in liqueur. Transfer to bowl; cover and refrigerate for 1 hour or until thickened and cold.

❧ Using whisk (not electric mixer), beat chocolate mixture just until creamy and lighter in color. Do not overbeat or mixture will separate.

❧ Using pastry bag fitted with 1/2-inch (1 cm) plain tip, pipe filling into 1-inch (2.5 cm) diameter rounds on two waxed paper-lined baking sheets. Cover and refrigerate for 30 minutes or until firm.

❧ Working with rounds of filling from one baking sheet at a time, lightly roll in icing sugar. Gently roll each round between fingertips to round off tips. Return to waxed paper-lined sheet and freeze for 1 hour or until hard and almost frozen.

❧ COATING: In top of double boiler over hot (not boiling) water, melt chocolate. Remove from heat and let cool slightly. Sift cocoa into pie plate. Using two forks, dip balls from one baking sheet at a time into chocolate, letting excess drip off. (If chocolate thickens, rewarm gently over hot water.) Place balls in cocoa.

❧ Using two clean forks, roll truffles in cocoa; refrigerate on waxed paper-lined baking sheet until hardened. Place truffles in candy cups and store in airtight container in refrigerator until just before serving . (*Truffles can be refrigerated for up to 1 week or frozen for up to 3 months.*) Makes about 50 truffles.

VARIATION

❧ CHOCOLATE ORANGE TRUFFLES: In ganache filling, substitute orange-flavored liqueur or orange juice for chocolate liqueur; add 1 tbsp (15 mL) finely grated orange rind. Do not roll chocolate-coated truffles in cocoa. Garnish with strips of orange rind just before serving.

Tip: Piping rather than spooning a delicate filling cuts down on handling. If you don't have a pastry bag, make your own from a small, sturdy plastic bag by snipping off a little piece of one corner.

Chocolate Truffles in chocolate box

Meringue Turtles

While there's lots of serious baking done at Christmas, it's a pleasure to take time for a fun project like these chocolate button and pecan turtles.

24	chocolate buttons	24
2 cups	pecan halves (about 8 oz/250 g)	500 mL
3	egg whites	3
Pinch	each cream of tartar and salt	Pinch
3/4 cup	instant dissolving (fruit/berry) sugar	175 mL
1/2 tsp	vanilla	2 mL
	Unsweetened cocoa powder	

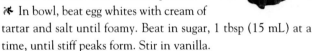

Line two baking sheets with foil or parchment paper. Position 1 chocolate button for head and 4 pecans for feet of each turtle on baking sheet, leaving about 1 inch (2.5 cm) between pecans.

❧ In bowl, beat egg whites with cream of tartar and salt until foamy. Beat in sugar, 1 tbsp (15 mL) at a time, until stiff peaks form. Stir in vanilla.

❧ Pipe or spoon meringue over pecans, partially covering nuts and buttons; smooth top with finger. Bake in 225°F (110°C) oven for 1 hour. Turn off oven; leave meringues in oven for 1 hour longer. Dust with cocoa. (*Turtles can be layered between waxed paper in airtight container and stored at room temperature for up to 3 weeks.*) Makes about 2 dozen turtles.

TOASTING NUTS

Toasting nuts before using them in a recipe intensifies their flavor and makes every dish they are in taste that much better.

❧ IN OVEN: Spread shelled pecans, walnuts, almonds, hazelnuts, peanuts, pistachios, cashews or Brazil nuts on baking sheet or in cake pan and toast in 350°F (180°C) oven for 10 minutes or until lightly browned and fragrant.

❧ For hazelnuts only, transfer toasted nuts to tea towel. Rub vigorously to remove most of the skins.

❧ IN MICROWAVE: Spread nuts on microwaveable plate and microwave, uncovered, at High for 8 to 10 minutes (5 to 7 minutes for cashews or Brazil nuts) or until lightly browned and fragrant, stirring every 2 minutes.

Chocolate Peanut Mounds

These delicious morsels are extra-easy to make — and even easier to eat!

1 cup	semisweet chocolate chips	250 mL
1/2 cup	butterscotch chips	125 mL
1 tsp	butter	5 mL
2 cups	Spanish peanuts	500 mL

In top of double boiler over hot (not boiling) water, melt together chocolate and butterscotch chips and butter; remove from heat.

❧ With wooden spoon, stir until smooth and blended. Stir in peanuts to coat completely.

❧ Drop rounded teaspoonfuls (5 mL) onto waxed paper-lined baking sheets. Refrigerate until firm. (*Mounds can be layered between waxed paper in airtight container and refrigerated for up to 3 weeks.*) Makes 48 pieces.

White Chocolate Almond Bark

This is the perfect last-minute homemade gift. Just toast almonds, melt chocolate and wait for the chocolate to firm up before layering between waxed paper in festive boxes.

1-1/2 lb	white chocolate, finely chopped	750 g
1 cup	unblanched whole almonds, toasted and cooled (see sidebar, this page)	250 mL

In bottom of double boiler, bring water to simmer; remove from heat. Add chocolate to top of double boiler and stir frequently until melted. Stir in almonds.

❧ Spread evenly onto waxed paper-lined 15- x 11-inch (40 x 28 cm) jelly roll pan. Refrigerate for 1 hour or until firm. Break into pieces. (*Bark can be layered between waxed paper in airtight container and refrigerated for up to 3 weeks.*) Makes 1-3/4 lb (875 g).

Tip: Bark is just as delicious made with semisweet or bittersweet (not unsweetened) chocolate, or with a combination of white and semisweet chocolate swirled together.

Eggnog Fudge

Here's an imaginative and tasty way to use the vanilla-scented commercial eggnog found in grocery stores at this time of year.

3 cups	granulated sugar	750 mL
1 cup	eggnog	250 mL
1 tbsp	corn syrup	15 mL
2 tbsp	butter	25 mL
1 tsp	vanilla	5 mL
1/2 cup	chopped walnuts	125 mL

Glaze

1/4 cup	semisweet chocolate chips	50 mL
1 tsp	butter	5 mL

Grease side of large heavy saucepan. Add sugar; stir in eggnog and corn syrup. Cook over medium heat, stirring constantly, until boiling.

❧ Cook, stirring only if necessary to prevent sticking, until candy thermometer reaches soft-ball stage of 238° (115°C), and when 1/2 tsp (2 mL) syrup dropped into very cold water forms soft ball that flattens on removal from water.

> *Tip: If fudge sets too quickly before spreading in pan, reheat gently over low heat just until soft enough to spread.*

❧ Immediately remove from heat; let cool to lukewarm, 110°F (43°C), without stirring.
❧ Using wooden spoon, beat in butter and vanilla, beating until very thickened and no longer shiny. Quickly stir in nuts. Spread in greased 8-inch (2 L) square cake pan.

❧ GLAZE: Melt together chocolate chips and butter. Drizzle over fudge.
❧ Score into 1-inch (2.5 cm) squares while warm; let cool completely and cut into squares. *(Fudge can be layered between waxed paper in airtight container and stored for up to 2 weeks.)* Makes 64 pieces.

Sesame Toffee

A chunk of sesame-sprinkled toffee is a delicious Christmas goodie, appreciated especially by people who like to savor their sweets.

1 cup	sesame seeds	250 mL
1 cup	butter	250 mL
1 cup	granulated sugar	250 mL
1/2 cup	packed brown sugar	125 mL
3 tbsp	water	50 mL
3/4 tsp	baking soda	4 mL

Spread sesame seeds on baking sheet; bake in 350°F (180°C) oven for 15 minutes or until golden. Reserve half of the seeds; sprinkle remaining seeds over well-greased 13- x 9-inch (3.5 L) cake pan. Set aside.

❧ In saucepan, bring butter, white and brown sugars and water to boil, stirring constantly. Cook, stirring often, until candy thermometer reaches soft-crack stage of 285°F (140°C), and when 1/2 tsp (2 mL) syrup dropped into very cold water separates into threads that are hard but not brittle.

❧ Immediately remove from heat; stir in baking soda. Pour over sesame seeds in prepared pan. Let cool for 5 minutes.
❧ Sprinkle with reserved sesame seeds, pressing lightly into toffee. Let cool until firm. Break into pieces. *(Toffee can be layered between waxed paper in airtight container and stored for up to 1 month.)* Makes about 30 pieces.

CANDY MAKING TIPS

Since successful candy making depends on the temperatures at which different crystallizations of sugar occur, an accurate candy thermometer is invaluable. Before making confections, check the accuracy of your thermometer.
❧ Place thermometer in pot of water and bring slowly to boil (to avoid breakage). Keep thermometer in gently boiling water for 10 minutes. It should register 212°F (100°C).
❧ If there is any variation, add or subtract the number of degrees necessary to make its reading conform to a standard scale and take this difference into account when testing the temperature of a syrup.

GIFTS FROM THE KITCHEN

❧

SOMETHING HOMEMADE MEANS SOMETHING PRECIOUS,
WHETHER IT'S A PRETTY JAR OF JAM OR AN EASY PASTA OR COOKIE MIX
THAT BUSY FRIENDS WILL APPRECIATE.

Microwave Cranberry Marmalade

❧

*A tangy-sweet red marmalade makes a very
special breakfast spread for Christmas morning.
Be sure to make enough for your own table,
and to give to friends, hosts and hostesses.*

2	oranges	2
1	lemon	1
1-1/2 cups	water	375 mL
4 cups	cranberries	1 L
6-1/2 cups	granulated sugar	1.625 L
1	pouch (3 oz) liquid pectin	1

Cut oranges and lemon into quarters; slice crosswise into very thin slices. In 12-cup (3 L) microwaveable casserole, combine oranges, lemon and water; microwave, covered, at High for 20 to 25 minutes or until rind is tender, stirring twice.

❧ Stir in cranberries; microwave, covered, at High for 2 minutes. Stir in sugar; microwave, uncovered, at High for 12 to 14 minutes or until boiling, stirring occasionally to prevent boil over. Add pectin; stir for 5 minutes, skimming off foam.

❧ Pour into hot sterilized canning jars, leaving 1/4-inch (5 mm) headspace; seal with prepared lids and screw on bands. *(Marmalade can be refrigerated for up to 1 month or processed in boiling water bath for 5 minutes for longer storage. See Preserving Basics, p. 34.)* Makes 8 cups (2 L).

Cranberry Raspberry Jam

❧

*Cranberries and frozen raspberries
make a festive last-minute preserve.*

6 cups	cranberries	1.5 L
1	lemon, cut in wedges	1
1 cup	water	250 mL
2	pkg (each 10 oz) unsweetened frozen raspberries, thawed (undrained)	2
4-1/2 cups	granulated sugar	1.125 L

Place two plates in freezer to chill for testing setting point.

❧ In large shallow saucepan, bring cranberries, lemon and water to boil; reduce heat to medium, cover and cook for 15 minutes. Press through sieve or food mill. Discard lemon.

❧ Return purée to pan; add raspberries and crush. Stir in sugar. Bring to boil, stirring constantly; boil for 2 minutes, stirring often.

❧ Remove from heat and test for setting point by dropping teaspoonful (5 mL) onto one chilled plate; let stand for 1 minute. Run fingertip through jam; if surface wrinkles, jam is ready. If too syrupy, continue boiling, repeating test every few minutes with clean chilled plate until setting point is reached.

❧ Ladle into hot sterilized canning jars, leaving 1/4-inch (5 mm) headspace. Seal with prepared lids and screw on bands. *(Jam can be refrigerated for up to 1 month or processed in boiling water bath for 5 minutes for longer storage. See Preserving Basics, p. 34.)* Makes about 7 cups (1.75 L).

A basketful of delicious gifts from the kitchen

Winter Chili Sauce

꙳

Whether it's for a bazaar or for gifts, chili sauce made with canned tomatoes is quicker to make and just as piquant as the summer stuff.

2	cans (each 28 oz/796 mL) tomatoes (undrained)	2
1	can (5 oz/156 mL) tomato paste	1
2 cups	chopped peeled apples	500 mL
2 cups	chopped onions	500 mL
1-1/2 cups	packed brown sugar	375 mL
1-1/2 cups	cider vinegar	375 mL
1 cup	chopped sweet green peppers	250 mL
1 cup	chopped celery	250 mL
2 tsp	mustard seeds	10 mL
2 tsp	cinnamon	10 mL
1-1/2 tsp	salt	7 mL
1 tsp	ground cloves	5 mL
1 tsp	ginger	5 mL
1/2 tsp	hot pepper flakes	2 mL

*I*n large heavy saucepan or Dutch oven, crush tomatoes; stir in tomato paste, apples, onions, sugar, vinegar, green peppers, celery, mustard seeds, cinnamon, salt, cloves, ginger and hot pepper flakes. Bring to boil; reduce heat to medium-low and cook, stirring often, for 55 to 65 minutes or until thickened.

꙳ Pour into hot sterilized canning jars, leaving 1/2-inch (1 cm) headspace. Seal with prepared lids and screw on bands. Process in boiling water bath for 10 minutes (see Preserving Basics, below). Makes about 10 cups (2.5 L).

Cold-Weather Salsa

꙳

Salsa is today's trendy relish of choice. With this easy recipe, you can put up a winter supply that will last you — and your friends —until next summer.

1	can (28 oz/796 mL) tomatoes (undrained), chopped	1
1	can (14 oz/398 mL) tomato sauce	1
3	stalks celery, diced	3
2	onions, finely chopped	2
2	cloves garlic, minced	2
1 tbsp	finely chopped pickled jalapeño pepper	15 mL
1/3 cup	granulated sugar	75 mL
1/4 cup	cider vinegar	50 mL
1/4 cup	lime juice	50 mL
1-1/2 tsp	crushed dried coriander	7 mL
1-1/2 tsp	salt	7 mL

*I*n large heavy saucepan or Dutch oven, combine tomatoes, tomato sauce, celery, onions, garlic and jalapeño pepper. Bring to boil; cook for 5 minutes or just until onions are translucent.

꙳ Stir in sugar, vinegar, lime juice, coriander and salt. Reduce heat and boil gently, stirring frequently, for 45 minutes or until slightly thickened.

꙳ Pour into hot sterilized canning jars, leaving 1/2-inch (1 cm) headspace. Seal with prepared lids and screw on bands. Process in boiling water bath for 10 minutes (see Preserving Basics, below). Makes 5 cups (1.25 L).

PRESERVING BASICS

1 Heat clean canning jars in 225°F (110°C) oven for 15 minutes; leave in oven until needed. Boil discs for 5 minutes just before filling jars.

2 Fill boiling water bath canner about two-thirds full of water; bring to gentle boil.

3 Fill jars, leaving about 1/4-inch (5 mm) headspace for jams, jellies, marmalades and conserves, and 1/2-inch (1 cm) headspace for pickles, relishes and chutneys.

4 Center prepared disc on jar and apply screw band until fingertip tight.

5 Add filled jars to canner; pour in enough boiling water to cover by 2 inches (5 cm). Process for time indicated. Let cool on rack. Check seals. If disc or lid is curved down, the seal is good. If not, store jar in refrigerator and use contents within 3 weeks.

6 Store jars in cool, dark, dry place. Once jars are opened, store in refrigerator.

Spiced Brandied Fruit Sauce

It takes about five minutes to put this sensational sauce together and four days for it to mellow into a great little hostess gift.

1 cup	chopped mixed candied peel	250 mL
1 cup	red candied cherries, quartered	250 mL
1 cup	dark seedless raisins (Thompson)	250 mL
1/4 cup	diced preserved ginger	50 mL
3	each whole allspice and cloves	3
1	stick cinnamon, broken in pieces	1
1-1/2 cups	(approx) brandy or rum	375 mL

In sterilized 4-cup (1 L) jar, stir together candied peel, cherries, raisins and ginger until well mixed.

❧ Tie allspice, cloves and cinnamon in cheesecloth and bury in fruit mixture. Pour in brandy, adding more if necessary to cover fruit. Seal and store in cool, dark, dry place for 4 days.

❧ Remove and discard spice bag. Spoon sauce into gift jars. (*Sauce can be stored in cool, dark, dry place for up to 3 months.*) Makes about 3 cups (750 mL).

Orange Hot Pepper Jelly

Give a jar of this zesty jelly with cream cheese and crackers for instant snacks or hors d'oeuvres. A food processor is the best way to chop the peppers quickly and evenly.

2 cups	finely chopped sweet red peppers	500 mL
1-1/4 cups	white vinegar	300 mL
1/4 cup	coarsely grated orange rind	50 mL
1/4 cup	orange juice	50 mL
5 cups	granulated sugar	1.25 L
1/2 tsp	hot pepper sauce	2 mL
2	pouches (each 3 oz) liquid pectin	2

In large saucepan, bring red peppers, vinegar, orange rind and juice to boil; reduce heat and simmer, covered, for 10 minutes or until rind is softened.

❧ Stir in sugar. Return to full rolling boil over high heat. Boil hard, stirring often, for 5 minutes; remove from heat. Add hot pepper sauce and pectin; stir for 5 minutes, skimming off any foam.

❧ Pour into hot sterilized canning jars, leaving 1/4-inch (5 mm) headspace; seal with prepared lids and screw on bands. Process in boiling water bath for 5 minutes (see Preserving Basics, p. 34). Makes about 5 cups (1.25 L).

Spiced Brandied Fruit Sauce

MINCEMEAT PIES AND TARTS

To make mincemeat pie: Combine 3-1/2 cups (875 mL) mincemeat, 1/2 cup (125 mL) chopped pears or apples and 2 tbsp (25 mL) rum. Fill pastry-lined 9-inch (23 cm) pie plate with mincemeat mixture; moisten pastry rim with water. Cover with top layer of pastry; trim edges and crimp. Brush top crust with cream or milk; slash Christmas tree design in pastry for steam vents.

To make tarts: Line 2 dozen tart shells with pastry cut to fit with crinkle-edged cutter. Fill three-quarters full with mincemeat mixture (as for pie, at left). If desired, using a smaller crinkle-edged cutter, cut out circles of pastry to fit over mincemeat but not touch edges. Brush top crust with cream or milk.

To bake pie and tarts: Bake in 425°F (220°C) oven for 15 minutes; reduce heat to 350°F (180°C) and bake pie for about 30 minutes, tarts for about 10 minutes, or until pastry is golden brown.

Pear Mincemeat

This delicious mincemeat is a new twist on an old tradition. Made from juicy ripe Anjou pears, it's nicely spiced with ginger, cinnamon and nutmeg and studded with candied cherries and peel. Add a dash of rum before sealing jars.

1	large clementine or mandarin (unpeeled), cut in chunks	1
Half	lemon (unpeeled), cut in chunks	Half
10 cups	grated peeled pears (about 5-1/2 lb/2.5 kg)	2.5 L
2 cups	golden raisins	500 mL
2 cups	seeded raisins (Lexia)	500 mL
2 cups	granulated sugar	500 mL
3/4 cup	chopped mixed candied peel	175 mL
3/4 cup	white wine	175 mL
1/2 cup	halved candied cherries	125 mL
1/4 cup	butter	50 mL
1 tsp	each cinnamon, ginger and nutmeg	5 mL
3/4 tsp	allspice	4 mL
1/2 tsp	cloves	2 mL
1/4 cup	dark rum	50 mL

In food grinder and using coarse blade, or in food processor and using on/off motion, coarsely chop clementine and lemon.

In large heavy saucepan, combine clementine mixture, pears, golden and seeded raisins, sugar, peel, wine, cherries, butter, cinnamon, ginger, nutmeg, allspice and cloves. Bring to simmer over medium heat; reduce heat to low and simmer, stirring frequently, for 45 minutes or until thickened and caramel brown. Stir in rum.

Pack into hot sterilized canning jars, leaving 1/2-inch (1 cm) headspace. Seal with prepared lids and screw on bands. *(Mincemeat can be refrigerated for up to 3 weeks or processed in boiling water bath for 25 minutes for longer storage. See Preserving Basics, p. 34.)* Makes about 10 cups (2.5 L).

WHAT A GREAT IDEA!

MINCEMEAT MAGIC

Pies and tarts aren't the only way to enjoy a fruity mincemeat made without suet. Mincemeat makes a grand sauce, thinned with rum, brandy or apple juice and served warm over ice cream. You can also layer it in an ice-cream pie (p. 107) or in a trifle, cut it with pears or apples in a crumble (p. 103), or wrap it in crêpes (p. 166) or strudel dough.

Herbed Beer Bread Mix

❧

With this easy bread mix, it takes just minutes to make a golden, crusty quickbread.
All you need to do is stir in a can of beer!
For gift-giving, pack the mix and can of beer in a loaf pan and tie with a ribbon.

2-3/4 cups	all-purpose flour	675 mL
2 tbsp	granulated sugar	25 mL
2 tbsp	baking powder	25 mL
1 tsp	salt	5 mL
1/4 tsp	each dried oregano and thyme	1 mL
Pinch	dried dillweed	Pinch

*I*n large bowl, stir together flour, sugar, baking powder, salt, oregano, thyme and dillweed. Pack into airtight container or bag. *(Mix can be stored at room temperature for up to 1 month.)* Makes enough for 1 loaf.

Herbed Beer Bread

	Herbed Beer Bread Mix	
1	can (12 oz) beer (at room temperature)	1
1 tsp	butter, melted	5 mL

Place Herbed Beer Bread Mix in large bowl. With wooden spoon, stir in beer just until incorporated. Scrape into greased 8- x 4-inch (1.5 L) loaf pan.

❧ Bake in 375°F (190°C) oven for 45 to 50 minutes or until crusty and golden brown. Let stand in pan for 5 minutes; remove to rack and brush with butter. Makes 1 loaf.

Old-Fashioned Oatmeal Cookie Mix

❧

Along with a big jar of our no-fuss cookie mix and the recipe, include a couple of good-quality baking sheets,
a metal rack, oven mitts and parchment paper for perfect cookies every time.

6 cups	rolled oats	1.5 L
4 cups	all-purpose flour	1 L
3 cups	packed brown sugar	750 mL
2 tsp	cinnamon	10 mL
2 tsp	baking powder	10 mL
1-1/2 tsp	salt	7 mL
1 tsp	baking soda	5 mL
1 lb	shortening	500 g
2 cups	raisins	500 mL
1-1/2 cups	shredded coconut	375 mL
1 cup	chocolate chips	250 mL
1 cup	chopped pecans	250 mL

*I*n large bowl, stir together oats, flour, sugar, cinnamon, baking powder, salt and baking soda. With pastry blender, cut in shortening until crumbly.

❧ Stir in raisins, coconut, chocolate and pecans. *(Mix can be refrigerated in airtight container for up to 10 weeks.)* Makes about 20 cups (5 L), enough for 5 batches of cookies.

Old-Fashioned Oatmeal Cookies

4 cups	Oatmeal Cookie Mix	1 L
1	egg, lightly beaten	1
2 tbsp	milk	25 mL
2 tsp	vanilla	10 mL
	Granulated sugar	

In bowl, combine Oatmeal Cookie Mix, egg, milk and vanilla until dough forms; shape into 1-1/2-inch (4 cm) balls. Place on parchment paper-lined or greased baking sheets; flatten with fork dipped in sugar.

❧ Bake in 375°F (190°C) oven for 15 to 18 minutes or until golden. Remove to racks and let cool. Makes 24 cookies.

Caesar Salad Mix

🍃

*Wrap up this mix, a bag of croutons, a tube
of anchovy paste and our recipe for
Caesar salad — and you've got an imperial gift.*

1 tbsp	grated lemon rind	15 mL
2/3 cup	freshly grated Parmesan cheese	150 mL
1 tbsp	dried oregano	15 mL
1-1/2 tsp	dry mustard	7 mL
1 tsp	black pepper	5 mL
1 tsp	garlic powder	5 mL
1/4 tsp	cayenne pepper	1 mL

Spread lemon rind on paper towel; microwave at High for
4 to 4-1/2 minutes or until dry, stirring several times, or dry for
1 day at room temperature.

🍃 In airtight container, combine lemon rind, cheese, oregano,
mustard, pepper, garlic powder and cayenne. (*Mix can be refrigerated for up to 1 month.*) Makes 3/4 cup (175 mL), enough for
3 salads.

Quick Caesar Salad

1/3 cup	vegetable oil	75 mL
1/4 cup	Caesar Salad Mix	50 mL
3 tbsp	lemon juice	45 mL
2 tbsp	light mayonnaise	25 mL
1 tsp	anchovy paste	5 mL
12 cups	torn romaine lettuce	3 L

Whisk together oil, Caesar Salad Mix, lemon juice, mayonnaise
and anchovy paste; toss with romaine in salad bowl. Makes 6 to
8 servings.

Spicy Mulled Cider Mix

Package this fragrant mix in an attractive glass jar and include the recipe for Spicy Mulled Cider. A warming gift for all the skiers and skaters on your list. For an alcoholic version, substitute red wine for the apple juice and add honey to taste.

3/4 cup	crushed cinnamon sticks	175 mL
3/4 cup	chopped dried orange rind	175 mL
1/3 cup	whole allspice	75 mL
1/4 cup	whole cloves	50 mL

In jar, combine cinnamon, orange rind, allspice and cloves. Makes about 2 cups (500 mL).

Spicy Mulled Cider

4 cups	apple juice (or half apple and half cranberry juice)	1 L
2 tbsp	Spicy Mulled Cider Mix	25 mL

In saucepan, combine apple juice and Spicy Mulled Cider Mix; cover and bring to simmer. Gently simmer for 20 minutes; strain into mugs. Makes 4 servings.

Herbed Cheese Ball

A nippy herbed-topped cheese blend, rolled in a ball or packed in a crock and surrounded with crackers, is a welcome gift during the Christmas entertaining season.

1 lb	old Cheddar cheese, shredded	500 g
4 oz	cream cheese	125 g
1/4 cup	port, brandy or sherry	50 mL
1 tbsp	crumbled dried tarragon, marjoram or oregano	15 mL
Pinch	dried dillweed	Pinch
1/4 cup	chopped fresh parsley	50 mL

In food processor or in bowl with fork, blend Cheddar and cream cheeses, port, tarragon and dillweed until smooth. Shape into ball.

Spread chopped fresh parsley on waxed paper; roll cheese ball in parsley to coat. Wrap in plastic wrap and refrigerate until chilled. *(Pâté can be refrigerated for up to 2 weeks.)* Makes 1 ball (1-1/4 lb/625 g).

Sun-Dried Tomato Pasta Sauce Mix

Make enough batches of this sun-dried tomato and herb mix for gifts — and include the recipe for cooking it into an easy tomato-rich pasta sauce.

1 cup	sun-dried tomatoes (2 oz/50 g)	250 mL
2 tbsp	dried parsley	25 mL
1 tbsp	dried basil	15 mL
2 tsp	dried marjoram	10 mL
1/2 tsp	hot pepper flakes	2 mL

With scissors, sliver tomatoes; combine in airtight container with parsley, basil, marjoram and pepper flakes. Makes about 1 cup (250 mL).

Pasta Sauce

2 tbsp	olive oil	25 mL
1	onion, chopped	1
2	cloves garlic, minced	2
1/2 cup	Sun-Dried Tomato Pasta Sauce Mix	125 mL
1	can (19 oz/540 mL) tomatoes (undrained)	1
	Salt and pepper	

In saucepan, heat oil over medium heat; cook onion and garlic for 3 minutes or until softened.

Add Sun-Dried Tomato Pasta Sauce Mix and tomatoes, breaking up with spoon; simmer for 15 minutes or until thickened. Season with salt and pepper to taste. Makes 3 cups (750 mL), enough for 4 servings.

Ice-Cream Sundae Makings

Tuck some old-fashioned sundae glasses, an ice-cream scoop and a jar each of these superlative sauces into a wicker basket. A perfect gift for all the ice-cream lovers on your list!

Milk Chocolate Fudge Sauce

8 oz	sweet or milk chocolate	250 g
1/2 cup	whipping cream	125 mL
1/4 cup	brewed coffee	50 mL
1/2 cup	packed brown sugar	125 mL
1/4 cup	corn syrup	50 mL
2 tbsp	orange, apricot or cherry liqueur	25 mL

In heavy saucepan, combine chocolate, cream and coffee; heat over medium heat, stirring, until chocolate has melted and mixture is smooth.

❧ Stir in sugar and corn syrup; bring to boil, stirring until sugar has dissolved. Reduce heat and boil gently, stirring once or twice, for 8 minutes. Stir in liqueur.

❧ Pour into hot sterilized jar; seal with prepared lid and screw on band. Store in cool, dark, dry place for up to 3 months. Refrigerate once opened. Serve warm. Makes about 1-1/2 cups (375 mL).

Pineapple Peach Sauce

1	can (14 oz/398 mL) crushed pineapple, drained	1
1	can (14 oz/398 mL) peach slices, drained and finely chopped	1
1 cup	granulated sugar	250 mL
1/4 cup	frozen orange juice concentrate	50 mL
1 tbsp	orange liqueur (optional)	15 mL

In heavy saucepan, combine pineapple, peaches, sugar and orange juice concentrate; bring to boil. Boil, stirring occasionally, for 12 minutes or until slightly thickened. Stir in liqueur (if using).

❧ Pour into hot sterilized jar; seal with prepared lid and screw on band. Store in cool, dark, dry place for up to 3 months. Refrigerate once opened. Makes 2 cups (500 mL).

Popcorn Crunch

Here's an easy last-minute treat for the Christmas bazaar.

4 cups	popped corn	1 L
1 cup	mixed salted nuts	250 mL
3/4 cup	dried banana chips	175 mL
3/4 cup	granulated sugar	175 mL
1/4 cup	corn syrup	50 mL
2 tbsp	water	25 mL
1/4 cup	butter	50 mL

Grease two wooden spoons; set aside. On lightly greased rimmed (preferably nonstick) baking sheet, combine popcorn and nuts. Break up banana chips; add to popcorn mixture. Place in 200°F (100°C) oven to keep warm.

❧ Meanwhile, in saucepan, bring sugar, corn syrup and water to boil; cover and cook for 3 minutes. Uncover and boil for 4 minutes or until candy thermometer reaches hard-ball stage of 250° to 263°F (121° to 128°C), and when 1/2 tsp (2 mL) syrup dropped into very cold water forms hard ball that holds its shape yet is pliable.

❧ Add butter; cook, stirring, for 1 minute. Pour over popcorn mixture; toss quickly with prepared spoons to coat. Spread to let dry. Break into pieces. *(Crunch can be stored in airtight container for up to 1 week.)* Makes about 6 cups (1.5 L).

Spicy Nuts

Package this nut blend in pretty cellophane bags.

2 cups	salted peanuts	500 mL
1-1/2 cups	mixed nuts	375 mL
1/2 cup	shelled pistachio nuts	125 mL
1 tbsp	vegetable oil	15 mL
1 tbsp	Worcestershire sauce	15 mL
2 tsp	granulated sugar	10 mL
2 tsp	teriyaki sauce	10 mL
1 tsp	dry mustard	5 mL
1/4 tsp	hot pepper sauce	1 mL

In bowl, combine salted, mixed and pistachio nuts. Combine oil, Worcestershire, sugar, teriyaki sauce, mustard and hot pepper sauce; mix into nuts. Let stand for 10 minutes.

❧ Spread nut mixture on nonstick baking sheet. Bake in 350°F (180°C) oven, stirring every 5 minutes, for 15 minutes or until slightly sticky. *(Nuts can be stored in airtight container for up to 2 weeks.)* Makes 4 cups (1 L).

WRAP UP
A LITTLE
CHRISTMAS

Special gifts from the
kitchen — whether for
friends or for the bazaar —
deserve extra-special packaging.
Here are some easy ways to add
pizzazz to your holiday offerings.

❧ Fill and tie festive food bags (in photo)
with pretty ribbon and add pinecones, dried
flowers or Christmas baubles.

❧ Line an inexpensive purchased basket with tissue
paper, or with florist's moss or shavings, and fill with
treats. Overwrap with plastic wrap and tissue, or colored
cellophane (available at craft shops.)

❧ Personalize cookie and coffee tins with wrapping paper,
bows, spray paint or stickers.

❧ Look for inexpensive reusable containers, such as large new canning
jars for cookies and mixes, or pretty bowls or mugs for truffles and fudge.

(left) Popcorn Crunch; Spicy Nuts

DECK THE HALLS
WITH BOUGHS OF HOLLY

❧

'TIS THE SEASON TO ADORN OUR HOMES
WITH EVERGREEN, HOLLY AND ALL THE SYMBOLS OF CHRISTMAS
THAT PROCLAIM OUR OWN GLAD TIDINGS OF JOY.

Twig Basket Wreath

❧

A grapevine basket bedecked with berries, birds and bright plaid bows offers the warmest country welcome.

You need:

Grapevine wreath, 40 cm
   (16-inch) diameter
Grapevines, pliable tree shoots
   or rushes
Piece of chicken wire, approx
   40 x 30 cm (16 x 12 inches)
Plastic ice cream or margarine
   container, or plastic half
   basket (available at garden
   centers)
Green or Spanish moss, birch
   bark and German statice
Evergreen branches, real or
   artificial
3 or 4 red berry picks
3 or 4 pheasant feathers
   (available at millinery
   supply stores)
Bird's nest with 2 red birds and
   wooden bird's eggs
Assorted nuts in the shell
1.5 m (1.5 yards) wired plaid
   ribbon, 8 cm (3 inches) wide
Florist wire
Glue gun

To make:

1 Lay chicken wire over bottom half of wreath. Bend edges around vines to hold in place at back of wreath.

2 Lay plastic container on chicken wire inside wreath. Loosely weave grapevines over container from side to side and in and out of wreath at each side, so container is held securely in place and is well hidden. Reinforce with wire, if needed. Fill in any small gaps with moss.

3 Twist a length of vine into a bow. Secure with wire. Wire and glue vine bow to top of wreath, slightly off center.

4 Insert evergreen branches into basket.

5 Make one large bow and one small bow from wired ribbon. Wire and glue large one to edge of basket just off center and small one on top of vine bow. Arrange bow tails and glue in place.

6 Wire birds and nest to basket. Glue sprigs of statice, nuts, berries and feathers in place.

*A wreath on the door is a sure sign
that Christmastime is here!*

Holly and Ivy Wreath

❧

Traditional greens, velvet ribbons and brass bells recreate the spirit of an old-fashioned Christmas.

You need:

Grapevine wreath, 30 cm (12-inch) diameter

Dried baby's breath, German statice, small pinecones, 20 to 30 cm (8- to 12-inch) twigs

3 or 4 artificial ivy trails

3 or 4 artificial holly picks

6 small jingle bells

.75 m (1 yard) burgundy velour ribbon, 7 cm (3 inches) wide

.80 m (1 yard) burgundy grosgrain ribbon, 7 cm (3 inches) wide

Dark red acrylic spray paint

Fine gauge florist wire

Pipe cleaners

Glue gun

To make:

1 Glue and insert twigs around outside of wreath to protrude irregularly. Spray paint wreath dark red.

2 Cut a 34 cm (13-1/2-inch) length of velour ribbon for bow, leaving the rest for tails. Cut a 44 cm (17-1/4-inch) length of grosgrain ribbon for second bow, leaving the rest for tails. Fold the 34 and 44 cm lengths into single bows.

3 Place small bow on top of larger bow on top of both tails. Pinch in center and secure with pipe cleaner. Wrap and glue a scrap of ribbon around middle of bow, covering pipe cleaner. Wire complete bow to vines at bottom of wreath. Reinforce with glue.

4 Twine ivy through wreath starting at either side of bow, securing with glue where needed.

5 Insert holly picks. Wire together small bunches of baby's breath and statice; glue and insert into wreath.

6 Wire several jingle bells together and attach at center of bow.

CANDLES AND GREENS

The flicker of candlelight and the scent of fresh greens and apples combine to make an appealing, inexpensive and easy arrangement.

❧ *Fill hollowed-out apples with votive candles and insert into floral-foam base with floral picks. Arrange greens. Accent with little red birds and bright plaid ribbon.*

Easy Christmas Dress-Ups

This unique porch decoration (left) is a charming alternative to a wreath at the front door — and is every bit as welcoming!

❧ *Spray twigs white and nestle them in a ceramic umbrella stand. Adorn with strands of tiny twinkle lights, red bows and stars cut out of acetate and strung with nylon thread.*

Even a tiny alcove (below) can be prettied up for the holidays.

❧ *String silver balls with sequin ribbon and hang from a spring-loaded shower rod.*

❧ *Stand assorted scented candles in a bed of fresh greens and let the glow and the pleasing aroma fill the space with warmth and Christmas cheer.*

Dining Table Centerpiece

❧

Natural and artificial materials blend beautifully in this versatile table decoration.

You need:

Styrofoam wreath, 36 cm (14-inch) diameter
Fern pins
Spanish moss
Artificial or fresh greenery, cut into 15 cm (6-inch) lengths
Decorations such as ornamental pineapples, pinecones, red grapes, red apples, artificial Queen Anne's lace sprayed gold, dried pomegranates, artificial ivy, corkscrew hazel branch, parchment roses tipped with gold spray paint, bear grass, tiny birds, wire-edged ribbon
18-gauge floral wire or floral picks
Glue gun
Candles

To make:

1 Cut Styrofoam ring in half, cutting on a diagonal. Re-form in S shape and secure halves together with fern pins.

2 Pin moss to form. Insert greenery at random and at an angle, being careful not to obscure the S shape.

3 Pare base of candles or pineapples into a point to insert easily into Styrofoam. Insert decorations as desired, securing with floral wire, floral picks or hot glue.

Apple Tree Centerpiece

❧

Grand in scale yet homey in feeling, this centerpiece is ideal for a holiday buffet table.

You need:

Large bowl, approx 40.5 cm (16-inch) diameter
10 blocks of floral foam
Chicken wire
Floral tape
Fern pins
1 bushel of apples (about 45 lb/20 kg)
Fresh Christmas greenery
Small ornamental birds
Ribbon, for bow
Wooden skewers

To make:

1 In bowl, pile floral foam into a cone tree shape. Wrap chicken wire around foam tree to hold in place.

2 Wet floral foam. Insert greenery so it lies flat against chicken wire; hold in place with fern pins.

3 Poke wooden skewers into apples and, starting at base of tree and working upward, poke skewers into foam, completely covering it.

4 Trim with sprigs of greenery, birds and ribbon bow.

FRAGRANT PAPERWHITES

Pots of fragrant paperwhites on mantels, tables, windowsills or in hallways brighten the holiday season with springtime fragrance — and contrast beautifully with the reds and greens of Christmastime. It's fun to watch them grow, too — from the time the first stem peeks through until the flowers burst forth into beautiful snowy blooms.

❧ Growing them indoors is easy. All you need are the bulbs, pebbles, sand or soil and traditional flowerpots, or china or glass containers without drainage holes. For an attractive display, consider soup tureens, glass bowls or vegetable dishes that are at least 10 cm (4 inches) in diameter.

❧ Plant the bulbs about six weeks before you want them to bloom. If using pebbles, leave 7.5 cm (3 inches) below the bottom of the bulbs for rooting. Include several pieces of horticultural charcoal among the pebbles. Place bulbs close together, even touching, and pack the pebbles around them to hold the bulbs in place. Add water until it touches the bottom of the bulbs and keep the water at this level at all times.

❧ Place pots in a cool, low-light area. Move them to a bright windowsill once green leaves appear. The cooler and more humid the room, the more fragrant the blooms and the longer they will last.

❧ If the plants are blooming too quickly, return them to a cool, dark area for a few days.

Holiday Plants and Greenery

❧

Flowering plants and natural wreaths and garlands are one of the easiest *and* prettiest ways of dressing up your home for the holiday season. They also make great gifts that will last all winter long.

❧ To keep them looking their festive best, follow these simple tips for care and watering. Remember to keep plants in cool temperatures (50° to 60°F/10° to 14°C) and high humidity. Keep them away from direct sources of heat, too.

Flowering Plants

❧ AMARYLLIS: Place in full direct sunlight to help it flower. Water when dry.

❧ AZALEA: Place in filtered sun (behind a translucent curtain or blind). For continuous flowering, keep soil permanently moist.

❧ CHRISTMAS CACTUS: Best in full sunlight but can tolerate filtered light. Water thoroughly when very dry. Needs cool nighttime temperatures and natural wintertime light and dark to flower.

❧ CYCLAMEN: Place in full sun. Keep soil evenly moist.

❧ HOLLY PLANT: Place in full sun during the winter. Water when dry. Mist regularly. Needs high humidity.

❧ NORFOLK ISLAND PINE: Needs filtered or diffused light. Will not tolerate low light. Water sparingly during the winter rest period. Keep moist the rest of the year. Likes high humidity.

❧ POINSETTIA: Place in unobstructed direct sunlight. Water moderately. Needs high humidity.

*In photo: Paperwhites in full bloom (far left)
and growing in small clay pot, bowl and basket*

Holiday Greenery

❧ For garlands and wreaths, choose white pine (its long needles retain moisture) or cedar (for its fragrance).

❧ Keep your garlands or greenery outside or, better yet, bury them in snow (no wind, great moisture) until you're ready to bring them indoors and use them.

❧ Mist wreaths and garlands daily with cool water.

Candles in the Kitchen

❧ Muffin-tin candles add homey Christmas warmth to any corner of the kitchen.

❧ To make, cut red votive candles in half horizontally, setting the upper half in the center of each muffin cup. Melt remaining wax and pour it around each candle. Decorate the tin by gluing or wiring a small spray of ribbon-trimmed greenery through the hole at one end.

Easy Ways to Make it Christmas all through the House

❧ Garland doorways, stairs and windows with cedar boughs, giant pinecones and red ribbons.

❧ Fill wooden bowls and baskets with nuts, pinecones and cinnamon sticks and place on side tables or in hallways. The rich muted colors and nostalgic fragrances will delight the senses.

❧ Arrange clementines in pretty glass or ceramic bowls and tie with bright ribbons.

❧ Invite family and friends to relax and linger over an assortment of unshelled nuts set by the fire.

❧ Cheer up kitchen windows with colorful jars of preserves.

❧ Fill a basket with rose hips and white-sprayed birch branches. Tie with a bright plaid ribbon and you'll have an natural arrangement that will last all winter long!

CANDLE HOLDERS

Let flickering candlelight cast a warm glow around your home this holiday. If you don't have enough candlesticks to go around, here are some quick and easy alternatives. Add decorative greenery, ribbon or pinecones and be sure to use dripless candles.

❧ Place several sizes of pillar candles or miniature tree-shaped candles on a mirror or in a shallow glass dish. Surround them with coarse salt to look like snow. Sprinkle sugar glitter over salt.

❧ Spray paint a tiny flowerpot in a festive color. Insert votive candle.

❧ Carve a hole in the top of an orange. For base, cut a slice of peel off the bottom. Stud the orange with whole cloves and insert taper candle into hole.

❧ With hammer and nail, punch decorative pattern in the side of a small tin can. Spray paint. Insert votive or short pillar candle.

❧ Spray paint a brick that has holes through it. Insert taper candle in holes.

❧ With a sharp knife, cut a slice off the bottom of a 7.5 cm (3-inch) Styrofoam ball, so it will sit securely. Cover ball in white craft glue and roll in crushed Christmas potpourri. Push taper candle into top.

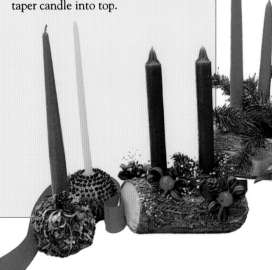

Ornaments to make

Even the simplest handmade tree trims add a special touch to holiday decorating. A fun activity for the entire family, these charming ornaments also make great gifts.

Calico Ball

You need:

Scraps of coordinating
    calico
Styrofoam ball, 6 cm
    (2-3/8-inch)
    diameter
1 m (1 yard) ribbon, 6 mm
(1/4-inch) wide Fern
pin or U-shaped hairpin
Tiny slot screwdriver
    (e.g., optician's or
    sewing-machine
    screwdriver) or nail file

To make:

1 Cut calico into 8 or 9 small assorted shapes and sizes to cover ball. Round off all corners of each piece.

2 Smooth one piece over section of ball. With head of screwdriver, poke at least 6 mm (1/4-inch) edge of fabric into ball, cutting into Styrofoam as you work.

3 Poke one edge of second piece of calico into slit along one edge of first piece. Poke remaining edges of second piece into Styrofoam.

4 Continue poking calico pieces into ball until completely covered, recutting pieces to fit if necessary.

5 Cut 35.5 cm (14-inch) length of ribbon; fold in half and tie ends together to form hanging loop. To make bow, wind remaining ribbon around four fingers; remove and pinch in middle. Place pinched middle over folded end of hanging loop. Slip fern pin over bow and hanging loop; push securely into a slit in ball.

Pinecone Ornament

You need:

Pinecone, approx 7.5 cm
    (3 inches) long
18 cm (7 inches) florist ribbon,
    13 mm (1/2-inch) wide
Artificial greenery and
    fruit, for decoration
Glue gun or white
    craft glue
Spray varnish

To make:

1 Varnish pinecone. Allow to dry thoroughly.

2 Overlap and glue ends of ribbon together to form loop. Glue to top of pinecone.

3 Glue greenery and decorations to inside ribbon loop at top of pinecone.

Snowman

You need:

Styrofoam ball, 6.5 cm
(2-1/2-inch) diameter,
for head

Styrofoam ball, 3.8 cm
(1-1/2-inch) diameter,
for body

Scrap of plaid wool fabric,
approx 30 x 1.5 cm
(11-7/8 x 5/8 inches),
for scarf

Piece of black bristol board,
approx 15 cm (6 inches)
square, for hat

Two small branching twigs,
approx 9 cm
(3-1/2 inches) long,
for arms

Celluclay (available at craft
supply stores)

Gesso (available at art
supply stores)

Black and orange acrylic
paint

Invisible nylon thread

Fine-gauge wire

Five tiny stones

Paintbrush

Compass

Glue gun

To make:

1 From wire, cut three
5 cm (2-inch) lengths;
push up into head and
down into body, to attach.

2 With Celluclay, coat
snowman and form
carrot-shaped nose on
head. Push arms into body.
Let dry.

3 Apply gesso to
snowman. Let dry. Glue
stones in place for eyes and
buttons. Paint eyes, nose
and buttons. Let dry.

4 From bristol board,
cut 5 cm (2-inch) diameter
circle, for hat brim; 3 cm
(1-1/8-inch) diameter
circle, for top; rectangle
11 x 2 cm (4-3/8 x 3/4
inches), for sides. Overlap
short ends of rectangle
approx 6 mm (1/4 inch) to
make cylinder; glue. Glue
top and brim in place. Glue
hat to head.

5 Fringe ends of scarf; tie
around neck. Loop
thread under scarf at back;
tie ends to make hanging
loop. Glue scarf in place.

Country Star

You need:

Piece of corrugated
cardboard, 35.5 x
20.5 cm (14 x 8 inches)

Large star-shaped cookie
cutter

White craft glue or glue gun

Xacto knife

Dried berries, leaves and
tiny pinecones,
for decoration

Twine

To make:

1 Trace cookie cutter
onto cardboard and cut
out 2 stars. Glue flat sides
of stars together. Glue
decoration midway down
1 point of star.

2 Make hanging loop
from twine; glue to
front of star above
decoration.

WHAT A GREAT IDEA!

WOODEN BASKET

Fill a tiny wooden basket (available at flower or wicker
shops) with moss and baby's breath. Spray several tiny
pinecones gold and secure to front of basket using florist's
wire or glue gun. Attach a 3 mm-wide red satin bow.

(top) Snowman; (bottom) Country Star

Choosing the Perfect Christmas Tree

*Christmas just wouldn't be Christmas without a tree,
but it isn't always easy to find just the right one. Here are some helpful hints that will take
the prickles out of Christmas tree picking.*

BEFORE LEAVING HOME:

❧ Decide where you'll display the tree. Do you want a tree that's full on all sides, or will it fit better if it's flat on one side?

❧ To determine how tall your tree should be, measure the height available. Allow about 20 cm (8 inches) for the stand, plus the height of your treetop decoration.

❧ Decide on the variety you want. If you like to leave your tree up for several weeks, a Scotch pine or a balsam fir might be best.

❧ Call the tourist office for information on local cut-your-own tree farms.

❧ Don't forget to take along a measuring tape.

PINE, FIR OR SPRUCE?

❧ **Scotch pine**, as it grows, is a squat, rounded tree, but may be pruned to a slim-downed silhouette for the Christmas tree market. Its long needles cling to the tree so that shedding is not a problem.

❧ **Fir** (balsam fir in the east, Douglas fir in the west) trees are

prized for their wonderful aroma and classic conical shape, making them a delight to decorate. Their needles grow along the sides of branches and are flat, short and prickly.

❧ **Spruce** (black, white or Norway) trees are similar to fir in shape and aroma. Their needles (short, prickly, and growing all around the branches) will not shed if the trunk is kept immersed in water.

❧ For good needle retention in *any* tree, keep the trunk immersed in water. This is also a fire prevention factor.

WHEN YOU GET TO THE LOT:

❧ Look for a tree that is green and fresh. If you purchase a tree that is dried out, it will be a naked and extremely flammable skeleton by Christmas.

❧ Pull off a needle and bend it; if it breaks, the tree is dried out. Crush and smell a needle — there should be a strong, fresh aroma. Look along the branches and close to the stalk for loose needles. Pull your hand firmly along a branch — do a lot of needles come off? Finally, bang the tree down hard on the stump end and watch for needles falling off.

❧ If you decide to cut your own at a tree farm, allow lots of time to find the perfect tree. Remember, it gets dark by 4:30 at this time of year.

*(right) A Christmas tree in
all its splendor.*

ARTIFICIAL TREES

Over the past few years, artificial trees have become immensely popular. They're easy to put up and take down, most are hypoallergenic, they'll last for many years and when you take them down, there are no needles to clean up.

❧ Look for a tree that has been made in North America — many come with a 10-year warranty.

❧ As a rule, the higher the number of tips (branch tips) per foot, the fuller the tree will look. Be sure you check the package for information on tree height and the number of tips.

❧ If you opt for a secondhand tree, make sure that it is flame retardant.

CHRISTMAS IS FOR KIDS

❧

GINGERBREAD HOUSES, COOKIES BAKED FOR SANTA,
"I MADE IT MYSELF!" ORNAMENTS... IT'S THE STUFF MEMORIES ARE MADE OF
AND IT'S ALL HERE — ESPECIALLY FOR KIDS!

Cinnamon Christmas Tree Ornaments

❧

When these delightful non-edible ornaments are hung on the boughs, your tree will give off a delicious cinnamon fragrance.

❧ Mix applesauce and cinnamon together in a bag and — presto! — you have a magic dough that rolls out easily and hardens beautifully.

❧ Use cookie cutters to cut out desired shapes and let everyone in the family have fun decorating them with glitter, sequins, fabric paint or colored beads.

To make:

1 In sturdy plastic bag, combine applesauce and cinnamon; seal bag. Knead until consistency of cookie dough. If too crumbly, knead in more applesauce, 1 tsp (5 mL) at a time.

2 Roll out dough to about 3 mm (1/8-inch) thickness. With cookie cutters, cut out Christmas shapes. Using straw, make hole in tops of shapes for ribbon.

3 Place on paper towel-lined baking sheet. Let dry for 24 to 48 hours or until completely hardened, turning several times. Decorate as desired.

(Ornaments can be stored in airtight container and reused. About 2 weeks before hanging, add open packet of cinnamon to container to enhance fragrance.) Makes about 18 ornaments.

You need:
125 mL (1/2 cup) unsweetened store-bought applesauce
(approx) 125 mL (1/2 cup) ground cinnamon
Plastic bag
Cookie cutters
Drinking straw or skewer
Ribbon

WHAT A GREAT IDEA!

EDIBLE COOKIE ORNAMENTS

Create delicious edible Christmas tree decorations with Gingerbread Dough (recipe, p. 60).

❧ Make dough as directed and roll out. With cookie cutters, cut out desired shapes; place on prepared baking sheets. Using straw, poke hole in tops of shapes for ribbon. Bake; repunch holes while cookies are still warm. Decorate with Easy Icing Paint (p. 63), if desired.

Cinnamon Christmas Tree Ornaments

Let's Have a Gingerbread Party!

Kids, candies and gingerbread are a dynamite idea for an afternoon of holiday fun.
You'll find everything you need on the next four pages — from a pre-party checklist to full-size pattern pieces and
nifty decorating ideas. Best of all, our easy gingerbread dough is make-and-bake-ahead.

You need:

1 batch Gingerbread Dough
(recipe, p. 60)
1 batch Royal Icing
(recipe, p. 61)

DECORATIONS:
3/4 lb (375 g) M&M's
2 pkg (each 100 g) multi-
colored jelly beans
1 pkg (4 oz/113 g)
cinnamon hearts
1 pkg (4 oz/113 g) multi-
colored candy shot
2 pkg (each 4 oz/113 g) red
and green sugar sprinkles
1 jar (2 oz/50 g) silver
dragées
12 green gumdrops
12 mini candy canes

12 gummy bear candies
12 licorice Allsorts
1 pkg (200 g) peppermints
1 pkg (250 g) colored mini
marshmallows
1 pkg (200 g) spearmint
leaves
Other candies, as desired

ACCESSORIES:
5 sturdy paper plates
Waxed paper and plastic
wrap
10 Popsicle sticks
5 paper cups
2 sq m (20 square feet)
tinted cellophane
5 m ribbon

To make:

1 Dip one Popsicle stick into Royal Icing and coat bottom of base so it sticks to paper plate.

2 Coat bottom and side edges of front piece and one side piece with icing; join together and stick onto base.

3 Repeat with back and remaining side piece. Let dry completely, about 20 minutes. (This is a good time for a refreshment break or outside play!)

4 Coat top edges of walls with icing and attach one roof piece. Coat top edge of roof; attach remaining roof piece and let dry, about 10 minutes.

5 Decorate with candies, attaching each with dab of Royal Icing.

PREPARING FOR THE PARTY

SEVERAL DAYS BEFORE:
❧ Prepare Gingerbread Dough.
❧ While dough chills, cut out waxed paper pattern pieces (p. 61).
❧ Bake gingerbread pieces; store in airtight containers for up to 3 weeks.
❧ Make Royal Icing; refrigerate in airtight container for up to 3 days.

JUST BEFORE THE PARTY:
❧ Protect table with plastic or disposable cover. Set out a waxed paper place mat for each child.
❧ Assemble kit for each child consisting of one house base, two sides, one front and one back cookie piece. (Reserve roof pieces to give out once walls have dried.) Place kits on paper plates and set at each place.
❧ Divide Royal Icing among paper cups; cover with plastic wrap and set out at each place, along with two Popsicle sticks.
❧ Place candy decorations in bowls in center of table.
❧ Cut ribbon lengths and 60 cm (2-foot) squares of tinted cellophane to wrap finished gingerbread houses in, so they can be carried home.
❧ Have damp cloths and paper towels available for wiping hands.

EASY DECORATING IDEAS

Making gingerbread houses isn't just for kids! Enlarge our pattern pieces to make a family-size house — then gather everyone together for an afternoon of pre-Christmas fun. Here are some easy decorating ideas to get you started.

❧ FOR VARIOUS COLORS: Tint Royal Icing with food coloring. Paste colors, available at cake-decorating stores, produce the most vivid colors.

❧ TO PAINT WITH ROYAL ICING PAINT: Thin a little icing, tinted to desired shade, with a few drops of water until consistency of heavy cream. Use small watercolor brush to paint onto gingerbread. (This icing paint is ideal for decorating cookies as shown in photo, p. 21.)

❧ TO MAKE SHINGLES: Pipe interlocking scallops of icing onto roof pieces.

❧ TO SIMULATE BRICKWORK: Pipe small rectangles of icing onto wall pieces.

❧ TO FINISH EDGES: Pipe scallops or rosettes of icing along house seams.

❧ TO MAKE WREATHS: Pipe circle of icing on door or wall. Pipe connecting rosettes of contrasting color over circle. Let dry. Pipe dots of red icing and bow onto wreath.

❧ TO MAKE ICICLES: Dribble small lines of white icing from eaves of roof.

❧ TO MAKE LAMPPOST: Cut black licorice twists for post; insert toothpick or bamboo skewer for support. Using icing, stick bubble-gum ball on top; let dry.

❧ TO MAKE DRIVEWAY: Brush thinned icing over driveway area; sprinkle with colored sugar.

Gingerbread Dough
❧

This easy dough is equally good for small and large houses. It also bakes into several dozen fragrant cookies, depending on size and shape of cookie cutters.

1 cup	shortening	250 mL
1 cup	granulated sugar	250 mL
2	eggs, lightly beaten	2
3/4 cup	fancy molasses	175 mL
1/2 cup	blackstrap or cooking molasses	125 mL
5-1/2 cups	all-purpose flour	1.375 L
2 tsp	ginger	10 mL
1 tsp	each baking soda, salt, cloves and cinnamon	5 mL

In large bowl and using electric mixer, beat shortening with sugar until light; beat in eggs and fancy and blackstrap molasses.

❧ Stir together flour, ginger, baking soda, salt, cloves and cinnamon; using wooden spoon, gradually stir into molasses mixture. Mix well, working with hands if necessary.

❧ Divide dough into four discs; wrap each in plastic wrap and refrigerate for at least 2 hours or until firm, or for up to 1 week.

❧ Meanwhile, referring to measurements on diagrams (next page), draw pattern pieces on waxed paper; label and cut out.

❧ Between sheets of waxed paper, roll out one disc at a time to 1/4-inch (5 mm) thickness. Remove top sheet of paper; arrange pattern pieces on dough. Using tip of knife, trace and cut out shapes. Freeze on waxed paper-lined baking sheet for 20 minutes or until hard.

❧ Transfer cutouts to parchment paper-lined or lightly greased baking sheets, reserving dough scraps for rerolling. Bake in 325°F (160°C) oven for 12 to 15 minutes or until golden and firm to the touch. Transfer gingerbread to racks and let cool completely. Makes enough for 1 large or 5 small gingerbread houses.

Royal Icing

Since this icing dries out very quickly, it's important to keep it covered with plastic wrap or a damp towel.

4 cups	icing sugar	1 L
1/2 tsp	cream of tartar	2 mL
3	egg whites	3

*I*n bowl, sift together icing sugar and cream of tartar. Using electric mixer, beat in egg whites for 7 to 10 minutes or until icing is thick enough to hold its shape. Makes about 2-1/2 cups (625 mL).

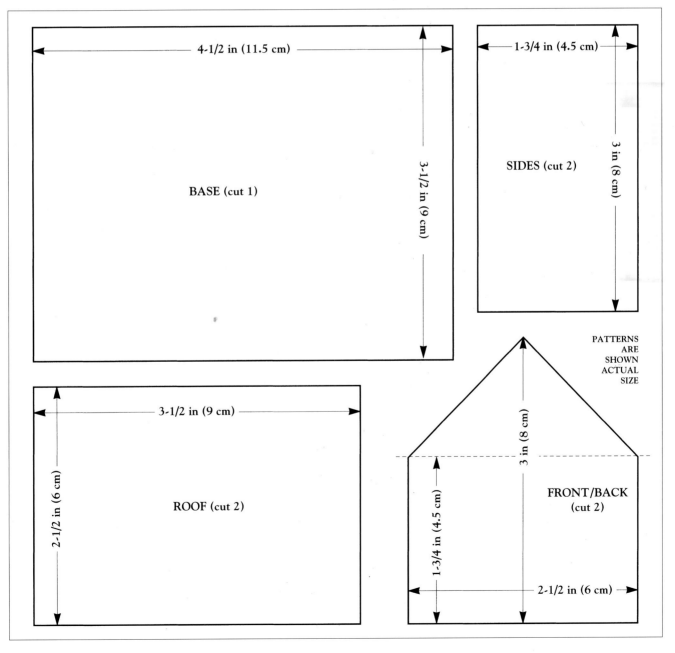

BASE (cut 1)

4-1/2 in (11.5 cm)

3-1/2 in (9 cm)

SIDES (cut 2)

1-3/4 in (4.5 cm)

3 in (8 cm)

ROOF (cut 2)

3-1/2 in (9 cm)

2-1/2 in (6 cm)

FRONT/BACK (cut 2)

3 in (8 cm)

1-3/4 in (4.5 cm)

2-1/2 in (6 cm)

PATTERNS ARE SHOWN ACTUAL SIZE

Chocolate Mice

❄

Cute and eye-catching, these little critters are fun to make — especially if you can round up some kids to snip licorice whips into tails and choose the most ear-shaped sliced almonds to press into the very malleable chocolate "dough."

4 oz	semisweet chocolate, melted	125 g
1/3 cup	sour cream	75 mL
1 cup	fine chocolate wafer crumbs (about 24)	250 mL
1/3 cup	icing sugar or fine chocolate wafer crumbs	75 mL

Garnish
Gold or silver dragées
Slivered almonds
Licorice

𝒥n bowl, combine chocolate and sour cream. Stir in 1 cup (250 mL) chocolate wafer crumbs; mix well. Cover and refrigerate until firm, about 1 hour.

❄ Roll scant tablespoonfuls (15 mL) of chocolate mixture into small balls slightly pointed at one end. Roll lightly in icing sugar. Place on waxed paper-lined tray.

❄ GARNISH: Insert dragées for eyes, almond slivers for ears and small bits of licorice for tails. Refrigerate until firm, about 2 hours. *(Chocolate mice can be refrigerated in airtight container for up to 1 week.)* Makes about 24 chocolates.

Sugar and Spice Cookies

❄

With this easy dough and an assortment of cookie cutters, children can have hours of fun making delicious decorated cookies, place cards and special treats for Santa.

𝒥n bowl, beat together butter and sugar until smooth; beat in egg and vanilla. Stir together flour, baking powder, cinnamon, nutmeg and cloves; gradually stir into batter until blended. Gather dough into ball; wrap and refrigerate for at least 1 hour or for up to 3 days.

❄ On lightly floured surface, roll out dough to 1/8-inch (3 mm) thickness. Cut into 2-inch (5 cm) round cookies or desired shapes. Transfer to parchment paper-lined, lightly greased baking sheets. Decorate as desired.

❄ Bake in 350°F (180°C) oven for 10 to 12 minutes or until edges just begin to brown. Remove to racks immediately and let cool. *(Cookies can be stored in airtight containers for up to 2 weeks.)* Makes about 50 cookies.

1/2 cup	butter, softened	125 mL
1 cup	packed brown sugar	250 mL
1	egg	1
1/2 tsp	vanilla	2 mL
1-3/4 cups	all-purpose flour	425 mL
1 tsp	baking powder	5 mL
1 tsp	cinnamon	5 mL
1/4 tsp	nutmeg	1 mL
Pinch	ground cloves	Pinch

❄ SANTA COOKIES: Decorate crinkle-cut cookies with decorator gel, silver dragées, candies and coarse red sugar crystals (see photo, left).

❄ PLACE CARD COOKIES: Cut out desired shapes and write the names of guests with decorator gel.

❄ SNOWFLAKE COOKIES: Place snowflake cutout on top of 3-inch (8 cm) cookie rounds; dust liberally with unsweetened cocoa powder (photo, p. 21). Carefully remove cutout.

Fat Teddies

❧

Delightful two-tone teddies are dark with chocolate and light with peanut butter dough, favorite flavors of all kids. Mix and match the two doughs to form arms, legs, ears and bodies.

1/2 cup	butter, softened	125 mL
1 cup	packed brown sugar	250 mL
1/2 cup	smooth peanut butter	125 mL
1/2 tsp	vanilla	2 mL
1	egg	1
2 oz	semisweet chocolate, melted	60 g
2 cups	all-purpose flour	500 mL
1/2 tsp	baking soda	2 mL
	Raisins or currants (optional)	

*I*n bowl, beat together butter, sugar, peanut butter and vanilla until smooth. Beat in egg, beating well. Remove about 1 cup (250 mL) of the batter to separate bowl; combine with melted chocolate.

❧ Stir together 1 cup (250 mL) of the flour and 1/4 tsp (1 mL) of the baking soda; gradually add to chocolate batter, blending thoroughly. Add remaining flour and baking soda to plain batter, blending thoroughly.

❧ Working with small pieces of dough at a time and keeping remainder covered with plastic wrap, shape 1-inch (2.5 cm) balls for bodies and heads; press together. Place 2 inches (5 cm) apart on lightly greased baking sheets; press lightly to flatten.

❧ Shape and add small bits of dough for ears, arms and legs, pressing together. Add raisins (if using) or tiny bits of contrasting dough for eyes, mouth, buttons and paws. Cover with plastic wrap and refrigerate for 30 minutes.

❧ Bake in 350°F (180°C) oven for 12 to 15 minutes or until firm to the touch and lightly browned. Let cool on sheets for 5 minutes; remove to racks and let cool completely. (*Cookies can be stored in airtight containers in refrigerator for up to 1 week or frozen for up to 3 months.*) Makes about 16 cookies.

WHAT A GREAT IDEA!

EASY ICING PAINT

*T*his fast-to-make icing paint spreads beautifully and is ideal for young children to use.

❧ In bowl, whisk together 4 cups (1 L) sifted icing sugar and 1/3 cup (75 mL) water, adding up to 2 tbsp (25 mL) more water if necessary to make spreadable. With pastry brush, paint some of the icing over cookies; let dry, about 30 minutes, covering bowl with damp towel.

❧ Divide remaining icing among 5 bowls; tint each with different food color paste, thinning slightly with more water if necessary. Paint decoratively onto cookies; let dry completely before storing in airtight containers. Makes enough to decorate 48 cookies.

Just-slice-and-bake Cookies

❧

When the little ones just can't wait to decorate cookies, rolls of this dough are ideal to have on hand in the freezer.

1/2 cup	butter or shortening	125 mL
1 cup	granulated sugar	250 mL
1/2 cup	smooth peanut butter	125 mL
1	egg	1
1-3/4 cups	all-purpose flour	425 mL
1/2 tsp	baking powder	2 mL
1/4 tsp	salt	1 mL

*I*n bowl, beat together butter, sugar and peanut butter until smooth; beat in egg, beating well. Mix together flour, baking powder and salt; gradually stir into creamed mixture until smooth dough forms.

❧ Gather dough into ball; divide in half. Place each half on sheet of waxed paper; using paper, shape dough into logs, each about 2 inches (5 cm) in diameter. Wrap paper around logs; chill in refrigerator for at least 4 hours or until firm. (*Dough can be refrigerated for up to 1 week or overwrapped and frozen for up to 6 weeks; thaw before baking.*)

❧ Slice dough into 1/4-inch (5 mm) thick slices; place on lightly greased baking sheets. Decorate as desired.

❧ Bake in 350°F (180°C) oven for 12 minutes or until firm to the touch and lightly browned. Remove to rack and let cool. (*Cookies can be stored in airtight containers for up to 1 week.*) Makes 40 cookies.

After the Santa Claus Parade

This kid-pleasing menu will delight grown-ups, too. It's also perfect winter fare after a day of skating or tobogganing.

Pizza Tortilla Turnovers

Fill the tortillas with cheese for the kids, and let the grown-ups enjoy the added taste of the pesto salsa.

4	10-inch (25 cm) flour tortillas	4
3 cups	shredded fontina or mozzarella cheese (6 oz/175 g)	750 mL

Pesto Salsa

1	tomato, seeded, diced and drained	1
1/4 cup	chopped fresh basil or parsley	50 mL
1 tbsp	chopped green onion	15 mL
1	clove garlic, minced	1
1 tbsp	freshly grated Parmesan cheese	15 mL
	Salt and pepper	

PESTO SALSA: In bowl, combine tomato, basil, onion, garlic, Parmesan, and salt and pepper to taste.

❦ On work surface, arrange tortillas in single layer; sprinkle half of each evenly with half of the fontina cheese, leaving thin border.

❦ Spoon salsa over cheese, spreading evenly; top with remaining cheese. Fold tortilla over to cover filling, pressing gently but firmly to seal.

❦ Cook turnovers on greased grill on medium-high setting, or broil, for about 2 minutes per side or until golden brown. Let cool for 5 minutes. Cut each turnover into 4 pieces. Makes 8 servings.

MENU

Pizza Tortilla
Turnovers

❦

Spaghetti with
Meatballs

❦

Crunchy Veggies
and Dip

❦

Triple
Chocolate Angel
Food Cake
(recipe, p. 107)

Spaghetti with Meatballs; Crunchy Veggies and Dip

Spaghetti with Meatballs

This family favorite is updated with Italian sausage. Offer the kids the option of plain spaghetti with a little butter and cheese. If you like, you can make the meatballs with all beef.

1-1/2 lb	spaghetti	750 g
1/4 cup	freshly grated Parmesan cheese	50 mL
1/4 cup	chopped fresh basil or parsley	50 mL
	Hot pepper flakes (optional)	

Meatballs

1/2 lb	sweet Italian sausage	250 g
1-1/2 lb	ground beef	750 g
2	eggs	2
1/2 cup	dry bread crumbs	125 mL
1 tsp	salt	5 mL
1/4 tsp	pepper	1 mL

Sauce

2 tbsp	olive oil	25 mL
1	large onion, chopped	1
2	cloves garlic, minced	2
1	carrot, diced	1
1	stalk celery, diced	1
3 cups	sliced mushrooms (1/2 lb/250 g)	750 mL
2	cans (each 28 oz/796 mL) tomatoes (undrained)	2
	Salt and pepper	

MEATBALLS: Remove sausage meat from casings. In bowl, combine sausage meat, beef, eggs, crumbs, salt and pepper; form into 4 dozen 1-inch (2.5 cm) balls. Bake on rimmed baking sheets in 400°F (200°C) oven for 15 to 20 minutes or until no longer pink inside; drain off fat.

❧ SAUCE: Meanwhile, in large saucepan, heat oil over medium-high heat; cook onion, garlic, carrot, celery and mushrooms, stirring occasionally, for 10 minutes or until just beginning to brown.

❧ Add tomatoes, mashing with fork; cook for about 20 minutes or until thickened, stirring occasionally. Add meatballs; reduce heat and simmer for 15 minutes. Season with salt and pepper to taste. *(Sauce can be cooled, covered and refrigerated for up to 1 day; reheat before continuing.)*

❧ In large pot of boiling salted water, cook spaghetti for 8 to 10 minutes or until tender but firm; drain well and arrange on plates. Top each serving with sauce; sprinkle with cheese, basil, and hot pepper flakes (if using). Makes 8 servings.

Crunchy Veggies and Dip

Children love raw vegetables and dip, so why not serve their favorite crisper crunchies at this informal family party. For an adults-only dip, increase the anchovy paste to 1 tbsp (15 mL).

1	head cauliflower, broken in florets	1
1	bunch broccoli, cut in florets	1
3	carrots, cut in sticks	3
1/2 lb	green beans, trimmed	250 g
1	each sweet red, green and yellow pepper, sliced	1
2	Belgian endives, separated	2

Dressing

1/2 cup	plain yogurt	125 mL
1/4 cup	mayonnaise	50 mL
2 tbsp	chopped fresh parsley	25 mL
1 tbsp	lemon juice	15 mL
1 tsp	anchovy paste	5 mL
1 tsp	Dijon mustard	5 mL
1	small clove garlic, minced	1
	Salt and pepper	

In large pot of boiling water, cook cauliflower for 4 minutes. With slotted spoon, remove and chill in cold water; drain and pat dry. Repeat with broccoli, blanching for 3 minutes.

❧ In rows of different colors, arrange cauliflower, broccoli, carrots, beans, peppers and endive leaves on serving platter.

❧ DRESSING: In bowl, combine yogurt, mayonnaise, parsley, lemon juice, anchovy paste, mustard and garlic; season with salt and pepper to taste. Serve with vegetable platter. Makes 8 servings.

KID-STYLE PARTIES

Children enjoy having a hand in organizing the party. Let them set the table, make place cards or decorate the house.

❧ Cook familiar foods you know children enjoy.

❧ To make sure children have room for the main course, keep appetizer snacks to a minimum.

❧ If you serve foods with sauces, be sure to leave some plain.

❧ Don't make anything too spicy.

❧ Don't force kids to eat. If they are hungry, they'll find something they like. Always have some bread and fruit on hand, just in case.

Children's Christmas Party

*Whether it's a holiday party for kindergarten chums or a special kids'
table at a neighborhood open house, this festive fare is sure to delight little ones.*

Sandwich Wreath

*Sandwiches rolled and cut into pinwheels (recipe follows)
add pizzazz to a kid-style party platter. For eight children,
prepare about 32 sandwiches (three or four different kinds).
Use an assortment of breads — party rye or pumpernickel,
long skinny loaves thinly sliced, or thin slices of bread cut
with round cookie cutters. For variety, use two different
breads for each sandwich.*

Pinwheels

1	sandwich loaf, unsliced	1
	Butter, softened (optional)	
	Fillings (recipes follow)	

Garnish

Evergreen sprigs
Radish roses or carved vegetables

Trim bottom crust from loaf; slice loaf lengthwise into 1/3-inch (8 mm) thick slices. Trim remaining crusts.

❧ With rolling pin, gently flatten bread slices and spread with butter (if using); spread with filling. Roll up jelly roll-style, starting at narrow end. Cover and refrigerate until ready to serve. Cut into 6 or 8 slices.

❧ TO SERVE: Place assorted sandwiches around rim of circular plate in wreath shape or arrange attractively to fill entire plate. Decorate with evergreen sprigs, radish roses or carved vegetables.

FILLINGS

❧ CHRISTMAS PINWHEELS: Combine 4 oz (125 g) softened cream cheese with 1 tbsp (15 mL) maraschino cherry juice. Spread thin layer on bread slice. Place row of whole maraschino cherries across narrow end of bread (or stir chopped maraschino cherries into cream cheese mixture); roll up.

❧ PEANUT BUTTER AND BANANA PINWHEELS: Spread bread slice with smooth or crunchy peanut butter. Place small peeled banana across narrow end; roll up.

❧ OTHER FAVORITE FILLINGS FOR THE YOUNGER CROWD: Tuna, egg or salmon salad; chopped chicken or turkey with mayonnaise; ham and mozzarella cheese slices; deviled ham or mild salami.

MENU

Apple Cider
❧
Sandwich Wreath
❧
Christmas Cookies
❧
Ice Cream with
Chocolate Sauce

GIFTS FROM THE HEART

Christmas gift giving shouldn't only mean dollars and cents: gifts from the heart are special, too. Let your children experience the wonderful feeling that the joy of giving can bring — without spending any money.

❧ Give each child some colored paper and pencils and let them make a "coupon" book for the special people on their list, with a "gift" on each page to be redeemed later.

❧ Let them decorate the pages, then punch two holes in one side. Create a cover for the coupons, add a gift tag, then tie them all together with ribbon.

❧ Here are some ideas to help youngsters get started. Once they begin, you'll be surprised at how generous they can be.

- *Two weeks of drying the dishes for Mom.*
- *A winter's worth of shovelling snow from the front walk for a favorite neighbor.*
- *Ten little kindnesses to a brother or sister.*
- *Four car washes for Dad.*
- *Ten errands for Grandpa.*
- *Twenty hugs (to be cashed in when least expected).*

Clementine Wreath

❧

"I made it all by myself!" will be the proud declaration when your child presents the teacher with this cheerful Christmas wreath.

You need:

Crêpe paper or cellophane
6 clementines or mandarin oranges
Ribbon

To make:

1 Cut crêpe paper into 70 x 40 cm (27-1/2- x 15-3/4-inch) rectangle.

2 Place clementines in row down center of paper. Roll paper around clementines sausage-style. Tie ribbon bow around paper between each clementine.

3 Bend roll into wreath shape. Overlap ends and secure with ribbon bow.

Saucy Santas

Whimsical little cone-shaped Santas are the perfect project for the kindergarten crowd.

You need:

Red construction paper
White typing paper
Black and red felt-tip markers
Red thread

White craft glue
Clothespin
Needle
Geometry compass

To make:

1 Using compass, draw 29 cm (11-1/2-inch) diameter circle on red construction paper. Cut out. Cut circle into four equal pie-shaped wedges.

2 Using photo as guide, cut Santa face and beard from white paper. Draw eyes and mouth. Glue to center of one wedge.

3 Roll up sides of wedge to form cone, overlapping edges 13 mm (1/2 inch). Glue in place.

Hold together with clothespin until glue dries.

4 Thread loop of red thread through tip of cone.

5 Make Santas from three remaining wedges in the same manner.

Picture Perfect Hang-Ups
❧

Simple dough frames require only flour, salt and water.
A little photo makes them special.

You need:

250 mL (1 cup) all-purpose flour	Acrylic paint and paintbrush
125 mL (1/2 cup) salt	Wallet-size photograph
125 mL (1/2 cup) water	Construction paper
Cookie cutters	String or ribbon
Drinking straw or skewer	White craft glue

To make:

1 Mix together flour, salt and water to form soft dough; divide in half. Working with one portion at a time and keeping remaining half covered with plastic wrap, knead dough on floured surface until smooth, 8 to 10 minutes.

2 Roll out dough to 5 mm (1/4-inch) thickness. Cut out shape with large cookie cutter; cut out hole in middle with smaller cutter.

3 Place frame on foil-lined baking sheet. With straw, poke hole at top of frame. Bake in 250°F (120°C) oven for 4 to 5 hours or until thoroughly dry. Let cool.

4 Paint frame and let dry. Place photograph behind center opening, trimming off any excess. Glue to back of frame. Trace around frame onto construction paper. Cut out paper just inside traced line. Glue to back of frame; poke hole through paper to line up with hole at top of frame. Poke ribbon through hole and tie in bow or loop.

Tissue Paper Decorations
❧

Tissue paper transforms simple shapes, such as snowmen and trees, into festive decorations.

You need:

Cardboard	Pom-poms
White, green and red tissue paper	White craft glue
	Red and green pipe cleaners

To make:

1 Cut out Christmas tree and snowman shapes from cardboard.

2 Cut colored tissue into many 5 cm (2-inch) squares. Center each square over pointer finger and fold down; scrunch together at fingertip. Glue to cardboard to cover shape completely.

3 Decorate tree with little red tissue-paper balls or pom-poms for berries.

4 Decorate snowman with pipe-cleaner mouth and bow, paper hat and pom-poms for eyes and buttons.

Candy Garlands

❧

Candy and colored yarn are all you need to make a nifty Christmas tree garland.

You need:

Sugar candies wrapped in clear cellophane and twisted at each end
Colored yarn

To make:

1 Cut yarn into 15 cm (6-inch) lengths.

2 Place candies end to end, overlapping twisted ends of cellophane wrappers. Tie ends together with strand of yarn. Continue until garland is desired length.

Glitter Gift Bag

❧

Brown bags never looked this good!

You need:

Small brown paper lunch bag
Shirt cardboard
Glitter in assorted colors
Poster paints or markers
Paintbrushes
Small sponge
Scraps of ribbon or yarn
Hole punch
Pinking shears
White craft glue

To make:

1 To make stencil: Draw simple shape, such as a star, tree or heart, on cardboard. Cut out shape *inside* the drawn line.

2 Place stencil on front of bag. With sponge, dab glue over cut-out area. Remove stencil. Sprinkle glitter over glue. Shake off excess. Let glue dry. Stencil as many motifs as you want on all sides of bag.

3 Write greeting with paint or marker on front of bag. Trim top edge with pinking shears. Fold pinked edge down and punch two holes 4 to 5 cm (1-5/8 to 2 inches) apart through all layers.

4 Put gift in bag. Thread ribbon through holes and tie in bow at center front.

BALLOON CHRISTMAS TREE

Make this delightful tree the star of a children's holiday party.

❧ Secure broom handle in Christmas-tree stand. Cut cardboard circle approx 122 cm (4 feet) in diameter. Cut small center hole in circle; slip over broom handle to cover stand. Along length of string, tie approx 75 green balloons, blown up to various sizes, leaving 1.5 cm (5/8 inch) between each.

❧ Beginning at edge of cardboard circle, tape string of balloons around circle, filling up space with loose balloons. Continue in a spiral to center of circle and up around trunk to form cone shape. With double-sided tape, tape each balloon to its neighbors.

❧ Decorate with tree-top ornament, multi-colored balloons, party hats and streamers.

WHAT A GREAT IDEA!

CANDY CANE REINDEER

Twist long colored pipe cleaner around curved end of candy cane. Bend ends into shape of funny antlers. Glue on little red pom-pom nose and two rolly eyes. Tie fancy bow around neck.

Sparkle Wrap

Because glitter and glue tend to stiffen paper, wrap the present before decorating the package.

You need:
Wrapped gift
Sheet of clean paper
White craft glue
Glitter

To make:

1 With pencil, draw desired design on all sides of package. Young children may find it easier to trace around a cookie cutter.

2 Squeeze line of glue along traced lines on one side of package. Sprinkle glitter over glued areas, then shake off excess onto clean paper. Let dry.

3 Repeat this process on all sides of package and with as many colors of glitter as you like.

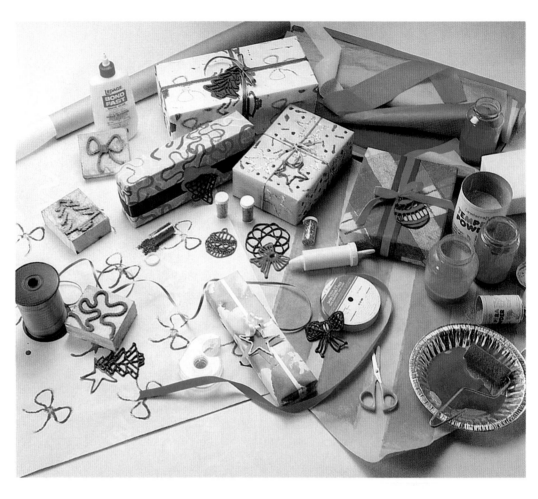

WHAT A GREAT IDEA!

REINDEER GIFT TAG *Cut small diamond from construction paper. Fold in half to make triangle. Cut two holly-shaped antlers from green paper; glue to top of triangle head along fold. Draw two eyes with marker; glue on tiny red pom-pom nose.*

String Print Wrap

A simple festive motif works best.

You need:

Large sheet of paper	**Block of wood**
Tempera paint	**White craft glue**
Thick cord or string	**Foil pie plates**

To make:

1 Draw desired motif on one side of wood block. Glue cord along traced design. Let glue dry overnight.

2 Fill plate with paint. Dip stamp into paint to saturate cord. Stamp several times on scrap paper to remove excess paint, then print on paper. Let dry.

3 Wash stamp in soap and water. Print more colors, if desired.

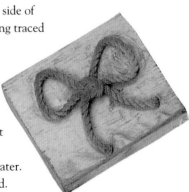

Lacy Glue Ornament and Gift Tag

A decoration to add sparkle to the tree — and to all the presents underneath!

You need:

White craft glue
Powdered tempera paint
Plastic cake decorator tube
  with round tip
Disposable cup and
  stir stick

Clear plastic bag
Colored paper
Ribbon

To make:

1 Draw simple Christmas motif on paper and place on flat surface. Cover with flattened plastic bag.

2 Pour approx 50 mL (1/4 cup) white glue into cup; stir in enough tempera powder to obtain desired color. Powder will thicken glue to consistency of stiff icing. Add a few drops of water if too thick. Fill cake decorator tube with colored glue and insert plunger.

3 Squeeze glue out of tube onto plastic, following traced lines of pattern underneath. Add circle of glue at top to form hole for ribbon. Fill in center of design with interconnecting lines, so ornament looks lacy and will stay rigid when dry. Let glue dry for 24 hours.

4 Peel off plastic. To hang, thread loop of ribbon through hole at top of ornament.

5 GIFT TAG: With pencil, lightly trace around ornament onto colored paper. Cut out. Write greeting on back of paper shape and punch hole to correspond to hole in ornament. Thread ribbon through holes. Tie to package.

Palm Print Package and Tag

Definitely Christmas packaging with a personal touch!

You need:

Empty cereal, detergent
  or tea bag box
White, red and green acrylic
  paint
Paintbrushes
2 foil pie
  plates

Scraps of ribbon
White cardboard, for
  gift tags
Xacto knife
Hole punch
Newspaper

To make:

1 Cover work surface with lots of newspaper.

2 If using detergent or cereal box, draw handle shape at top of both sides of box. Carefully cut around outline and cut out center of handle with sharp scissors or Xacto knife (parental assistance will be needed).

3 Paint box white. Let dry. Apply 2 or 3 more coats if necessary to completely cover printing on box.

4 Mix red paint in one pie plate and green in the other. Dip palm of hand in one of the colors. Blot off excess and practise printing on newspaper. Print as many hands as you want on all sides of box, supporting it from inside with clean hand. Let paint dry. Wash hands. Repeat printing process with other color of paint.

5 For splatter marks, thin out paint with a little water. Dip paintbrush in paint and flick it at box. Let dry.

6 GIFT TAG: Cut piece of white cardboard 10 x 6 cm (4 x 2-3/8 inches). Using process described above, hand-paint and splatter-paint card. Let dry. Punch hole in corner. Thread ribbon through hole. Write greeting on card. Line box with tissue paper; tuck in gift and attach tag.

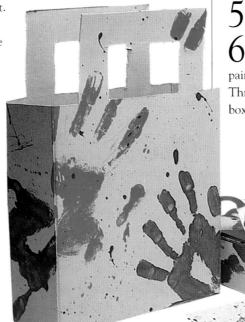

hands off!
don't touch
til Dec.25

do not touch
til Dec.25

HOLIDAY ENTERTAINING

✿

OPEN YOUR HOME AND HEART THIS HOLIDAY SEASON
WITH A TEMPTING ARRAY OF DISHES FOR EVERY FESTIVE OCCASION.

Leek and Brie Pizza Fingers

*Bite-size pizza fingers with a ready-made crust and
creamy topping make very pleasing holiday party fare.*

3 tbsp	butter	50 mL
6 cups	thinly sliced leeks	1.5 L
2/3 cup	whipping cream	150 mL
1/3 cup	freshly grated Parmesan cheese	75 mL
Pinch	each salt and pepper	Pinch
1	long flat bread, cut in half	1
1/4 lb	Brie cheese, cut into bits	125 g
	Chopped fresh parsley	

*I*n large heavy pan, melt butter over medium-low heat; cook leeks for 15 minutes or until softened but not browned. Add cream and bring to boil; boil, stirring frequently, for 2 minutes or until thickened and reduced by half. Stir in Parmesan, salt and pepper.

✿ Spread leek mixture over bread; scatter Brie over top. Bake on baking sheets in 400°F (200°C) oven for about 12 minutes or until crust is crisped and cheese melted. Sprinkle with parsley. Cut into fingers to serve. Makes about 30 hors d'oeuvres.

WHAT A GREAT IDEA!

BLACK BEAN AND SALSA NACHOS

*D*rain 2 cups (500 mL) chunky salsa through fine sieve *to make 1 cup (250 mL); combine with 1 cup (250 mL) drained canned black beans.*

✿ On baking sheet, arrange 34 round nachos in single layer; top each with 2 tsp (10 mL) bean mixture. Shred old white Cheddar cheese to make 3/4 cup (175 mL); sprinkle 1 tsp (5 mL) over each nacho. Bake in 400°F (200°C) oven for 4 minutes or until cheese melts. Serve immediately. Makes 34 hors d'oeuvres.

Savory Phyllo Tartlets

*Crisp little pastry cups filled with cream cheese are accented
with the pleasurable warmth of pepper jelly.*

8	sheets phyllo pastry	8
1/3 cup	butter, melted	75 mL

Filling

3/4 cup	cream cheese (6 oz/175 g)	175 mL
2 tbsp	butter, softened	25 mL
1/2 cup	jalapeño or homemade hot pepper jelly (recipe, p. 35)	125 mL
	Dill sprigs	

*P*lace one sheet of phyllo on work surface, keeping remaining phyllo covered with damp towel to prevent drying out. Brush phyllo sheet lightly with butter. Lay second sheet on top; brush with butter. Repeat with remaining phyllo.

✿ Cut into 2-inch (5 cm) squares and press into 1-3/4-inch (4.5 cm) miniature tart tins. Bake in 350°F (180°C) oven for 10 to 15 minutes or until crisp and golden. Let cool. (*Pastry shells can be stored in airtight containers for up to 3 days.*)

✿ FILLING: In food processor or bowl, blend cream cheese with butter until smooth; pipe or spoon into pastry shells. Top each with about 1/4 tsp (1 mL) jalapeño jelly; garnish with dill. (*Tartlets can be covered and refrigerated for up to 24 hours; let stand at room temperature for 45 minutes before serving.*) Makes about 50 hors d'oeuvres.

VARIATION

✿ SMOKED SALMON TARTLETS: Add about 2 oz (50 g) smoked salmon to cream cheese and butter; process until smooth. Omit jalapeño jelly.

*(clockwise from top) vegetables and dip; Black Bean and Salsa
Nachos; Savory Phyllo Tartlets and Smoked Salmon Tartlets*

(bottom left) Mushroom Shrimp Toast Cup; (center) Salmon Roll; (right) Pâté Cutout

Salmon Rolls

❧

Roll slices of smoked salmon into tiny cornucopias. Pipe softened cream cheese, blended with minced fresh parsley, into centers. Dot each with red caviar.

Mushroom Shrimp Toast Cups

❧

In large skillet, cook 3-1/2 cups (875 mL) sliced mushrooms in 2 tbsp (25 mL) butter over high heat, stirring often, for 5 minutes or until browned and excess moisture has evaporated. Remove from heat; blend in 3 tbsp (50 mL) sour cream. Season with salt and pepper to taste.

Spoon into toast cups. Top each with a cooked salad shrimp and sprig of fresh parsley or dill. Makes 20 hors d'oeuvres.

❧ TO MAKE TOAST CUPS: With rolling pin, roll 20 slices of white or whole wheat bread to 1/4-inch (5 mm) thickness. Using 3-inch (8 cm) circle or square cookie cutter, cut shape from each slice, reserving trimmings for bread crumbs. Tuck into 2-inch (5 cm) tart or muffin pans; brush lightly with vegetable oil. Bake in 350°F (180°C) oven for 10 to 15 minutes or until lightly toasted. Remove from pans; let cool on racks.

Pâté Cutouts

❧

Spread your favorite liverwurst or homemade pâté on slices of peeled cored apple or peeled white turnip. Brush surfaces of both apple and liverwurst with lemon juice to prevent browning. Cut into Christmassy shapes and decorate.

For our photo, we tied a green onion bow on a bell and added a red pepper clapper. The flower has green pepper "holly" and red pepper "berries."

Italian Mushroom Antipasto

*This fresh-tasting tomato and mushroom relish is a
handy one to spoon into toast cups (see p. 76),
store-bought pastry cups or onto crackers.*

1 tbsp	olive oil	15 mL
5 cups	sliced mushrooms (about 1 lb/500 g)	1.25 L
2 tbsp	lemon juice	25 mL
1/2 cup	chopped onion	125 mL
2	large cloves garlic, minced	2
1	bay leaf	1
1/4 tsp	each dried marjoram, thyme and pepper	1 mL
Pinch	cayenne pepper	Pinch
1	can (19 oz/540 mL) tomatoes, drained	1
2 tbsp	red wine vinegar	25 mL
Pinch	granulated sugar	Pinch
2 tbsp	chopped fresh parsley	25 mL
	Salt	

*I*n skillet, heat oil over medium-high heat; cook mushrooms for
7 to 10 minutes or until liquid is released. Drain, reserving liquid.
In bowl, toss mushrooms with lemon juice; set aside.

❧ Add onion, garlic and 2 tbsp (25 mL) mushroom liquid to
skillet; cook over medium heat for 3 to 5 minutes or until softened. Add bay leaf, marjoram, thyme, pepper and cayenne; cook,
stirring, for 1 minute.

❧ Stir in tomatoes, breaking up with spoon, remaining mushroom liquid, vinegar and sugar; bring to boil. Reduce heat to low;
cover and simmer for 25 minutes. Uncover and increase heat to
medium-high; cook for 2 minutes or until liquid is reduced by
half. Discard bay leaf.

❧ Add tomato mixture and parsley to mushrooms, stirring to
mix well. Season with salt to taste. Refrigerate until chilled or for
up to 5 days. Serve at room temperature. Makes 2 cups (500 mL).

Smoked Salmon Spirals

*Keep a roll or two of this impressive
last-minute appetizer on hand in the freezer.*

1/2 lb	thinly sliced smoked salmon	250 g
1/2 lb	light cream cheese, softened	250 g
1 tbsp	chopped fresh dill	15 mL
1 tbsp	capers	15 mL
1	English cucumber, sliced	1
	Red onion strips and dill sprigs	

*A*rrange salmon on plastic wrap in 12- x 8-inch (30 x 20 cm)
rectangle. Mix cheese with dill; spread over salmon.

❧ Press row of capers into cheese along one long edge; beginning at edge with capers, roll up jelly roll-style to enclose capers
in center. Wrap in plastic wrap, squeezing to form smooth cylinder; twist ends closed. Freeze for at least 4 hours. *(Roll can be
frozen for up to 1 month.)*

❧ To serve, thaw roll for 10 minutes; slice thinly and arrange
on cucumber slices. Garnish with onion and dill. Let stand at
room temperature for 10 minutes. Makes 60 hors d'oeuvres.

Mini Salsa Soufflés

*Salsa adds a new twist to puffy
cheesy-topped toast rounds.*

1/2 cup	shredded Swiss cheese	125 mL
1/2 cup	low-fat ricotta	125 mL
1/4 cup	spicy salsa	50 mL
1 tbsp	chopped fresh coriander	15 mL
1 tbsp	lime juice	15 mL
1/2 tsp	each ground cumin and paprika	2 mL
2	egg whites	2
1	baguette	1

*I*n bowl, combine Swiss and ricotta cheeses, salsa, coriander,
lime juice, cumin and paprika. Beat egg whites until stiff peaks
form; fold into cheese mixture.

❧ Slice baguette into 30 rounds; place on baking sheet and
broil for 1 minute. Spread untoasted side of each round right to
edge with 1 tsp (5 mL) cheese mixture; broil for 3 to 5 minutes
or until puffed and lightly browned. Makes 30 hors d'oeuvres.

Oriental Meatballs

❧

Some appetizers never go out of style, like this guaranteed crowd pleaser — baked nuggets of beef drenched in a tangy hoisin sauce. Serve them at late-afternoon events when everyone is hungry for something satisfying.

1/3 cup	ketchup	75 mL
2 tbsp	hoisin sauce	25 mL
2 tsp	lemon juice	10 mL
1/4 tsp	granulated sugar	1 mL
1-1/2 lb	lean ground beef	750 g
1/2 cup	minced green onions	125 mL
1/4 cup	dry bread crumbs	50 mL
1	egg, beaten	1
2	cloves garlic, minced	2
1 tbsp	minced gingerroot	15 mL
1/2 tsp	dry mustard	2 mL
1/2 tsp	salt	2 mL
1/4 tsp	pepper	1 mL

*I*n bowl, whisk together ketchup, hoisin sauce, lemon juice and sugar.

❧ In large bowl, combine beef, onions, bread crumbs, egg, garlic, gingerroot, mustard, salt, pepper and 1 tbsp (15 mL) of the ketchup mixture. Shape heaping tablespoonfuls (15 mL) into balls. *(Recipe can be prepared to this point, covered and refrigerated for up to 24 hours.)*

❧ Bake 1 inch (2.5 cm) apart on baking sheet in 400°F (200°C) oven for 20 to 25 minutes or until no longer pink inside, turning halfway through. Let cool for 2 minutes; toss gently with remaining ketchup mixture. Makes 36 hors d'oeuvres.

WHAT A GREAT IDEA!

QUICK SARDINE ROLL

*H*umble ingredients — sardines and cream cheese — combine for a heavenly taste. This is a wonderful appetizer to have in the refrigerator when unexpected company drops in for a holiday visit. It keeps for up to five days.

❧ *Blend together 1 drained can (4-3/8 oz/124 g) sardines, 1/2 lb (250 g) softened cream cheese, 4 tsp (20 mL) lemon juice, 1 tsp (5 mL) brandy and dash Worcestershire sauce until smooth and creamy; chill until firm.*

❧ *Shape mixture into roll or ball; roll in 3/4 cup (175 mL) finely chopped fresh parsley. Wrap in waxed paper and chill. Serve surrounded with melba toast. Makes about 2 cups (500 mL).*

Christmas Quiche Wedges

❧

Sweet red and green pepper strips turn custardy quiche into festive Christmas fare.

1-2/3 cups	all-purpose flour	400 mL
Pinch	salt	Pinch
1/2 cup	cold butter	125 mL
1/4 cup	cold water	50 mL
1	egg yolk	1
1 tbsp	vegetable oil	15 mL

Filling

1/3 cup	shredded mozzarella cheese	75 mL
1/2 cup	each thin strips sweet green and red pepper	125 mL
2	eggs	2
1 cup	milk or light cream	250 mL
1/2 tsp	each dried oregano and salt	2 mL
1/4 tsp	pepper	1 mL

*I*n bowl, combine flour and salt; with pastry blender or two knives, cut in butter until mixture resembles fine crumbs with a few larger pieces. Beat together water, yolk and oil; stir into flour mixture until moistened. On floured surface, knead into ball. Cover and refrigerate for 1 hour or up to 5 days.

❧ On lightly floured surface, roll out pastry to 1/8-inch (3 mm) thickness; cut out five 6-inch (15 cm) rounds. Fit each into 4-inch (10 cm) quiche or tart pan with removable bottom. Refrigerate for 30 minutes.

❧ Line each shell with foil; weigh down with pie weights or dried beans. Bake on baking sheet in 375°F (190°C) oven for 15 minutes; remove weights and foil. Prick pastry with fork; bake for 10 minutes longer or until golden brown. *(Shells can be cooled, covered and stored at room temperature for up to 1 day.)*

❧ FILLING: Divide mozzarella evenly among shells; top with sweet peppers. In bowl, whisk eggs; whisk in milk, oregano, salt and pepper. Pour into shells.

❧ Bake tarts for 35 to 40 minutes or until knife inserted into centers comes out clean. Let stand for 10 minutes; cut each tart into 6 wedges. Makes 30 hors d'oeuvres.

Prosciutto Roll-Ups

❧

Rolled in from both ends like a scroll, this puff-pastry appetizer can be assembled and waiting in the refrigerator for last-minute baking to crisp and delicious perfection.

1	pkg (14 oz/397 g) frozen puff pastry, thawed	1
2 tbsp	sweet mustard	25 mL
1/4 cup	freshly grated Parmesan cheese	50 mL
1/4 lb	thinly sliced prosciutto (or 6 oz/175 g sliced smoked ham)	125 g
1	egg, beaten	1

*O*n lightly floured surface, roll out half of the pastry to 12- x 10-inch (30 x 25 cm) rectangle.

❧ Spread with half of the mustard, leaving 1/2-inch (1 cm) border. Sprinkle with half of the cheese; arrange half of the prosciutto in single layer over cheese. Brush border with water.

❧ Starting at short end, roll up jelly roll-style just to center of rectangle. Roll up other end to meet in center; turn over. Using serrated knife, trim ends; cut into 1/2-inch (1 cm) thick slices. Place on parchment paper-lined baking sheets; press lightly.

❧ Repeat with remaining ingredients. Cover and refrigerate for 1 hour. *(Roll-ups can be prepared to this point and refrigerated for up to 1 day.)*

❧ Brush egg over roll-ups. Bake in 400°F (200°C) oven for 15 to 18 minutes or until puffed and lightly golden. Makes about 34 hors d'oeuvres.

Almond Cheeseballs

❧

Crisp and crunchy, these tasty morsels are best made just a few hours before serving.

1/2 cup	chopped blanched almonds	125 mL
1/3 cup	crushed unsalted soda crackers	75 mL
1 cup	shredded Swiss cheese	250 mL
1 cup	shredded old Cheddar cheese	250 mL
1/4 cup	all-purpose flour	50 mL
1/4 tsp	each cayenne and black pepper	1 mL
Pinch	salt	Pinch
2	egg whites	2
1/2 cup	vegetable oil	125 mL

*O*n waxed paper, combine almonds and crackers; set aside.

❧ In bowl, toss together Swiss and Cheddar cheeses, flour, cayenne, black pepper and salt. In separate bowl, beat egg whites until stiff peaks form; fold into cheese mixture.

❧ Scooping out 1 tbsp (15 mL) at a time, form cheese mixture into balls. Roll each ball in nut mixture to coat. Cover and refrigerate for 1 hour or up to 24 hours.

❧ In skillet, heat oil over medium-high heat for 5 minutes; cook balls, in batches, for 2 to 3 minutes or until golden, turning often. With slotted spoon, transfer to paper towels and let drain. Serve warm. *(Cheeseballs can be cooled, covered and refrigerated for up to 4 hours; heat in 400°F/200°C oven for 8 to 10 minutes or until heated through.)* Makes about 18 hors d'oeuvres.

(clockwise from top left) snow peas piped with cream cheese; Prosciutto Roll-Ups; Oriental Meatballs; Almond Cheeseballs; (in center) Christmas Quiche Wedges and Savory Phyllo Tartlets (p. 74)

Blue Cheese and Walnut Spread

❧

This blend of blue cheese and nuts is an all-purpose pleaser — for casual events with crackers, fruit and a video, or as an easy make-ahead for fancier cocktail occasions.

1/4 lb	Gorgonzola or other creamy blue cheese	125 g
1/4 lb	cream cheese	125 g
1/2 cup	coarsely chopped walnuts	125 mL
2 tbsp	brandy	25 mL
	Pepper	
	Walnut halves	

*I*n bowl or food processor, beat Gorgonzola and cream cheese until smooth, being careful not to overmix.

> **Tip**: *For a tasty dip, blend in 1 cup (250 mL) sour cream along with the cheese.*

❧ Fold in chopped walnuts, brandy, and pepper to taste. Transfer to attractive 1-cup (250 mL) dish, smoothing top; garnish with walnut halves. (*Spread can be covered and refrigerated for up to 10 days.*) Makes about 1 cup (250 mL).

NUTCRACKER DELIGHTS

The holiday season finds stores stocked with freshly harvested nuts in their shells — pecans and peanuts from the American south, walnuts, almonds, hazelnuts and pistachios from the west coast and Brazil nuts from its rainforest. A heaping bowl of nuts is a great natural decoration, and a must for holiday entertaining. And, unlike shelled salted nuts that can be popped into the mouth a handful at a time (adding an amazing number of calories with each munch!), nuts in the shell slow partiers down long enough to let them savor the flavor of each freshly cracked morsel.

MARINATED HERRING AND APPLE SPREAD

*S*erve thin rye crackers or Scandinavian flat bread with this piquant fresh-tasting spread. You can find jars of herring tidbits pickled with onions in delis and supermarkets. Drain, reserving herrings and onions for the spread.

❧ In bowl, blend 6 oz (175 g) softened cream cheese with 1/4 cup (50 mL) sour cream. Mix in 2/3 cup (150 mL) finely chopped marinated herring, 2/3 cup (150 mL) finely chopped (unpeeled) red apple, 2 tbsp (25 mL) chopped pickled onion, and pepper to taste. Transfer to serving dish; cover and refrigerate for up to 3 days. Makes about 1-3/4 cups (425 mL).

Onion and Sun-Dried Tomato Bruschetta

❧

Balsamic vinegar gives these mellow onion-topped bread rounds a wonderful flavor.

5 cups	thinly sliced onions (about 1 lb/500 g)	1.25 L
1 cup	chicken stock	250 mL
1/4 cup	chopped sun-dried tomatoes	50 mL
1/3 cup	freshly grated Parmesan cheese	75 mL
1/4 cup	chopped fresh parsley	50 mL
4 tsp	balsamic vinegar	20 mL
	Salt and pepper	
Half	baguette	Half
4 tsp	olive oil	20 mL
1	clove garlic, minced	1

*I*n skillet, bring onions, chicken stock and tomatoes to boil; reduce heat to low and simmer for 45 minutes or until onions are tender and only 1 tbsp (15 mL) liquid remains. Sprinkle with half of the Parmesan, the parsley, vinegar, and salt and pepper to taste; mix well. Set aside.

❧ Cut baguette into 1/2-inch (1 cm) thick slices; place on baking sheet. Mix together oil and garlic; brush over bread. Toast in 350°F (180°C) oven for 5 minutes or until crisp.

❧ Spread about 1 tsp (5 mL) onion mixture over each round; sprinkle with remaining Parmesan. Broil for 2 to 3 minutes or until hot. Makes about 36 hors d'oeuvres.

Thai Beef Skewers

ік

*Thin slices of lean beef make a satisfying
cocktail snack. For an extra shot of flavor,
serve with peanut dipping sauce (p. 170).*

1 lb	flank, round or sirloin steak	500 g
3 tbsp	chopped fresh coriander or parsley	50 mL
2 tbsp	dry sherry or lime juice	25 mL
1 tbsp	wine vinegar	15 mL
1 tbsp	fish sauce or hoisin sauce	15 mL
1 tbsp	dark sesame oil	15 mL
1 tbsp	liquid honey	15 mL
1 tbsp	soy sauce	15 mL
1 tbsp	minced gingerroot	15 mL
1	large clove garlic, minced	1
Pinch	hot pepper flakes	Pinch

Trim fat from beef; slice beef across the grain into 1/4-inch (5 mm) thick strips.

ік In bowl, combine coriander, sherry, vinegar, fish sauce, sesame oil, honey, soy sauce, gingerroot, garlic and hot pepper flakes. Add beef, stirring to coat. Cover and marinate in refrigerator for at least 2 hours or up to 8 hours.

ік Soak wooden skewers in water for about 15 minutes to prevent scorching. Thread marinated beef strips onto skewers. Broil for 3 to 5 minutes or until browned. Makes 30 hors d'oeuvres.

*(on plate) Onion and Sun-Dried
Tomato Bruschetta (p. 80) and Thai
Beef Skewers; (above plate) white
sangria punch; Kir Fruit
Spritzers (p. 84)*

(from left) Christmas Cran-Raspberry Punch Bowl with Frozen Holly Wreath (p. 84); Double-Salmon Terrine; Guacamole Pâté with Salsa; Creamy Chèvre Dip

Guacamole Pâté with Salsa

⁂

A spicy fresh salsa tops this gently flavored avocado pâté.

1/4 oz	gelatin	
1/4 cup	cold water	50 mL
2	ripe avocados, peeled and pitted	2
1 cup	sour cream	250 mL
1/2 cup	mayonnaise	125 mL
3 tbsp	lemon juice	50 mL
1/2 tsp	salt	2 mL
1/4 tsp	pepper	1 mL
Dash	hot pepper sauce	Dash
1	clove garlic, minced	1
1	small tomato, seeded and chopped	1
1	small jalapeño pepper, seeded and finely chopped	1
1/4 cup	chopped fresh coriander or parsley	50 mL
2	green onions, finely chopped	2

Salsa

1	each tomato, sweet red pepper and jalapeño pepper, seeded and chopped	1
2 tbsp	chopped fresh coriander or parsley	25 mL
2	green onions, chopped	2
1	clove garlic, minced	1

*I*n small saucepan, sprinkle gelatin over cold water; let stand for 1 minute. Heat gently over low heat for 2 to 3 minutes or until dissolved.

⁂ In food processor, purée avocados, sour cream, mayonnaise, lemon juice, salt, pepper, hot pepper sauce and garlic until smooth; blend in dissolved gelatin. Stir in tomato, jalapeño pepper, coriander and onions.

⁂ Line 8- x 4-inch (1.5 L) loaf pan with plastic wrap; spoon in avocado mixture and cover with plastic wrap. Refrigerate for 3 hours or until set. *(Pâté can be refrigerated for up to 1 day.)*

⁂ SALSA: Combine tomato, red pepper, jalapeño pepper, coriander, onions and garlic.

⁂ Unmold pâté onto serving plate; serve in slices with some salsa spooned down center of each. Makes 10 to 12 servings.

Double-Salmon Terrine

Speckled with salmon, onion and parsley,
this rich-tasting country-style pâté is delicious
with slices of pumpernickel and French bread.

2	cans (each 7 oz/213 g) salmon, drained	2
1/2 lb	smoked salmon, diced	250 g
2 tbsp	chopped fresh parsley	25 mL
3	green onions, chopped	3
1 tsp	dried tarragon	5 mL
1/2 cup	butter, softened	125 mL
1/2 cup	mayonnaise	125 mL
1 tbsp	each Dijon mustard and lemon juice	15 mL
1/2 tsp	pepper	2 mL

Flake salmon, discarding skin and bones. In bowl, gently combine flaked and smoked salmon, parsley, onions and tarragon.

✷ In separate bowl, beat together butter, mayonnaise, mustard, lemon juice and pepper; add salmon mixture and gently combine.

✷ Line 8- x 4-inch (1.5 L) loaf pan with plastic wrap; spoon in salmon mixture and cover with plastic wrap. Refrigerate for about 3 hours or until firm. *(Terrine can be refrigerated for up to 5 days or wrapped and frozen for up to 1 month.)* Unmold and serve in slices. Makes 12 to 15 servings.

Creamy Chèvre Dip

Surround this creamy dip with a colorful bouquet
of crunchy fresh vegetable sticks — carrots,
celery, fennel, red pepper and green beans.

6 oz	chèvre (cream-style goat cheese)	175 g
1-1/2 cups	sour cream	375 mL
1	clove garlic, minced	1
1/2 tsp	crumbled dried rosemary	2 mL
1/2 tsp	dried thyme	2 mL
Dash	hot pepper sauce	Dash
3 tbsp	chopped sun-dried tomatoes	50 mL
2 tbsp	chopped fresh parsley	25 mL
2	green onions, chopped	2

In food processor or using electric mixer, blend chèvre, sour cream, garlic, rosemary, thyme and hot pepper sauce until smooth.

✷ Stir in tomatoes, parsley and onions. Taste and adjust seasoning if necessary. *(Dip can be refrigerated for up to 2 days; let stand at room temperature for 30 minutes before serving.)* Makes about 2 cups (500 mL).

Caesar Dip

Caesar leaves the salad bowl and finds a delicious new role as an appetizer. The pale green heart leaves of romaine
make great dippers, as do larger leaves, rolled lengthwise into tight cylinders.

1/3 cup	mayonnaise	75 mL
2 tbsp	lemon juice	25 mL
1 tbsp	Worcestershire sauce	15 mL
1 tsp	Dijon mustard	5 mL
1/4 tsp	pepper	1 mL
2	anchovy fillets, minced (or 1 tsp/5 mL anchovy paste)	2
Dash	hot pepper sauce	Dash
1	clove garlic, minced	1
1/4 cup	olive oil	50 mL
1/2 cup	sour cream	125 mL
1/4 cup	freshly grated Parmesan cheese	50 mL

In bowl, whisk together mayonnaise, lemon juice, Worcestershire sauce, mustard, pepper, anchovies, hot pepper sauce and garlic; gradually whisk in oil until blended.

✷ Stir in sour cream and Parmesan cheese. Taste and adjust seasoning if necessary. *(Dip can be covered and refrigerated for up to 1 day.)* Makes 1-1/4 cups (300 mL).

Christmas Cran-Raspberry Punch Bowl

❧

This ruby red showstopper is sure to please everyone. Both the spirited and nonalcoholic versions are a snap to prepare, and gorgeous to look at (see photo, p. 82).

2	cans (each 12 oz) frozen Cranberry Cocktail concentrate	2
1	can (12 oz/341 mL) frozen raspberry concentrate	1
3	bottles (each 40 oz/1.14 L) Cranberry Cocktail, chilled	3
2	bottles (each 2 L) Raspberry Ginger Ale, chilled	2
3	pkg (each 10 oz) frozen raspberries in light syrup, thawed	3
	Frozen "Holly" Wreath (recipe, this page)	

Shortly before serving, partially thaw Cranberry Cocktail concentrate and raspberry concentrate until slushy.

❧ In punch bowl, combine Cranberry Cocktail and raspberry concentrates and chilled Cranberry Cocktail.

❧ Just before serving, add chilled Raspberry Ginger Ale and raspberries in syrup, being careful to keep raspberries whole. Float Frozen "Holly" Wreath, rounded side up, on top. Makes 40 servings, each about 3/4 cup (425 mL).

VARIATION

❧ SPIRITED CRAN-RASPBERRY PUNCH: Substitute 4 bottles (each 750 mL) chilled sparkling rosé wine for the Raspberry Ginger Ale.

WHAT A GREAT IDEA!

KIR FRUIT SPRITZER

This apple juice-based spritzer, with a blush of black currant nectar (Ribena), is totally sans alcohol yet totally festive.

❧ In wine glass, stir together 2 tbsp (25 mL) black currant nectar concentrate and 1 tbsp (15 mL) each lemon juice and apple juice. Add 1/4 cup (50 mL) soda water and some crushed ice. Makes 1 serving.

Frozen "Holly" Wreath

❧

It takes a little time to make an ice ring but you'll be able to chill a punch without diluting it the way ice cubes do. Never use real holly: it is poisonous.

	Water, boiled and cooled	
	Fresh or frozen cranberries	
1	bunch fresh mint sprigs	1
2	lemons	2

In 10-inch (25 cm) ring mold, freeze 1/4 inch (5 mm) water until solid. Pour 1/8 inch (3 mm) water over top; arrange 8 clusters of 3 cranberries each around inner edge of mold and freeze until solid.

❧ Repeat with second 1/8-inch (3 mm) layer of water and berries around outer edge of mold; freeze.

❧ Repeat water layer; arrange tiny clusters of mint and single mint leaves face down among cranberry clusters to look like holly. Freeze.

❧ Using citrus stripper and working from top to bottom, cut 8 evenly spaced ridges out of rind of each lemon; cut each lemon into 8 thin slices. Pour 1/8 inch (3 mm) water into mold; arrange overlapping lemon slices all around mold, bringing slices up slightly against outer edge. Freeze.

❧ Repeat water layer; arrange solid ring of cranberries against inside edge of mold. Tuck in mint leaves, face down; freeze.

> *Tip: It's important to freeze this ring in stages so decorations don't all float to top of wreath.*

❧ Repeat, pouring in water; arrange ring of cranberries against outer edge of mold and freeze. If necessary, pour in water to top of mold; freeze. (*Ring can be stored in freezer for up to 3 days.*)

❧ To unmold, dip ring into cold water for 30 seconds; invert onto plate and unmold. Slide into punch, rounded side up. Makes 1 ring.

Tree-Trimming Fruit Punch

White grape juice adds the flavor to this refreshing nonalcoholic drink.

In large punch bowl, combine grape juice, soda water, lemon and lime slices and bitters. Gently add ice ring. Makes 30 servings, each 1/2 cup (125 mL).

1	bottle (64 oz) white grape juice, chilled	1
1	bottle (1 L) seltzer or club soda, chilled	1
1	lemon, sliced	1
1	lime, sliced	1
1 tbsp	angostura bitters	15 mL
	Ice ring	

Tip: To make a simple ice ring, pour a thin layer of water into a ring mold. Attractively arrange lemon and lime slices around ring. Freeze until firm. Cover with about 1 inch (2.5 cm) water and freeze until solid.

Moroccan Beef Stew

❧

Moroccan spices add a tasty new twist to an old favorite. Go authentic and serve with couscous or enjoy with a herbed rice pilaf. Round out the menu with a salad of mixed greens.

3 lb	chuck steak	1.5 kg
1/3 cup	all-purpose flour	75 mL
3 tbsp	vegetable oil	50 mL
1	large onion, chopped	1
3	cloves garlic, minced	3
3	large carrots, chopped	3
1	can (19 oz/540 mL) tomatoes, drained and chopped	1
1 tsp	each ground coriander and cumin	5 mL
3/4 tsp	ginger	4 mL
1/2 tsp	turmeric	2 mL
1/2 tsp	each salt and pepper	2 mL
1/4 tsp	cinnamon	1 mL
2 cups	beef stock	500 mL
2 tbsp	liquid honey	25 mL
3	cinnamon sticks	3
1 cup	each dried apricots and pitted prunes	250 mL
	Chopped fresh parsley	

*C*ut beef into 1-inch (2.5 cm) cubes; toss with 1/4 cup (50 mL) of the flour.

❧ In Dutch oven, heat half of the oil over medium heat; brown beef, in batches and adding remaining oil as necessary. Remove to bowl and set aside.

❧ To pan, add onion, garlic and carrots; cook, stirring, for 3 minutes or until softened. Stir in tomatoes, coriander, cumin, ginger, turmeric, salt, pepper and cinnamon; cook, stirring, for 30 seconds. Stir in remaining flour. Stir in stock, honey and cinnamon sticks; bring to boil.

❧ Return meat and any accumulated juices to pan; reduce heat, cover and simmer for 2-1/2 to 3 hours or until meat is just tender. Add apricots and prunes; simmer, partially covered, for 35 to 45 minutes or until fruit is tender. (*Stew can be cooled, covered and refrigerated for up to 2 days or frozen for up to 2 weeks, then thawed in refrigerator for 36 hours. Heat over low heat for 25 to 30 minutes or until heated through, stirring occasionally and adding up to 1/2 cup/125 mL additional beef stock if necessary.*) Makes 8 servings.

Herbed Seafood Casserole

A rice crust holds a delectable blend of scallops, shrimp and crab in a herbed cream sauce.

1 cup	long grain rice	250 mL
1	egg, beaten	1
1/3 cup	chopped fresh parsley	75 mL
1/3 cup	butter	75 mL
1	onion, chopped	1
3	cloves garlic, minced	3
1	large carrot, finely chopped	1
1-1/2 cups	chopped fennel or celery	375 mL
1 tbsp	chopped fresh dill (or 1-1/2 tsp/7 mL dried dillweed)	15 mL
1 tsp	each salt and pepper	5 mL
1 lb	scallops	500 g
1 lb	raw shrimp	500 g
1	pkg (7 oz/200 g) frozen crabmeat, thawed	1
1/4 cup	all-purpose flour	50 mL
1-1/2 cups	milk	375 mL
1/2 lb	cream cheese	250 g
1/4 tsp	dried thyme	1 mL

Topping

1-1/2 cups	fresh bread crumbs	375 mL
2 tbsp	butter, melted	25 mL
	Chopped fresh parsley	

In saucepan, combine rice with 2 cups (500 mL) salted water; bring to boil. Reduce heat to low, cover and simmer for 15 to 20 minutes or until tender and water is absorbed. Stir in egg and 2 tbsp (25 mL) of the parsley. Set aside.

Meanwhile, in large skillet, melt 1 tbsp (15 mL) of the butter over medium heat; cook onion, garlic, carrot and fennel, stirring occasionally, for 3 to 5 minutes or until softened. Stir in 1/2 tsp (2 mL) of the dill and 1/4 tsp (1 mL) each of the salt and pepper; transfer to large bowl.

Wipe skillet clean. Pour in 2 cups (500 mL) water and bring to gentle simmer; poach scallops until just opaque, 1 to 3 minutes. Using slotted spoon, add scallops to bowl.

Poach shrimp for about 3 minutes or until just firm and pink. Drain, reserving 1 cup (250 mL) liquid. Shell and devein shrimp; add to bowl. Chop crabmeat into bite-size chunks; add to bowl.

In same skillet, melt remaining butter over medium heat; whisk in flour and cook, whisking, for 2 minutes, without browning. Gradually whisk in reserved poaching liquid and milk; cook, stirring, for about 5 minutes or until thickened. Whisk in cream cheese, remaining dill, salt, pepper and thyme until cheese has melted. Stir into seafood mixture along with remaining parsley.

Line bottom of greased 13- x 9-inch (3.5 L) baking dish with rice; spoon seafood mixture over top. *(Recipe can be prepared to this point, cooled, covered and refrigerated for up to 2 days or frozen for up to 2 weeks, then thawed in refrigerator for 48 hours. Let stand at room temperature for 30 minutes before continuing.)*

TOPPING: Mix bread crumbs with butter; sprinkle over casserole. Bake in 325°F (160°C) oven for 40 to 50 minutes or until heated through and topping is golden and crunchy. Garnish with chopped fresh parsley. Makes 8 servings.

FREEZER FARE

Here are a few tips for any casserole or side dish that can be frozen after cooking.

FREEZING
Let cooked dish cool thoroughly in the refrigerator overnight.

When chilled, cover well with plastic wrap, then foil, and freeze.

THAWING
Place still-wrapped dish on baking sheet in refrigerator until thawed. Casserole should no longer be frosty inside and tip of a knife should glide through the food without resistance.

Once thawed, unwrap and let dish stand at room temperature for 30 minutes.

Sprinkle casserole with topping just before reheating.

In photo:
(left) Herbed Seafood Casserole; Moroccan Beef Stew

Holiday Buffet

❧

Texas Black Bean Caviar*

❧

Feta-Stuffed Mushrooms*

❧

Chicken and Shrimp Jambalaya*

❧

Salad Greens with Garlic Vinaigrette

❧

Whole Wheat Rolls

❧

Light Berry Trifle
(*recipe, p. 101*)

❧

Recipes included

SETTING A BUFFET TABLE

When there are more friends and family than places at the table, a buffet is the answer. The key to success is choosing an easy-to-serve-and-eat menu and arranging it on the table so guests can help themselves without fuss. Then, provide enough chairs, or even a few small tables, for guests to eat comfortably.

❧ Choose food that is easy to eat. Bite-size pieces and fork-only are best for guests to balance on their lap.

❧ If possible, place the serving table in the middle of the room so guests can move around it as they choose their food.

❧ Think logically about the placement of dishes, cutlery, napkins and food. Start with the stack of plates, then the main dish, already cut into serving portions. Follow with a starch dish, vegetables, salad and bread or rolls, placing appropriate serving forks and spoons beside platters

and bowls. Finish the round with any relishes or sauces, salt and pepper and, finally, cutlery and napkins.

❧ If the crowd is big, having someone helping to serve guests keeps the line moving and the food hot.

❧ Set beverages at a separate table if possible. When guests have helped themselves to the main course and the table has been cleared, set out dessert, coffee, tea, and liqueurs, if serving them.

Texas Black Bean Caviar

Serve with wedges of pita bread or Belgian endive. If using canned beans, don't soak and cook them, just warm them slightly.

3/4 cup	dried black beans (or one 14 oz/398 mL can, drained)	175 mL
3/4 cup	chunky salsa	175 mL
1/3 cup	each finely chopped sweet green and red pepper	75 mL
2 tbsp	finely chopped green onion	25 mL
1 tbsp	chopped fresh coriander (or 1/2 tsp/2 mL dried)	15 mL
1 tsp	lime juice	5 mL
1/2 tsp	salt	2 mL

*I*n saucepan, cover beans with 3 times their volume of cold water; let soak overnight. Drain and cover with same amount of fresh water; bring to boil. Reduce heat; simmer over medium-low heat for 1 hour or until tender. Drain and rinse.

In bowl, toss together warm beans, salsa, green and red pepper, onion, coriander, lime juice and salt. Makes 3 cups (1.5 L), enough for 8 servings.

Feta-Stuffed Mushrooms

This easy appetizer is low in calories and high in great taste.

30	mushrooms	30
2/3 cup	cottage cheese	150 mL
1/2 cup	finely crumbled feta cheese	125 mL
2 tbsp	chopped green onion	25 mL
1 tsp	lemon juice	5 mL
1/2 tsp	olive oil	2 mL
1/4 tsp	dried marjoram	1 mL
	Chopped fresh parsley or green onion	

*R*emove stems from mushrooms; wipe caps and set aside.

In small bowl, combine cottage cheese, feta cheese, onion, lemon juice, oil and marjoram; spoon heaping teaspoonful (5 mL) into each mushroom cap. Garnish with parsley. Makes 30 hors d'oeuvres.

Chicken and Shrimp Jambalaya

This Creole classic is an excellent choice for a lighter holiday buffet. If the crowd likes spicy food, choose a hot spicy sausage and splash in some hot pepper sauce.

1 tbsp	butter	15 mL
2 cups	each chopped onion and celery	500 mL
1	sweet green pepper, chopped	1
3 oz	smoked sausage or ham, diced	75 g
1-1/2 lb	boneless skinless chicken breasts, cubed	750 g
1	clove garlic, minced	1
2	bay leaves	2
2 tsp	dried oregano	10 mL
1 tsp	dried thyme	5 mL
1/2 tsp	each salt, cayenne and black pepper	2 mL
1	can (28 oz/796 mL) tomatoes (undrained)	1
1	can (7-1/2 oz/213 mL) tomato sauce	1
4 cups	chicken stock	1 L
2-1/2 cups	parboiled rice	625 mL
1 lb	raw shrimp	500 g
1	sweet red pepper, chopped	1
1/2 cup	each chopped green onions and fresh parsley	125 mL

*I*n Dutch oven, heat butter over medium-high heat; cook onion and celery for 3 minutes. Add green pepper, sausage, chicken, garlic, bay leaves, oregano, thyme, salt, cayenne and black pepper; cook, stirring, for 2 minutes.

Add tomatoes, tomato sauce and chicken stock; bring to boil. Stir in rice and shrimp; boil for 1 minute.

Bake, covered, in 350°F (180°C) oven for 25 minutes or until rice is tender. Discard bay leaves. Stir in red pepper and green onions; sprinkle with parsley. (*Jambalaya can be cooled, covered and refrigerated for up to 1 day. To reheat, stir in 1 cup/250 mL hot water; bake, covered, in 350°F/180°C oven for 1 hour and 15 minutes.*) Makes 8 servings.

In photo:
Chicken and Shrimp Jambalaya

Holiday Family Dinner

❦

Butternut Squash Soup

❦

Fruit-Stuffed Pork Loin

❦

Celebration Coleslaw

❦

Oven-Roasted Rosemary
Potatoes

❦

Eggnog Cheesecake
(recipe, p. 104)

Fruit-Stuffed Pork Loin

❦

*Pork is an excellent choice for a holiday family dinner.
Stuffed with orange- and ginger-accented dried fruit, the
glazed roast slices beautifully and appeals to all ages.*

3/4 cup	each chopped pitted prunes and dried apricots	175 mL
1 tbsp	grated gingerroot	15 mL
1 tsp	grated orange rind	5 mL
1-1/2 tsp	ground cumin	7 mL
1/2 tsp	cinnamon	2 mL
	Salt and pepper	
4 lb	boneless pork loin roast	2 kg
1/4 cup	packed brown sugar	50 mL
2 tsp	all-purpose flour	10 mL
2 tsp	cider vinegar	10 mL
1 tsp	dry mustard	5 mL
1 tsp	cornstarch	5 mL

*I*n bowl, combine prunes, apricots, gingerroot, orange rind, 1/2 tsp (2 mL) of the cumin, cinnamon, and salt and pepper to taste.

❦ Open out roast; spoon stuffing down center. Fold meat over and tie with kitchen string. Place on rack in roasting pan.

❦ Combine sugar, flour, vinegar, mustard and remaining cumin; spread over roast.

❦ Bake in 325°F (160°C) oven for 1-1/2 hours or until meat thermometer inserted into meat registers 160°F (70°C). Transfer roast to platter; tent with foil.

❦ Skim off fat in roasting pan; pour pan juices into saucepan and set aside.

❦ Add 1/2 cup (125 mL) water to roasting pan; cook over high heat, stirring to scrape up brown bits from bottom of pan. Pour into saucepan; bring to boil over medium-high heat.

❦ Mix cornstarch with 1 tbsp (15 mL) water; add to saucepan and cook, stirring, for 1 minute. Strain into gravy boat and serve with roast. Makes 8 servings.

Butternut Squash Soup

The velvety texture of this deep-orange soup suggest oodles of cream. Surprise! Yogurt and the squash deliver all the smoothness.

6 cups	cubed peeled butternut squash	1.5 L
3-1/2 cups	chicken stock	875 mL
1-1/2 cups	chopped onions	375 mL
1	bay leaf	1
1/2 tsp	nutmeg	2 mL
	Salt and pepper	
1 cup	plain yogurt	250 mL

In large saucepan, combine squash, stock, onions and bay leaf; bring to boil. Cover and reduce heat to low; simmer for about 20 minutes or until squash is tender. Remove bay leaf.

❧ In blender or food processor, purée soup in batches until smooth. Return to pan and reheat if necessary; season with nutmeg, and salt and pepper to taste. *(Soup can be cooled and frozen for up to 2 months; thaw and reheat.)*

❧ To serve, ladle into soup bowls; swirl 2 tbsp (25 mL) yogurt into each. Makes 8 servings, each about 3/4 cup (175 mL).

Oven-Roasted Rosemary Potatoes

Olive oil and dried rosemary add a lively Mediterranean touch to a simple yet satisfying dish.

3	large sweet potatoes	3
3	large Yukon gold potatoes	3
1/2 cup	water	125 mL
2 tbsp	olive oil	25 mL
2 tsp	dried rosemary	10 mL

Peel potatoes; cut into 1/8-inch (3 mm) thick slices.

❧ In 13- x 9-inch (3.5 L) baking dish, pack sweet and white potatoes tightly in alternating rows; sprinkle evenly with water. Drizzle with half of the oil; sprinkle with rosemary.

❧ Cover with foil and bake in 325°F (160°C) oven for 1 hour and 10 minutes. Uncover and baste with remaining oil; broil for 3 to 5 minutes or until crisp and browned. Makes 8 servings.

Celebration Coleslaw

When planning a get-together, it's nice to know that most of the dishes can be finished in the quiet time before guests arrive — like this colorful slaw that can be made up to one day ahead.

5	carrots	5
3 cups	cauliflower florets	750 mL
12 cups	finely shredded red and green cabbage	3 L
1 cup	chopped green onions	250 mL
1/2 cup	chopped fresh parsley	125 mL
1/3 cup	granulated sugar	75 mL
3/4 cup	cider vinegar	175 mL
1/3 cup	vegetable oil	75 mL
1 tbsp	dried tarragon	15 mL
2 tsp	dried basil	10 mL
1 tsp	salt	5 mL
1/2 tsp	pepper	2 mL

Cut carrots into 2- x 1/8-inch (5 cm x 3 mm) strips to make about 2 cups (500 mL).

❧ In saucepan of boiling water, cook carrots and cauliflower for 2 to 3 minutes or until tender-crisp. Drain and cool under cold water; drain again and pat dry.

❧ In large bowl, combine carrots, cauliflower, cabbage, green onions, parsley and sugar; cover and refrigerate for at least 1 hour or up to 8 hours.

❧ In small saucepan, combine vinegar, oil, tarragon, basil, salt and pepper; bring to boil. Pour over salad and toss well. Cover salad and marinate in refrigerator for at least 2 hours or up to 1 day. Makes 8 servings.

WHAT A GREAT IDEA!

DRESS UP A SOUP

Here's a chef's trick that's easy to do at home. Buy some inexpensive ketchup or mustard squirt bottles and fill with liquidy ingredients you can "paint" on food.

❧ For example, for the Butternut Squash Soup (this page) or the Quick Beet Soup with Yogurt (p. 93), fill the squirt bottle with yogurt and draw an attractive design over each bowlful. It's quick — and impressive!

Fireside Dinner Party

❧

Quick Beet Soup with Yogurt*

❧

Endive Salad

❧

Cornish Hens with Lemon and
Couscous*

❧

Spinach Timbales*

❧

Puréed Gingered Squash

❧

Irish Cream Parfaits
(recipe, p. 101)

*Recipes included

Spinach Timbales

❧

Spinach molded in muffin tins adds pizzazz to the holiday table.

3	pkg (each 10 oz) frozen spinach, thawed	3
3	eggs	3
2/3 cups	light cream	150 mL
1/2 cup	garlic-and-herb cream cheese	125 mL
2 tbsp	Dijon mustard	25 mL
1/2 tsp	salt	2 mL
1/4 tsp	hot pepper sauce	1 mL
	Sweet yellow and red pepper triangles	

*L*ine bottoms of 8 greased muffin cups with circles of waxed paper. Set aside.

❧ Squeeze out excess moisture from spinach. In blender or food processor, purée spinach, eggs, cream, cream cheese, mustard, salt and hot pepper sauce until smooth. *(Recipe can be prepared to this point, covered and refrigerated for up to 1 day.)*

❧ Spoon spinach mixture into muffin cups; place pan in larger pan and pour in enough hot water to come halfway up cups. Bake in 375°F (190°C) oven for 20 to 25 minutes or until firm to the touch.

❧ Remove from larger pan and let cool for 5 minutes. Run knife around timbales and invert onto serving plate; peel off paper. Garnish with yellow and red pepper. Makes 8 servings.

Quick Beet Soup with Yogurt

*Canned beets are a handy cupboard ingredient
and perfect for this modern borscht.*

2 tbsp	olive oil	25 mL
1	onion, finely chopped	1
2	cloves garlic, minced	2
2	cans (each 14 oz/398 mL) sliced beets (undrained)	2
1	can (14 oz/398 mL) tomatoes	1
1	can (10 oz/284 mL) beef broth	1
1 cup	water	250 mL
2 tbsp	apple cider vinegar or cider vinegar	25 mL
1 tsp	caraway seeds	5 mL
	Salt and pepper	
1/2 cup	plain yogurt	125 mL

*I*n large heavy saucepan, heat oil over medium-high heat; cook onion and garlic, stirring, for 3 minutes or until softened.

❧ Stir in beets, tomatoes, beef broth, water, vinegar and caraway seeds; bring to boil. Reduce heat to medium-low; cover and simmer for 15 minutes.

❧ In blender or food processor, purée soup in batches until smooth. Return to pan and reheat if necessary; season with salt and pepper to taste. *(Soup can be cooled and frozen for up to 1 month; thaw and reheat.)*

❧ To serve, ladle into soup bowls; swirl 1 tbsp (15 mL) yogurt into each. Makes 8 servings.

Cornish Hens with Lemon and Couscous

Even though Cornish hens are surprisingly easy to prepare, they still make a spectacular entrée for a special dinner party.

4 cups	chicken stock	1 L
1/4 cup	olive oil	50 mL
3 tbsp	grated lemon rind	50 mL
2-1/2 cups	couscous	625 mL
1/3 cup	finely chopped fresh parsley	75 mL
4	Cornish hens (each 1-1/4 lb/625 g)	4
	Salt and pepper	
1/3 cup	lemon marmalade	75 mL
2 tbsp	Dijon mustard	25 mL

*I*n large saucepan, combine chicken stock, oil and 4 tsp (20 mL) of the lemon rind; bring to boil. Add couscous; cover and remove from heat. Let stand for 5 minutes. Add parsley; fluff with fork. *(Couscous can be covered and refrigerated for up to 1 day.)*

❧ Meanwhile, cut wing tips from hens. Cut through backbones to divide hens in half; trim excess fat and skin. Gently loosen skin from each breast and leg, leaving skin attached at one side; rub remaining lemon rind over flesh under skin.

❧ Evenly space 8 mounds of couscous, 1 cup (250 mL) each, on lightly greased rimmed baking sheet; cover with hen halves, cut sides down. Sprinkle lightly with salt and pepper.

❧ Mix marmalade with mustard; brush over hens. Bake in 375°F (190°C) oven for 40 to 45 minutes or until browned, juices run clear when hens are pierced with fork, and meat thermometer registers 185°F (85°C). Makes 8 servings.

I'M DREAMING OF A SWEET CHRISTMAS

❧

IF DREAMS ARE SWEET, THESE CHRISTMAS DREAMS
ARE THE SWEETEST OF ALL — WITH LUSCIOUS TRIFLES, CREAMY CHEESECAKES,
CHOCOLATE DELIGHTS... AND MUCH MORE!

Chocolate Raspberry Ice-Cream Cake

❧

This spectacular layered cake can be made up to two weeks ahead — ready and waiting in the freezer for a special holiday dinner. Even the chocolate curls can be made in advance.

3 cups	chocolate ice cream	750 mL
2	pkg (each 10 oz) IQF (individually quick-frozen) raspberries	2
1/4 cup	raspberry liqueur or schnapps	50 mL
2 tbsp	granulated sugar	25 mL
6 cups	vanilla ice cream	1.5 L
	Chocolate curls (see p. 98)	

Crust

1-1/2 cups	chocolate wafer crumbs	375 mL
2 oz	semisweet chocolate, chopped	60 g
1/4 cup	butter, melted	50 mL
2 tbsp	granulated sugar	25 mL

CRUST: Stir together crumbs, chocolate, butter and sugar until well moistened. Press onto bottom of 9-inch (2.5 L) springform pan. Bake in 350°F (180°C) oven for 10 minutes. Let cool.

❧ Line inside of pan above crust with double thickness waxed paper extending 2 inches (5 cm) above pan and overlapping by 1 inch (2.5 cm). Tape or staple top edges together.

❧ Let chocolate ice cream stand at room temperature for 10 to 15 minutes or until softened; stir until smooth. Spread over crust and freeze.

❧ Meanwhile, reserve 24 raspberries in freezer for garnish. Cut 1 cup (250 mL) of the remaining berries in half; set aside in freezer. Thaw remaining berries and purée in food processor; press through sieve into bowl to remove seeds. Stir in raspberry liqueur and sugar.

❧ Soften 3 cups (750 mL) of the vanilla ice cream; stir in halved raspberries and 1-1/2 cups (375 mL) of the purée. Spread over chocolate layer and freeze for 1 hour.

❧ Soften remaining vanilla ice cream; spread over raspberry layer, smoothing top. Freeze for 15 minutes. Spread remaining purée over top; freeze until solid. (*Cake can be wrapped and stored in freezer for up to 2 weeks.*)

❧ Garnish with chocolate curls and reserved frozen raspberries. Let stand in refrigerator for 1-1/2 hours before serving. Makes about 12 servings.

*(left) Chocolate Raspberry Ice-Cream Cake;
Lemon Semifreddo (p. 97)*

IQF BERRIES

IQF is the answer to having frozen berries that not only taste as good as summer fresh, but also look good enough to use as an ingredient and garnish. IQF stands for "individually quick-frozen" and works particularly well with raspberries and blueberries.

❧ To make your own during berry season, arrange dry berries in single layer on tray; freeze until solid.

❧ Arrange in freezer bags or rigid-sided airtight containers and store in freezer where they will not be crushed.

Raspberry Cream Torte

❧

Round wafer cookies, layered with whipped cream and raspberry sauce, make a lavish entertaining dessert — especially at Christmas. To garnish the torte, cover the top wafer with a doily and dust with icing sugar to create a pretty pattern. Top with just-thawed or fresh berries.

2 cups	whipping cream	500 mL
1/3 cup	icing sugar	75 mL

Wafers

6	egg whites	6
1-1/2 cups	granulated sugar	375 mL
1 cup	all-purpose flour	250 mL
3/4 cup	unsalted butter, melted	175 mL
2 tbsp	water	25 mL
1 tbsp	vanilla	15 mL

Raspberry Sauce

2	pkg (each 10 oz) unsweetened raspberries, thawed	2
1/2 cup	instant dissolving (fruit/berry) sugar	125 mL
2 tsp	raspberry liqueur (optional)	10 mL

WAFERS: Trace two 8-inch (20 cm) circles on each of two pieces of parchment paper; invert and place on baking sheets.

❧ In large bowl, lightly whisk egg whites; gradually whisk in sugar, flour, butter, water and vanilla just until blended. Drop 1/3 cup (75 mL) batter onto each circle; gently spread to cover circle.

❧ Bake one sheet at a time in upper half of 400°F (200°C) oven for 8 to 10 minutes or until edges are just beginning to brown; let cool on baking sheet on rack for 2 minutes.

❧ Using metal spatula, transfer wafers to flat surface; let cool completely. Repeat with remaining batter to make 9 wafers. *(Wafers can be layered between waxed paper in airtight container and stored for up to 2 days.)*

❧ RASPBERRY SAUCE: In food processor or blender, purée raspberries until smooth; press through sieve into bowl to remove seeds. Whisk in sugar, and liqueur (if using). *(Sauce can be covered and refrigerated for up to 3 days.)*

❧ In bowl, whip cream with icing sugar. Place one wafer on serving plate; spread with 1/2 cup (125 mL) of the whipped cream. Drizzle with 1/4 cup (50 mL) of the raspberry sauce. Repeat layering with remaining wafers, cream and sauce. Top with remaining wafer.

❧ Cover and refrigerate for 1-1/2 to 2 hours or until wafers have softened just enough to cut into wedges. Makes 8 servings.

Lemon Semifreddo

A dome of cake holds a lusciously tart lemon cream filling that's served ice-cream cold. Garnish with candied violets (available in cake decorating shops) and a lemon zest bow (see below).

6	eggs, separated	6
1 cup	granulated sugar	250 mL
1 tbsp	grated lemon rind	15 mL
1 cup	sifted cake-and-pastry flour	250 mL
1/2 cup	ground almonds	125 mL

Lemon Syrup

1/3 cup	lemon juice	75 mL
1/4 cup	granulated sugar	50 mL

Lemon Filling

3	eggs, beaten	3
1 cup	granulated sugar	250 mL
1/2 cup	lemon juice	125 mL
1/4 cup	butter	50 mL
2 cups	whipping cream	500 mL

Topping

1-1/2 cups	whipping cream	375 mL
1/2 cup	sliced almonds, toasted (see p. 30)	125 mL

In large bowl and using electric mixer, beat egg yolks with 1/2 cup (125 mL) of the sugar and lemon rind for 6 to 8 minutes or until very pale and thickened.

In separate bowl and with clean beaters, beat egg whites until soft peaks form; gradually beat in remaining sugar until stiff peaks form.

Stir together flour and ground almonds. Fold one-third of the egg whites, then one-third of the flour mixture, into yolk mixture; repeat twice. Pour into greased and floured 10-inch (3 L) springform pan.

Bake in 350°F (180°C) oven for 25 to 30 minutes or until cake tester inserted near center comes out clean. Run knife around edge of cake. Let cool in pan on rack.

LEMON SYRUP: In saucepan, heat lemon juice with sugar until dissolved, stirring occasionally; set aside.

LEMON FILLING: In small heavy nonaluminum saucepan, combine eggs, sugar, lemon juice and butter; cook over low heat, stirring, for 15 to 20 minutes or until mixture coats spoon thickly. Transfer to bowl; place waxed paper directly on surface and refrigerate until chilled. Whip cream; fold into lemon mixture.

ASSEMBLY: Slice cake horizontally into three layers. Line 10-cup (2.5 L) bowl with plastic wrap, then fit in top layer of cake, cut side up. Trim off 1-inch (2.5 cm) strip around middle layer; place strip around edge over cake in bowl to meet rim.

Brush cake with one-third of the lemon syrup. Spoon in about one-third of the lemon filling; cover with middle layer of cake. Brush with one-third of the syrup; spoon in remaining filling. Top with third layer, cut side down, trimming if necessary to fit; brush with remaining lemon syrup. Cover with plastic wrap and refrigerate for at least 8 hours or up to 1 day.

TOPPING: Uncover cake and invert onto serving plate. Remove plastic wrap. Whip cream and spread over cake. Garnish bottom edge with toasted almonds. Freeze overnight or until solid. (*Semifreddo can be wrapped and stored in freezer for up to 2 weeks.*)

To serve, let stand in refrigerator for 4 hours to partially thaw. Makes 12 servings.

WHAT A GREAT IDEA!

LEMON ZEST BOWS

Pretty citrus peel garnishes add a sophisticated touch to any large lemon dessert.

With a stripper (cannel knife) and starting at blossom end of lemon, cut strip of yellow peel (zest) all around the lemon in spirals to get the maximum length. Tie loosely in bow.

To make neat strip with paring knife, peel lemon thinly in the same spiral fashion; trim edges of peel. Tie loosely in bow.

Zest bows can be wrapped in wet cloth and plastic bag and refrigerated for up to 4 hours.

Black Forest Trifle

*Red sour cherries are the secret to the great tart
taste of this sensational dessert.*

1	Chocolate Cake (recipe follows)	1
1/3 cup	chocolate liqueur, kirsch or cherry liqueur	75 mL
4 cups	drained canned cherries or drained thawed frozen cherries	1 L
1 cup	whipping cream	250 mL
2 tbsp	icing sugar	25 mL
1 tsp	vanilla	5 mL
	Chocolate curls (see below)	

Custard

3 cups	milk	750 mL
5	egg yolks	5
1/2 cup	granulated sugar	125 mL
1/4 cup	cornstarch	50 mL
1 tsp	vanilla	5 mL

CUSTARD: In saucepan, heat milk just until bubbles form
around edge. In heavy saucepan, beat egg yolks with sugar and
cornstarch until smooth; gradually whisk in milk. Cook over
medium heat, stirring constantly, for 3 to 5 minutes or until
thickened. Reduce heat to low and simmer, stirring, for
1 minute. Strain into bowl; stir in vanilla. Place plastic wrap
directly on surface; refrigerate until cooled or for up to 2 days.

❧ Break chocolate cake into chunks; arrange in bottom of
14-cup (3.5 L) trifle bowl. Drizzle with chocolate liqueur. Set
1/4 cup (50 mL) cherries aside; spoon in remaining cherries,
arranging attractively around side of bowl. Spoon in custard.
*(Trifle can be prepared to this point, covered and refrigerated for up
to 1 day.)*

❧ Whip cream with icing sugar; beat in vanilla. Spread over
trifle. Garnish with chocolate curls and reserved cherries. Makes
12 servings.

Chocolate Cake

1/2 cup	butter, softened	125 mL
1-1/3 cups	granulated sugar	325 mL
2	eggs	2
1 tsp	vanilla	5 mL
1-1/3 cups	all-purpose flour	325 mL
1/2 cup	sifted unsweetened cocoa powder	125 mL
1/2 tsp	baking powder	2 mL
1/2 tsp	baking soda	2 mL
1/4 tsp	salt	1 mL
3/4 cup	milk	175 mL

Line bottom of 9-inch (1.5 L) round cake pan with waxed
paper. Grease side.

❧ In large bowl, beat butter with sugar until fluffy; beat in eggs,
one at a time. Beat in vanilla. Stir together flour, cocoa, baking
powder, baking soda and salt. Add to creamed mixture alternately with milk, making three additions of flour mixture and
two of milk. Pour into pan.

❧ Bake in 350°F (180°C) oven for 30 to 35 minutes or until
cake tester inserted into center comes out clean. Let cool in
pan on rack for 10 minutes; turn out onto rack to let cool
completely. Makes 1 cake.

MAKING CHOCOLATE CURLS

Chocolate curls are an impressive
finishing touch for any dessert.
Here are several ways to make them.

WITH SQUARES OF CHOCOLATE

❧ The secret is warming the
chocolate to the right temperature,
and having enough chocolate. You
will need about 5 oz (150 g) to cover
the top of a 9-inch (23 cm) cake,
cream pie or other dessert.

❧ Microwave chocolate, 1-oz (30 g)
square at a time, at High for 30
seconds. Or, handhold wrapped square
for about 1 minute or until softened
but not melted.

❧ Hold the chocolate firmly and
use firm, even pressure. For wide curls,
slowly draw a vegetable peeler along
the underside of square; for smaller
curls, draw peeler along the
narrow side.

ON BAKING SHEETS

❧ Melt chocolate and spread evenly
and thinly with palette knife onto
clean baking sheet. Refrigerate until
set but not hard, about 5 minutes,
letting warm again at room
temperature if necessary.

❧ For small curls, hold spoon at

30° angle and scrape across chocolate
toward you, forming curls. For large
curls, scrape a knife or scraper across
chocolate in opposite direction,
forming curls of desired width.

GRATED CURLS

❧ These are the easiest to make, and
are especially pretty on chilled
desserts. You get the longest curls if
you use a large block of chocolate.

❧ Let block soften at room
temperature for about 1 hour before
grating. Use firm, even pressure and
grate long side of chocolate block
against coarse side of grater.

Raspberry Tiramisu

Whenever tiramisu, a superlative Italian trifle, is served, a silence of pleasure descends on the table as guests dip their spoons into layers of rich Italian cream cheese (mascarpone), whipped cream and espresso-soaked ladyfingers. Truly a dessert made in heaven!

2	pkg (each 10 oz) frozen unsweetened raspberries	2
2	tubs (each 8 oz) mascarpone or cream cheese	2
1/2 cup	granulated sugar	125 mL
2	egg yolks	2
1/4 cup	brandy	50 mL
1 tbsp	lemon juice	15 mL
1-1/2 tsp	vanilla	7 mL
1-1/2 cups	whipping cream	375 mL
2	pkg small soft ladyfingers, halved (or 1 pound cake, thinly sliced)	2
1 tbsp	(approx) unsweetened cocoa powder	15 mL
	Chocolate decorations (see below)	
1/2 cup	fresh raspberries	125 mL

In colander set over bowl, thaw raspberries, reserving juice; set aside.

❧ In large bowl, beat mascarpone with sugar. In separate bowl set over hot (not boiling) water, beat egg yolks with clean beaters for 5 minutes or until pale and thickened; beat into mascarpone mixture.

❧ Stir in brandy, lemon juice and vanilla. Whip 1/2 cup (125 mL) of the cream; fold into mascarpone mixture.

❧ Line bottom of 8-cup (2 L) glass trifle bowl with 12 ladyfinger halves; brush well with about 3 tbsp (50 mL) reserved raspberry juice. Spread with one-quarter of the mascarpone mixture. Sift 1 tsp (5 mL) of the cocoa over top. Sprinkle with one-third of the thawed raspberries, pressing some against glass to show through.

❧ Repeat mascarpone, cocoa and raspberry layers twice. Line bowl with remaining 12 ladyfinger halves; brush with juice and top with remaining mascarpone mixture. Cover lightly and refrigerate for at least 4 hours or overnight.

❧ Whip remaining 1 cup (250 mL) cream; mound over trifle, leaving rim of mascarpone mixture visible. Dust rim lightly with more sifted cocoa powder. Garnish with chocolate decorations, fresh raspberries, and gold dragées and rose geranium leaves, if desired. Makes 8 to 10 servings.

Tip: To make chocolate decorations, line baking sheet with waxed or parchment paper. Pipe 2 oz (60 g) melted semisweet chocolate onto sheets in festive decorations, such as stars, miniature Christmas trees or holly leaves. Refrigerate for 15 minutes or until firm. Slide thin sharp knife under decorations and transfer to top of trifle.

CHILLED CHESTNUT MOUSSE

For carefree holiday entertaining, serve this delicious make-ahead dessert. Look for cans of unsweetened chestnut purée in delis, specialty food shops and some supermarkets.

❧ In large bowl, beat one 15-oz (435 g) can of unsweetened chestnut purée until smooth; gradually beat in 1 cup (250 mL) icing sugar, 1/4 cup (50 mL) orange liqueur or frozen orange juice concentrate and 1 tsp (5 mL) vanilla. Set aside.

❧ Whip 2 cups (500 mL) whipping cream; fold into chestnut mixture. Spoon or pipe into eight 3/4-cup (175 mL) dessert dishes or wine glasses. Cover and refrigerate for at least 1 hour or until set. (Mousse can be refrigerated for up to 2 days or frozen for up to 1 week; transfer to refrigerator 3 hours before serving.) Garnish with more whipped cream, if desired. Makes 8 servings.

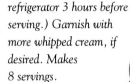

Christmas Custard with Fruit

❧

For a trifle without the cake, layer a silky smooth custard with raspberries and fragrant kiwifruit.

2/3 cup	granulated sugar	150 mL
1 tbsp	cornstarch	15 mL
Pinch	salt	Pinch
2 cups	milk	500 mL
2 cups	light cream	500 mL
3	eggs	3
6	egg yolks	6
1 tsp	vanilla	5 mL
1	pkg (10 oz) IQF raspberries (see p. 94)	1
3	kiwifruit	3
1/2 cup	whipping cream, whipped (optional)	125 mL

In large heavy saucepan, blend sugar, cornstarch and salt; whisk in milk and light cream. Bring to simmer over medium heat, stirring constantly; cook, stirring constantly, for 2 minutes or until slightly thickened. Reduce heat to low.

❧ In bowl, beat eggs with egg yolks; whisk in 1 cup (250 mL) of the hot milk mixture, then return to pan. Cook, whisking constantly, for about 4 minutes or until thickened and smooth. Strain into bowl. Stir in vanilla; let cool. (Custard can be covered with plastic wrap directly on surface and refrigerated for up to 2 days.)

❧ About 3 hours before serving, thaw raspberries, reserving any juice for another use. Set 15 aside on paper towel for garnish. Peel and slice kiwifruit; set 12 slices aside for garnish.

❧ In 8-cup (2 L) glass bowl, layer custard with raspberries and kiwifruit, finishing with custard. Decoratively garnish with reserved raspberries and kiwifruit. Pipe or spoon whipped cream (if using) among fruit. Makes 8 servings.

KIWIFRUIT

Kiwifruit, once exotic and expensive, have become more affordable recently and their perfumy flavor has earned the fuzzy-skinned fruit a regular spot in produce sections of supermarkets. Kiwifruit are great to eat out of hand and, because of their bright color, make a grand ingredient for holiday desserts.

❧ Choose kiwifruit a few days before serving and let them ripen, preferably enclosed in a paper bag, at cool room temperature out of sunlight. Kiwifruit now come to us from as near as British Columbia and California, and as far away as New Zealand and Italy.

Light Berry Trifle

We lightened this Christmas favorite by using angel food cake and a custard with 2% milk and fewer egg yolks. Even without the whipped cream topping, you'll still have a pleasing holiday trifle.

1	angel food cake or light pound cake	1
1/2 cup	dry sherry or raspberry juice	125 mL
1	pkg (10 oz) each frozen unsweetened blueberries and raspberries, thawed and drained	1
	Fresh mint	

Custard Sauce

3/4 cup	granulated sugar	175 mL
1/3 cup	cornstarch	75 mL
Pinch	salt	Pinch
4 cups	2% milk	1 L
4	egg yolks, beaten	4
2 tsp	vanilla	10 mL
Pinch	nutmeg	Pinch

CUSTARD SAUCE: In heavy saucepan, combine sugar, cornstarch and salt; stir in milk. Bring to boil over medium heat, stirring; cook for about 2 minutes, stirring constantly, or until slightly thickened.

❧ Whisk about 1/2 cup (125 mL) of the milk mixture into egg yolks; whisk yolks back into saucepan. Cook, stirring, over low heat for about 1 minute or until thickened. Strain into bowl. Stir in vanilla and nutmeg. Place plastic wrap directly on surface; refrigerate for at least 2 hours or up to 2 days.

❧ Cut cake into 1-inch (2.5 cm) thick slices. Line bottom of 10-cup (2.5 L) glass bowl with half of the cake; sprinkle with half of the sherry and all the blueberries. Repeat cake and sherry layers; spoon on half of the custard.

❧ Reserve 1/4 cup (50 mL) raspberries. Sprinkle remaining raspberries over custard; spoon on remaining custard. Refrigerate for at least 2 hours or up to 4 hours. Just before serving, garnish with reserved raspberries and mint. Makes 12 servings.

Christmas Pavlova

Crisp on the outside and meltingly soft on the inside, this holiday pavlova is smothered with whipped cream and fancied up with the season's colors — red strawberries and green kiwifruit.

6	egg whites	6
1/4 tsp	salt	1 mL
1/4 tsp	cream of tartar	1 mL
1-1/2 cups	granulated sugar	375 mL
2 tbsp	cornstarch	25 mL
1 tbsp	vinegar	15 mL
1-1/2 tsp	vanilla	7 mL
1-1/2 cups	whipping cream	375 mL
1 cup	raspberries or strawberries	250 mL
2	kiwifruit, sliced	2

Line baking sheet with parchment paper. Place bottomless 8-inch (2 L) or 9-inch (2.5 L) springform pan on top; set aside.

❧ In bowl, beat egg whites, salt and cream of tartar until soft peaks form. Gradually beat in sugar in thin steady stream until stiff glossy peaks form. Fold in cornstarch, vinegar and vanilla.

❧ Spoon batter into prepared pan; smooth top. Bake in 275°F (140°C) oven for 2 to 2-1/2 hours or until crisp and lightly browned on outside but still soft in middle. Let cool completely (meringue will deflate). Run knife around meringue; remove pan. Carefully remove paper. *(Meringue can be loosely covered and stored for up to 3 days.)*

❧ Remove loose bits from meringue. Whip cream; spread over top of meringue, swirling into peaks. Garnish with raspberries and kiwifruit. Makes 6 to 8 servings.

WHAT A GREAT IDEA!

IRISH CREAM PARFAITS

These easy parfaits are impressive, always pleasing and, best of all — make-ahead!

❧ With fork, drizzle some chocolate sauce from one 8-oz (250 mL) jar onto insides of eight 8-oz (250 mL) parfait glasses; freeze for 10 to 15 minutes or until slightly hardened.

❧ Using 6 cups (1.5 L) softened coffee ice cream, divide half among glasses; drizzle each with 1 tbsp (15 mL) sauce. Repeat with remaining ice cream and sauce. Freeze for 1 hour or until firm. (Parfaits can be frozen for up to 2 days. Let soften in refrigerator for about 20 minutes before garnishing.)

❧ In bowl, whip 1 cup (250 mL) whipping cream with 1/4 cup (50 mL) Irish cream liqueur; spoon over parfaits. Sprinkle with 1 oz (30 g) grated semisweet chocolate.

Makes 8 servings.

Holiday Eggnog Pudding

Rum-spiked eggnog, jelled in a pretty mold and garnished with whipped cream, makes a soothing melt-in-your-mouth dessert.

3/4 oz	unflavored gelatin	3/4 oz
1/4 cup	packed brown sugar	50 mL
1 cup	boiling water	250 mL
1 cup	ice water	250 mL
1 tbsp	rum	15 mL
2 cups	commercial eggnog	500 mL
	Whipped cream	

*I*n large bowl, combine gelatin and brown sugar; stir in boiling water until gelatin is dissolved. Stir in ice water and rum; refrigerate until chilled and thickened enough to mound when dropped from spoon.

❧ Beat at medium speed until light and fluffy; gradually beat in eggnog in thin steady stream.

❧ Rinse 4-cup (1 L) pudding mold with cold water but do not dry; pour in eggnog mixture. Cover with plastic wrap and refrigerate until firm, about 4 hours, or overnight.

❧ Invert onto serving plate; cover mold with hot damp tea towel and shake gently until pudding is released. Garnish with whipped cream. Makes 6 to 8 servings.

Zesty Lemon Mousse

Lemon mousse, served in pretty parfait glasses (photo above), is a refreshing finish to a satisfying dinner. For a larger gathering, make two batches of the recipe.

1	pkg (7 g) unflavored gelatin	1
1/4 cup	cold water	50 mL
1 tbsp	grated lemon rind	15 mL
1/2 cup	lemon juice	125 mL
1 cup	granulated sugar	250 mL
2/3 cup	plain yogurt	150 mL
1 cup	whipping cream	250 mL

*I*n saucepan, sprinkle gelatin over cold water; let stand for 1 minute to soften. Stir over low heat until gelatin dissolves. Stir in lemon rind, lemon juice and half of the sugar. Stir in yogurt.

❧ In bowl, whip cream with remaining sugar; fold into lemon mixture. Spoon into parfait glasses or serving dish. Cover and refrigerate for 2 hours or up to 1 day. Makes 6 to 8 servings.

HONEY-GINGER BAKED APPLES

Serve this comfy dessert with whipped cream or Easy Yogurt Topping (this page).

* In saucepan, heat 1/2 cup (125 mL) liquid honey and 1 tbsp (15 mL) chopped gingerroot over medium heat until boiling. Score line around 6 cored apples about one-third from top. Place in 8-inch (2 L) square baking dish. Mix together 1/2 cup (125 mL) golden raisins and 2 tbsp (25 mL) chopped crystallized ginger; spoon into centers of apples. Top each with 1/2 tsp (2 mL) butter; pour honey mixture over top. Bake in 375°F (190°C) oven, basting twice, for 45 to 50 minutes or until tender. Makes 6 servings.

Appleberry Crisp

In the dessert world of seasonal indulgence, it comes as a sigh of relief to be served a bowl of old-fashioned crisp, with a scoop of vanilla ice cream melting enticingly into the crunchy topping and tender fruit.

5 cups	sliced peeled cored apples	1.25 L
1 cup	each frozen raspberries and blueberries	250 mL
1 tbsp	packed brown sugar	15 mL
1 tbsp	all-purpose flour	15 mL
	Topping	
1/2 cup	packed brown sugar	125 mL
1/2 cup	all-purpose flour	125 mL
1/2 cup	rolled oats	125 mL
1 tsp	cinnamon	5 mL
1 tsp	finely grated orange rind	5 mL
1/4 cup	butter, softened	50 mL
1/3 cup	chopped hazelnuts	75 mL

*I*n buttered 8-inch (2 L) square baking dish, toss together apples, raspberries, blueberries, sugar and flour; set aside.

* TOPPING: In bowl, combine sugar, flour, rolled oats, cinnamon and orange rind. With pastry blender or fingertips, work in butter until crumbly; sprinkle over fruit. Sprinkle with hazelnuts.

* Bake in 350°F (180°C) oven for 45 to 50 minutes or until browned and fruit is fork-tender. Makes 4 to 6 servings.

Pear Mincemeat Crumble

Mincemeat turns an ordinary dessert into a festive finale. This crumble is so delicious you won't want to save it just for Christmas!

4 cups	sliced peeled pears (about 5)	1 L
1-1/2 cups	mincemeat	375 mL
2 tbsp	lemon juice	25 mL
1/2 cup	all-purpose flour	125 mL
1/3 cup	packed brown sugar	75 mL
1/3 cup	rolled oats	75 mL
1/3 cup	butter	75 mL
1/2 cup	slivered or sliced almonds	125 mL

*I*n 9-inch (2.5 L) square baking dish, combine pears, mincemeat and lemon juice.

* In bowl, stir together flour, sugar and rolled oats; cut in butter until mixture resembles coarse crumbs. Stir in almonds. Sprinkle evenly over pear mixture. Bake in 375°F (190°C) oven for 45 minutes or until pears are tender. Makes 6 servings.

Pear Mincemeat Crumble

EASY YOGURT TOPPING

Spoon 2 cups (500 mL) yogurt into cheesecloth-lined sieve set over large glass measure. Let drain in refrigerator for up to 12 hours or until reduced to about 1 cup (250 mL). If desired, sweeten to taste with honey or sugar and stir in a touch of vanilla or grated orange or lemon rind.

Chocolate Meringue Mousse Cake

🎄

This is definitely a dessert-lover's dessert!

2/3 cup	granulated sugar	150 mL
1 tbsp	unsweetened cocoa powder	15 mL
1 tbsp	cornstarch	15 mL
3	egg whites	3
1/2 tsp	vanilla	2 mL

Mousse

8 oz	unsweetened chocolate	250 g
1-1/2 cups	granulated sugar	375 mL
1/2 cup	water	125 mL
10	egg yolks	10
2 cups	whipping cream	500 mL
1 tsp	vanilla	5 mL

Garnish

Whipped cream

Unsweetened cocoa powder

Trace two 8-inch (20 cm) circles on parchment paper; invert and place on baking sheet. Combine 1/3 cup (75 mL) of the sugar, cocoa and cornstarch; set aside.

🎄 In large bowl, beat egg whites until soft peaks form; gradually beat in remaining sugar until stiff peaks form. Fold in vanilla and reserved sugar mixture. Spoon onto circles, spreading evenly and smoothing tops. Bake in 300°F (150°C) oven for 1-1/2 hours or until dry; let cool completely.

🎄 MOUSSE: In bowl over hot (not boiling) water, melt chocolate, sugar and water. In another bowl over hot (not boiling) water, beat egg yolks for 5 minutes or until pale and thickened; gently fold into chocolate. Let cool at room temperature for no longer that 10 minutes.

🎄 Meanwhile, whip cream and vanilla; whisk one-quarter into warm chocolate mixture. Fold in remaining whipped cream.

🎄 ASSEMBLY: Line side of 9-inch (2.5 L) springform pan with waxed paper extending 1 inch (2.5 cm) above pan. Place one meringue in pan, trimming to fit; pour in half of the chocolate mousse. Top with remaining meringue, trimming if necessary; pour in remaining mousse. (*Cake can be covered and refrigerated for up to 1 day or frozen for up to 2 weeks; thaw in refrigerator for 6 hours before continuing.*)

🎄 Garnish with whipped cream rosettes; dust with cocoa powder. Makes 12 to 16 servings.

Eggnog Cheesecake

🎄

Nutmeg and rum, the festive flavors of eggnog, are splendid in cheesecake, too.

1 cup	graham cracker crumbs	250 mL
2 tbsp	granulated sugar	25 mL
3 tbsp	butter, melted	50 mL

Filling

1-1/2 lb	cream cheese, softened	750 g
1 cup	granulated sugar	250 mL
1/2 cup	whipping cream	125 mL
3 tbsp	all-purpose flour	50 mL
3	eggs	3
2 tbsp	rum (or 2 tbsp/25 mL orange juice and 1 tsp/5 mL rum extract)	25 mL
1/2 tsp	nutmeg	2 mL

Garnish

2 oz	semisweet chocolate	60 g
	Round red candies	
	Gold or silver dragées	

Combine crumbs, sugar and butter; press onto bottom of 9-inch (2.5 L) springform pan. Bake in 325°F (160°C) oven for 10 minutes. Let cool on rack.

🎄 FILLING: In food processor or in bowl, beat together cream cheese, sugar, cream and flour until smooth; beat in eggs, rum and nutmeg. Pour over crust.

🎄 Bake in 425°F (220°C) oven for 10 minutes. Reduce heat to 250°F (120°C) and bake for 45 minutes longer or until edge is set but center still jiggles slightly. Turn oven off. Quickly run knife around edge of cake; let cool in oven for 1 hour. Remove to rack and let cool completely.

🎄 GARNISH: Melt semisweet chocolate and let cool slightly. Roll out between waxed paper to 1/8-inch (3 mm) thickness; place on baking sheet and refrigerate until firm. Cut out holly leaf shapes. Place on cheesecake. Remelt remaining chocolate and pipe onto cheesecake to form stems. Add candies and dragées for berries. Makes 10 to 12 servings.

Eggnog Cheesecake

Chocolate Cookie Cheesecake

*This dream of a dessert is a fabulous way to satisfy the urge
for something cool, creamy — and full of chocolate!*

1-1/2 lb	cream cheese	750 g
3/4 cup	granulated sugar	175 mL
3	eggs	3
1 tsp	vanilla	5 mL
1 cup	sour cream	250 mL
2 tsp	all-purpose flour	10 mL
15	chocolate sandwich cream cookies, broken	15

Crust

15	chocolate sandwich cream cookies	15
3 tbsp	butter, melted	50 mL

Garnish

Chocolate sandwich cream cookies

CRUST: In food processor or blender, crush cookies to fine crumbs; stir in butter until crumbs are moistened. With back of spoon, press onto bottom and 1/4 inch (5 mm) up side of lightly greased 8-1/2-inch (2.25 L) springform pan. Center pan on large piece of foil; press up to side of pan. Refrigerate.

In bowl, beat cheese; beat in sugar until fluffy. Beat in eggs, one at a time, beating well after each addition; beat in vanilla. Beat in sour cream and flour.

Pour one-third over prepared crust; sprinkle with half of the broken cookies. Repeat once. Top with remaining batter, smoothing top.

Set pan in larger pan; pour in hot water to come 1 inch (2.5 cm) up sides. Bake in 325°F (160°C) oven for 50 to 60 minutes or until edge is set but center still jiggles slightly. Turn oven off.

Quickly run knife around edge of cake; let cool in oven for 1 hour. Remove foil; let cool completely on rack. Cover and refrigerate overnight or for up to 3 days.

GARNISH: Just before serving, cut cookies in half and arrange on top. Makes 10 to 12 servings.

Triple Chocolate Angel Food Cake

❧

Light angel food cake contrasts beautifully
with a tunnel of ice cream and a gooey fudge sauce.
For a low-fat version, use a fruit sorbet in the
tunnel and a raspberry purée for the sauce.

4 cups	chocolate ice cream, softened	1 L
	Icing sugar	

Cake

1-3/4 cups	granulated sugar	425 mL
1 cup	cake-and-pastry flour	250 mL
1/3 cup	unsweetened cocoa powder	75 mL
2 cups	egg whites (about 16)	500 mL
1 tsp	cream of tartar	5 mL
Pinch	salt	Pinch
1 tsp	vanilla	5 mL

Fudge Sauce

6 oz	semisweet chocolate, chopped	175 g
1/3 cup	whipping cream	75 mL
1/3 cup	water	75 mL
3 tbsp	corn syrup	50 mL
2 tbsp	unsweetened cocoa powder	25 mL
1 tsp	vanilla	5 mL

CAKE: Into bowl, sift together 3/4 cup (175 mL) of the sugar, all of the flour and cocoa three times; set aside.

❧ In separate bowl, beat egg whites, cream of tartar and salt until soft peaks form; gradually beat in remaining sugar, 2 tbsp (25 mL) at a time, until stiff peaks form. Beat in vanilla.

❧ In three additions, sift flour mixture over egg whites, gently folding in each until blended. Gently turn into ungreased 10-inch (4 L) tube pan. Run knife through batter to eliminate any large air pockets; smooth top with spatula.

❧ Bake in 350°F (180°C) oven for 50 to 60 minutes or until cake springs back when lightly touched. Invert cake pan and let cake hang on legs attached to pan, or on inverted funnel or bottle, until completely cool. Run knife around edges and remove cake; cover and freeze for 2 hours or until firm.

❧ Working from bottom (wider, rougher side), gently scoop out tunnel about 3 inches (8 cm) deep, leaving 1-inch (2.5 cm) thick walls. Reserve cake pieces. Fill tunnel with ice cream; top with enough of the cake pieces to cover completely. Cover and freeze for 4 hours or until ice cream is firm. *(Cake can be frozen for up to 3 days.)*

❧ FUDGE SAUCE: In saucepan, combine chocolate, cream, water, corn syrup and cocoa; cook over medium heat, whisking, until smooth. Increase heat to medium-high and bring just to boil; remove from heat and stir in vanilla. Let cool. *(Sauce can be covered and refrigerated for up to 3 days; reheat gently in double boiler or in microwave just until pourable.)*

❧ To serve, invert cake onto serving plate; sprinkle with icing sugar. Serve each slice drizzled with sauce. Makes 10 to 12 servings.

Mincemeat Sundae Pie

❧

Choose a fruit-based mincemeat made without suet to layer with ice cream and caramel sauce in this festive dessert.

1-1/4 cups	vanilla wafer crumbs	300 mL
1/2 cup	finely chopped pecans	125 mL
1/4 cup	butter, melted	50 mL
2 tbsp	packed brown sugar	25 mL
1/2 tsp	cinnamon	2 mL

Filling

6 cups	vanilla ice cream	1.5 L
1 cup	mincemeat	250 mL

Caramel Sauce

1/2 cup	packed brown sugar	125 mL
1/2 cup	whipping cream	125 mL
1/2 tsp	vanilla	2 mL

Combine wafer crumbs, pecans, butter, sugar and cinnamon. Press onto bottom and 1-1/2 inches (4 cm) up side of 10-inch (3 L) greased springform pan; freeze for 30 minutes.

❧ FILLING: Place ice cream in bowl; let stand at room temperature for 10 to 15 minutes or until softened. Stir in mincemeat until evenly distributed. Pack into crumb crust. Cover and freeze overnight or for up to 4 weeks.

❧ CARAMEL SAUCE: In saucepan, bring sugar and cream to boil; cook, stirring occasionally, for 3 to 4 minutes or until thickened enough to coat spoon. Do not overcook. Stir in vanilla. Let cool for 3 minutes. *(Sauce can be cooled completely and stored in airtight container for up to 4 weeks; reheat over medium heat before serving.)*

❧ To serve, drizzle caramel sauce over pieces of pie. Makes 12 servings.

Dried Fruit Pie

When you're looking for a superb holiday dessert, don't let the words "dried fruit" persuade you to pass this recipe by. Dried apricots, prunes, raisins and apples — with a dash of rum and a sprinkle of cinnamon (memories of mincemeat without all its sweetness!) — bake in a pie that's simply wonderful served warm with whipped cream.

	Pastry for 9-inch (23 cm) double-crust pie	
1	egg, beaten	1

Filling

2 cups	dried apricots	500 mL
1-1/2 cups	pitted prunes	375 mL
1 cup	raisins	250 mL
1/2 cup	dried apples	125 mL
3/4 cup	packed brown sugar	175 mL
1/2 cup	chopped almonds	125 mL
1/2 cup	butter, melted	125 mL
1/4 cup	rum	50 mL
1 tsp	grated lemon rind	5 mL
1 tbsp	lemon juice	15 mL
1-1/2 tsp	cinnamon	7 mL

FILLING: In large saucepan, cover apricots, prunes, raisins and apples with water; bring to boil over medium heat. Reduce heat to medium-low; cover and simmer for 10 minutes. Drain fruit and let cool; coarsely chop. In large bowl, toss fruit with sugar, almonds, butter, rum, lemon rind and juice and cinnamon.

❧ On lightly floured surface, roll out half of the pastry and fit into 9-inch (23 cm) pie plate; spoon in filling. Trim and flute edge. Roll out remaining pastry; using star-shaped or other cookie cutter, cut out shapes and arrange in overlapping pattern over filling. (*Pie can be prepared to this point, wrapped and frozen for up to 2 weeks. Do not thaw.*)

❧ Brush stars with egg. Bake in 425°F (220°C) oven for 15 minutes. Reduce heat to 375°F (190°C); bake for 20 to 25 minutes (1 hour and 15 minutes for frozen pie, shielding edges of pastry with foil) or until golden. Makes 12 servings.

Double Walnut and Chocolate Tarte

Fresh walnuts lend their crunch to both the crust and the filling in this chocolate lovers' pie.

1-1/3 cups	all-purpose flour	325 mL
1/3 cup	ground walnuts	75 mL
2 tbsp	granulated sugar	25 mL
1/4 tsp	salt	1 mL
1/2 cup	butter	125 mL
1/4 cup	shortening	50 mL
1	egg yolk	1
2 tbsp	water	25 mL
2 oz	semisweet chocolate, melted	60 g

Filling

4	eggs	4
1 cup	granulated sugar	250 mL
1 cup	corn syrup	250 mL
2 tbsp	butter, softened	25 mL
2 tsp	vanilla or coffee liqueur	10 mL
3 oz	semisweet chocolate, coarsely chopped	90 g
1-1/2 cups	coarsely chopped walnuts	375 mL

In large bowl, combine flour, walnuts, sugar and salt. With pastry blender or two knives, cut in butter and shortening until mixture resembles fine crumbs with a few larger pieces.

❧ Combine egg yolk and water; drizzle over dry ingredients, tossing lightly with fork. Press into disc; wrap and refrigerate for 1 hour.

❧ On pastry cloth and using stockinette-covered rolling pin, or between two sheets of waxed paper, roll out pastry to 1/4-inch (5 mm) thickness. Ease into 11-inch (28 cm) flan pan with removable base; trim excess pastry. Refrigerate.

❧ FILLING: In large bowl, beat together eggs, sugar, corn syrup, butter and vanilla; stir in chocolate and walnuts. Spoon into tarte shell.

❧ Bake in 375°F (190°C) oven for about 45 minutes or until pastry is browned and tester inserted into center of filling comes out clean. Let cool on wire rack.

❧ Drizzle melted chocolate over tarte. Makes 10 to 12 servings.

Double Walnut and Chocolate Tarte

'TWAS THE NIGHT BEFORE CHRISTMAS

❧

WHETHER YOU CELEBRATE CHRISTMAS EVE RELAXING BY THE FIRE
OR RENEWING CHERISHED HERITAGE TRADITIONS AROUND THE SACRED TABLE,
WE HOPE YOU'LL ENJOY THIS MOST MAGICAL NIGHT OF THE YEAR!

By the Fire

❧

*Family, friends, a fondue pot and a fireplace — what
a lovely way to spend a relaxed Christmas Eve!*

❧

Cranberry Sangria

❧

Cheese Fondue with Dippers

❧

Tangy Tossed Greens

❧

Pear Mincemeat Crumble
(recipe, p.103)

Tangy Tossed Greens

❧

*Serve this refreshing salad after the last of the fondue has
disappeared. Choose your favorite greens — spinach,
romaine or Bibb — and add a contrasting color and taste
with peppy arugula, Belgian endive or watercress.*

8 cups	torn mixed greens	2 L
1/2 cup	slivered red or Spanish onion	125 mL
1/2 cup	toasted nuts (see p. 30)	125 mL
2 tbsp	white wine vinegar	25 mL
2 tsp	Dijon mustard	10 mL
1/2 tsp	brown sugar	2 mL
1/3 cup	vegetable oil	75 mL
	Salt and pepper	

*I*n salad bowl, combine mixed greens, onion and nuts.
❧ In small bowl, whisk together vinegar, mustard and sugar;
gradually whisk in oil. Pour over greens; toss to coat. Season
with salt and pepper to taste. Makes 6 servings.

Cheese Fondue with Dippers

❧

*For dipping, prepare a selection of the following
— blanched broccoli, broccoflower and
cauliflower florets, sweet pepper chunks, whole
mushrooms, cooked shrimp and chunks of crusty bread.*

1-1/2 cups	dry white wine	375 mL
1 tbsp	lemon juice	15 mL
1	clove garlic	1
4 cups	shredded Swiss cheese	1 L
2 cups	shredded Edam cheese	500 mL
1 tbsp	cornstarch	15 mL

*I*n saucepan, bring wine, lemon juice and garlic almost
to boil over medium heat. Reduce heat to medium-low;
remove garlic.
❧ In bowl, toss together Swiss and Edam cheeses and cornstarch; gradually add to saucepan, a handful at a time, whisking
constantly until cheese melts before adding more cheese. Cook
until thickened and starting to bubble; transfer to fondue pot
set over heat. Makes 6 servings.

WHAT A GREAT IDEA!

CRANBERRY SANGRIA

*I*t's easy to make this mildly alcoholic refresher nonalcoholic
by substituting Fresca or Five Alive for the wine and
skipping the liqueur.
❧ In serving pitcher, combine 1 can (275 mL) frozen
Cranberry Cocktail concentrate, 1 bottle (750 mL) dry white
wine, 2 tbsp (25 mL) orange liqueur (if using), and 1 each
sliced lime, lemon and orange; refrigerate for at least 1 hour
or until chilled.
❧ At serving time, add 2 cups (500 mL) soda water and
ice. Makes 6 servings, each about 2/3 cup (150 mL).

Baked Tuscan Vegetable and Bread Soup

This hearty dish from Tuscany starts with a rich chicken and vegetable minestrone that's layered in a casserole with crusty bread, then baked until steaming and tender inside, crusty and golden on top.

5 cups	chicken stock	1.25 L
1 lb	chicken breasts, skinned	500 g
2	bay leaves	2
3 tbsp	olive oil	50 mL
1	onion, chopped	1
2	cloves garlic, minced	2
2	carrots, diced	2
2	stalks celery, diced	2
1	sweet green pepper, diced	1
2 cups	chopped cabbage	500 mL
1 tsp	each dried thyme and rosemary	5 mL
1	can (19 oz/540 mL) tomatoes, coarsely chopped (undrained)	1
1/4 tsp	pepper	1 mL
1	pkg (10 oz/284 g) fresh spinach, chopped	1
1/2 cup	chopped fresh parsley	125 mL
1	small zucchini, thinly sliced	1
1	can (19 oz/540 mL) white kidney beans, drained and rinsed	1
8	thick slices stale Italian or French bread	8
1 cup	freshly grated Parmesan cheese	250 mL

Fireside Supper

With the house at its festive best and everything ready for the next day's Christmas feast, it's time to relax and reminisce over this satisfying make-ahead supper.

Baked Tuscan Vegetable and Bread Soup

Carrot and Celery Slaw

Chilled Chestnut Mousse (recipe, p. 100)

*I*n large saucepan, bring chicken stock, chicken breasts and bay leaves to boil; reduce heat, cover and simmer for about 20 minutes or until chicken is no longer pink inside. Remove chicken and discard bones; dice meat and set aside. Discard bay leaves. Keep stock warm.

❧ Meanwhile, in large skillet, heat 2 tbsp (25 mL) of the oil over medium heat; cook onion, garlic, carrots and celery for 10 minutes, stirring occasionally. Add remaining oil, green pepper, cabbage, thyme and rosemary; cook over low heat, stirring occasionally, for 10 minutes.

❧ Add vegetable mixture to stock in saucepan along with tomatoes and pepper; bring to boil. Reduce heat, cover and simmer for 30 minutes. Add spinach, parsley, zucchini, kidney beans and reserved diced chicken; cook for 5 minutes. Remove 1 cup (250 mL) of the soup and set aside.

❧ Ladle half of the remaining soup into 24-cup (6 L) Dutch oven or casserole; cover with four of the bread slices and 1/2 cup (125 mL) of the Parmesan cheese. Cover with remaining soup; layer with remaining bread. Drizzle reserved soup over top; sprinkle with remaining Parmesan cheese. *(Recipe can be prepared to this point, cooled, covered and refrigerated for up to 24 hours.)*

❧ Bake, covered, in 350°F (180°C) oven for 20 minutes (45 minutes if refrigerated); uncover and bake for 20 minutes longer (45 minutes if refrigerated) or until hot.

❧ Serve soup in large warmed bowls. Garnish with drizzle of olive oil and sprinkle of Parmesan cheese, if desired. Makes about 6 servings.

Carrot and Celery Slaw

❦

*This wintertime salad looks especially attractive served
on the tenderest Boston or romaine lettuce leaves.*

2-1/2 cups	grated carrots	625 mL
2 cups	thinly sliced celery	500 mL
1/4 cup	chopped fresh mint or parsley	50 mL
1/4 cup	vegetable oil	50 mL
1 cup	sliced red onion	250 mL
1 tsp	mustard seeds	5 mL
1/2 tsp	salt	2 mL
1/4 tsp	pepper	1 mL
3 tbsp	red wine vinegar	50 mL

In salad bowl, toss together carrots, celery and mint; set aside.

❧ In skillet, heat oil over medium-high heat. Add onion, mustard seeds, salt and pepper; cook, stirring often, for 3 minutes or until onion is softened.

❧ Stir in vinegar; immediately pour over salad and toss well. Taste and adjust seasoning. *(Salad can be covered and refrigerated for up to 2 hours.)* Makes about 6 servings.

Soft-Sided White Rolls

*These tender, buttery white rolls are easy to make — even if
you're not an old hand at bread, like most Maritimers are!*

2-3/4 cups	milk	675 mL
1/2 cup	butter	125 mL
1	pkg active dry yeast (or 1 tbsp/15 mL)	1
1/4 cup	warm water	50 mL
2	eggs	2
1/4 cup	granulated sugar	50 mL
1 tsp	salt	5 mL
7-1/2 cups	(approx) all-purpose flour	1.875 L

Glaze

2 tbsp	milk	25 mL

In saucepan, heat milk with butter until bubbles form around
edge; let cool until lukewarm.

In large bowl, sprinkle yeast into warm water; let stand for 10
minutes or until frothy. Stir in milk mixture, eggs, sugar and salt.

Using electric mixer, gradually beat in 3 cups (750 mL) of the
flour for 3 minutes or until dough is smooth. With wooden spoon,
gradually stir in enough of the remaining flour to make soft
dough. Turn out onto floured surface; knead for 10 minutes or
until smooth and elastic.

Place dough in greased bowl, turning to grease all over. Cover
and let rise for 1-1/2 hours or until doubled in bulk.

Punch down dough; divide into three portions. Divide each
portion into 9 pieces; form each piece into smooth ball. Place
balls, almost touching, in three greased 8-inch (2 L) square cake
pans; cover and let rise for 30 minutes or until almost doubled
in bulk.

GLAZE: Brush dough with milk. Bake in 400°F (200°C) oven
for 20 to 25 minutes or until golden brown and bottoms sound
hollow when tapped. Remove from pans and let cool on racks.
Makes 27 rolls.

Maritime Lobster Chowder

For special occasions, lobster is the seafood
of choice in chowder. You can make the chowder
earlier in the day and store it in the refrigerator.
When fresh lobster is not available, substitute canned
frozen lobster (thaw, drain and reserve juices).

6 cups	diced peeled potatoes (about 8)	1.5 L
2	large onions, diced	2
3 cups	lobster meat (about 4 lobsters, each 1-1/2 lb/750 g), cooked and juices reserved	750 mL
1/4 cup	butter	50 mL
2 cups	light cream	500 mL
1 cup	heavy cream	250 mL
1-1/2 cups	lobster juice, fish stock or canned clam juice	375 mL
	Salt and pepper	

In large pot, bring 3 cups (750 mL) water to boil over
medium-high heat; cook potatoes and onions, covered, for 5 to
10 minutes or just until potatoes are tender. Do not drain.

Meanwhile, cut lobster into bite-size pieces. In large skillet,
heat 2 tbsp (25 mL) of the butter over medium-high heat; cook
lobster, stirring occasionally, for 3 to 5 minutes or until light
golden.

Add lobster to potato mixture along with light and heavy
cream, lobster juice and remaining butter. Cook over medium
heat for 3 to 5 minutes or just until heated through but not
boiling. Season with salt and pepper to taste. (Chowder can be
cooled, covered and refrigerated for up to 8 hours; reheat gently to
serve.) Makes 12 servings.

COOKING LOBSTER

In large pot, bring to full rolling boil over high heat
enough water to cover lobster; add 1 tbsp (15 mL) salt
for every 4 cups (1 L) water. Plunge live lobster headfirst
into water; return to boil. Reduce heat to low; cover and
simmer for 10 to 12 minutes for first pound (500 g) of
lobster, adding 1 minute for each additional 1/4 lb
(125 g). Cooked lobster will be bright red, and small leg
will come away easily when pulled.

In photo:
During the holiday season, hundreds of Christmas lights
twinkle from the riggings of ships in the harbor.

Whole Roasted Salmon with Wild Rice

A whole salmon provides a luxurious feast for Christmas Eve
or any other special holiday entertaining.

1 cup	wild rice, rinsed	250 mL
1 tsp	(approx) salt	5 mL
2 tbsp	butter	25 mL
1 cup	finely chopped mushrooms	250 mL
1/2 cup	finely chopped onion	125 mL
1	clove garlic, minced	1
1/2 cup	slivered almonds or pine nuts	125 mL
1 tsp	crumbled dried thyme	5 mL
1/2 tsp	crumbled dried sage	2 mL
1/4 tsp	pepper	1 mL
2 tbsp	lemon juice	25 mL
1	fresh whole salmon (4 to 5 lb/2 to 2.2 kg)	1
1 tbsp	butter, melted	15 mL
	Watercress	
2	lemons, cut into wedges	2

In saucepan, combine 2 cups (500 mL) water, rice and 1/2 tsp
(2 mL) of the salt; cover and bring to boil. Reduce heat and simmer for 25 to 30 minutes or until rice is tender but not mushy.
If necessary, uncover and cook briefly just until no moisture
remains. Spread on baking sheet and let cool; transfer to bowl.

Meanwhile, in large skillet, melt butter; cook mushrooms,
onion, garlic, almonds, thyme, sage, pepper and pinch of salt
until onion is softened and nuts slightly browned. Add to rice
along with 1 tbsp (15 mL) of the lemon juice.

Wipe salmon cavity and exterior with damp cloth. Brush
cavity with remaining lemon juice; sprinkle with remaining
1/2 tsp (2 mL) salt. Fill with stuffing. Place any leftover stuffing
in heatproof dish and cover. Sew cavity closed.

Place fish on lightly greased rimmed baking sheet; brush
with melted butter. Bake in 450°F (230°C) oven for 10 minutes
per inch (2.5 cm) of thickness or until flesh is opaque and flakes
easily when tested with fork. Bake any extra stuffing along
with fish.

Let fish stand for 5 minutes. Transfer to heated platter;
carefully remove string and skin from top side of salmon.
Garnish with watercress and lemon wedges. Arrange extra
stuffing around cavity opening. Makes 8 to 10 servings.

Fireside Drinks

Easy-Sipping Eggnog

Based on a creamy cooked custard and spiked with brandy and rum, every sip of this homemade eggnog is worth savoring.

6	eggs	6
1/2 cup	granulated sugar	125 mL
2 cups	milk	500 mL
1	orange	1
2 cups	light cream	500 mL
1/2 cup	brandy	125 mL
1/2 cup	dark rum	125 mL
1 cup	whipping cream	250 mL
	Freshly grated nutmeg or shaved chocolate	

In large saucepan, whisk together eggs and sugar; gradually whisk in milk.

❧ Using vegetable peeler, thinly peel off strips of orange rind. Add to milk mixture; cook over medium-low heat, whisking constantly, for 10 to 15 minutes or until mixture coats back of spoon or until candy thermometer registers 160°F (70°C).

❧ Immediately strain into heatproof bowl; whisk in light cream. Let cool slightly; cover and refrigerate for at least 2 hours or up to 24 hours or until chilled. Stir in brandy and rum.

❧ Whip cream; fold into eggnog mixture. Serve in chilled punch bowl or individual glasses. Sprinkle with nutmeg. Makes 12 to 16 servings.

W H A T   A   G R E A T   I D E A !

ALL-AMERICAN COFFEE

A cup of this spirited coffee is the perfect ending to any relaxing meal by the fire.

❧ TOPPING: Whip 3/4 cup (175 mL) whipping cream with 4 tsp (20 mL) pure maple syrup just until soft mounds form; set aside.

❧ Divide 1/4 cup (50 mL) pure maple syrup and 1/2 cup (125 mL) whisky among 4 warmed heatproof glass mugs or goblets. Pour in 3 cups (750 mL) hot double-strength black coffee to within 1 inch (2.5 cm) of top; spoon topping over coffee. Makes 4 servings, each about 1 cup (250 mL).

Mocha with Whipped Cream

This Viennese chocolate coffee topped with whipped cream is dessert and after-dinner beverage all in one.

4 oz	bittersweet chocolate	125 g
1/4 cup	water	50 mL
4 cups	hot double-strength black coffee	1 L
1 tbsp	(approx) granulated sugar	15 mL
	Whipped cream	
	cinnamon sticks	4

In top of double boiler over hot (not boiling) water, melt chocolate with water. Remove from heat and whisk until slightly thickened.

❧ Gradually add hot coffee, whisking constantly. Sweeten with sugar, adding more if desired.

❧ Pour into heated mugs; top with dollop of whipped cream. Serve with cinnamon stick for stirring. Makes 4 servings, each about 1 cup (250 mL).

Nightcap Cocoa

Whether it's the 24th or any other cold winter's night, a cup of cocoa is a cosy way to finish the evening.

1/3 cup	granulated sugar	75 mL
1/4 cup	unsweetened cocoa powder	50 mL
4 cups	milk	1 L
1 tsp	vanilla	5 mL
	Brandy (optional)	
	Whipped cream	

In small bowl, whisk sugar and cocoa with just enough of the milk to make a paste; whisk in a little more milk to make pourable.

❧ In saucepan, combine cocoa mixture with remaining milk; heat over low heat just until bubbles form around edge, stirring occasionally. Stir in vanilla.

❧ Pour into heated mugs; add dash of brandy (if using). Top each with dollop of whipped cream. Makes 4 servings, each about 1 cup (250 mL).

Easy-Sipping Eggnog

Heritage Dishes

❧

Christmas is a celebration of the special foods of our North American heritage
— a cuisine that is as varied as the nationalities that enrich this great land of ours.
The ethnic kaleidoscope is especially bright on Christmas Eve when cherished recipes,
passed down from generation to generation and from old country to new,
are enjoyed once again.
Join us in sharing some of the great tastes of Christmas.

Portuguese King's Cake

❧

After midnight mass on Christmas Eve, Portuguese
families sit down to a festive dinner. The traditional dessert
is Bolo Rei, or King's Cake, a rich fruit-filled bread.

2 cups	finely chopped mixed candied fruit	500 mL
1 cup	seedless raisins	250 mL
2 tsp	each finely grated lemon and orange rind	10 mL
1/2 cup	port	125 mL
2	pkg active dry yeast (or 2 tbsp/25 mL)	2
3/4 cup	granulated sugar	175 mL
6 cups	(approx) all-purpose flour	1.5 L
3/4 cup	lukewarm water	175 mL
3/4 cup	butter, softened	175 mL
4	eggs	4
2/3 cup	lukewarm milk	150 mL
1 cup	chopped almonds or walnuts	250 mL
	Melted butter	

Topping

5	candied pineapple rings	5
1	egg	1
1/3 cup	candied cherries	75 mL
2 tbsp	corn syrup	25 mL
	Icing sugar	

*I*n small bowl, mix together candied fruit, raisins, lemon and orange rinds and port; cover and let stand while preparing dough.

❧ Meanwhile, in bowl, whisk together yeast, 1 tbsp (15 mL) of the sugar, 1 cup (250 mL) of the flour and water until smooth. Cover and let rise in warm spot for 30 minutes or until doubled in volume.

❧ In large bowl and using electric mixer, beat butter and remaining sugar until fluffy. Beat in eggs, one at a time, beating well after each addition. Beat in 1 cup (250 mL) of the flour and milk.

❧ Stir down yeast mixture; beat into egg batter. With wooden spoon, mix in fruit mixture and nuts. Stir in as much of the remaining flour, 1 cup (250 mL) at a time, as needed to make a soft, sticky dough.

❧ Transfer to large greased bowl; lightly brush top of dough with melted butter. Cover and let rise in warm spot for 1 hour or until doubled in volume.

❧ Punch down dough; divide in half. On floured surface and with floured hands, knead each half for 1 minute. Shape each half into ball; place on greased baking sheets.

❧ With two fingers, form hole in center of each ball and gently shape into 9-inch (23 cm) ring with 3-1/2 -inch (9 cm) hole in center. Grease outside of two empty 19-oz (540 mL) cans; place in center of each to ensure rings hold shape.

❧ TOPPING: Cut each pineapple ring in half horizontally to make 2 rings; cut in half again. Whisk egg; brush over top of each bread ring. Decorate with thin slices of pineapple and cherries, pressing lightly into dough.

❧ Cover lightly and let rise in warm spot for 1 hour or until doubled in volume. Bake in 375°F (190°C) oven for 35 to 40 minutes or until golden brown. Transfer to racks; brush with corn syrup and let cool. Before serving, dust with icing sugar. Makes 2 loaves.

A joyous abundance of fresh breads, cheeses, cold meats, smoked fish and enticing salads — including Chilled Potato Salad (at left, in glass bowl) — is typical of German Christmas Eve suppers.

Chilled Potato Salad

In German homes on Christmas Eve, as the night sky darkens, the door opens to the living room to reveal the lighted tree in all its glory, decorated by the parents and seen by the children for the first time. After the Christmas story from the Bible and carols, it's on to the presents awaiting everyone in individual piles — and then, the feast! Chilled Potato Salad is one of the stars.

2 lb	red-skinned potatoes	1 kg
1	anchovy fillet	1
2	hard-cooked egg yolks, chopped	2
1-1/3 cups	mayonnaise	325 mL
1/2 cup	finely chopped onion	125 mL
1/4 cup	diced gherkin pickles	50 mL
1/4 cup	minced fresh parsley	50 mL
2 tbsp	capers	25 mL
1 tbsp	chopped fresh chives or green onion	15 mL
3/4 tsp	salt	4 mL
1/4 tsp	pepper	1 mL
1/4 tsp	dried tarragon	1 mL

Scrub potatoes; quarter if large. In pot of boiling water, cook potatoes until tender but not mushy. Drain and let cool enough to handle; cut into cubes.

In large bowl, mash anchovy fillet; stir in egg yolks, mayonnaise, onion, gherkins, parsley, capers, chives, salt, pepper and tarragon.

Gently stir in potatoes; cover and refrigerate until chilled. Taste and adjust seasoning if necessary. Makes 8 servings.

Christmas Eve Dumplings

Spiritual values and cultural traditions make the gathering of Ukrainian families on Christmas Eve especially moving. For this holy supper, the table holds twelve symbolic meatless dishes — including savory dumplings, or varenyky.

2 tbsp	vegetable oil	25 mL
1	large onion, chopped	1

Filling

3 tbsp	vegetable oil	50 mL
1	onion, chopped	1
2 cups	sauerkraut	500 mL
	Salt and pepper	

Dough

3 cups	all-purpose flour	750 mL
1-1/2 tsp	salt	7 mL
1	egg	1
3/4 cup	(approx) water	175 mL
4 tsp	vegetable oil	20 mL

FILLING: In skillet, heat oil over medium heat; cook onion, stirring, for 5 minutes or until golden. Rinse, drain and chop sauerkraut. Add to skillet; cook for 15 minutes or until golden. Season with salt and pepper to taste. Set aside and let cool.

❧ DOUGH: Meanwhile, in bowl, combine flour with salt. Beat together egg, water and oil; stir into flour mixture to make soft, not sticky dough, adding more water, 1 tbsp (15 mL) at a time, if necessary. Turn out onto lightly floured surface; knead 10 times or until smooth. Halve dough and cover with plastic wrap; let rest for 20 minutes.

❧ Divide each half into three. Roll out each portion on lightly floured surface to 1/16-inch (1.5 mm) thickness. Using 3-inch (8 cm) round cookie cutter, cut into rounds.

❧ Place 1 tsp (5 mL) filling on each round; moisten edge of one-half of dough with water. Pinch edges to seal; crimp, if desired. Place on cloth; cover with damp towel to keep moist.

❧ In large pot of boiling salted water, cook dumplings, in batches, for 1-1/2 to 2 minutes or until they float to top, stirring gently to prevent sticking. Remove to colander to drain.

❧ Meanwhile, in skillet, heat oil over medium heat; cook onion, stirring occasionally, for 8 minutes, or until golden. In serving dish, toss dumplings gently with onions. Makes 36 dumplings.

Italian Seafood Antipasto

Antipasto is the appetizer prelude to the other fish courses in the traditional Italian Christmas Eve feast. Serve with crusty bread.

1	stalk celery, coarsely chopped	1
1	small onion	1
1	bay leaf	1
1/2 tsp	salt	2 mL
6	whole peppercorns	6
2	strips lemon rind	2
1 lb	small squid	500 g
1 lb	scallops	500 g
1 lb	uncooked small shrimp	500 g

Dressing

1/4 cup	extra virgin olive oil	50 mL
1/4 cup	lemon juice	50 mL
1	large clove garlic, minced	1
2 tbsp	chopped fresh Italian parsley	25 mL
1/2 tsp	salt	2 mL
1/4 tsp	pepper	1 mL

In saucepan, combine 6 cups (1.5 L) water, celery, onion, bay leaf, salt, peppercorns and lemon rind; bring to boil. Reduce heat, cover and simmer for 20 minutes. Strain and return liquid to saucepan; set aside.

❧ Hold squid under cold water and peel off skin. Squeeze out insides; pull off head and pull out center transparent bone. Wash squid well; cut into small strips or 1/4-inch (5 mm) rings. Cut tentacles in half or quarters, if desired. Halve or quarter each scallop if large. Peel and devein shrimp.

❧ Bring reserved cooking liquid to simmer; add squid and simmer for 3 minutes or until tender. Remove with slotted spoon; set aside. Return liquid to simmer; add scallops and simmer for 3 minutes or until opaque. Remove with slotted spoon; set aside. Repeat with shrimps. Transfer seafood mixture to bowl.

❧ DRESSING: In small screwtop jar or bowl, combine oil, lemon juice, garlic, parsley, salt and pepper; shake to mix well. Pour over seafood mixture and toss gently to coat.

❧ Cover and marinate in refrigerator for at least 1 hour or up to 4 hours, stirring occasionally. Toss just before serving mounded on platter. Makes 8 servings.

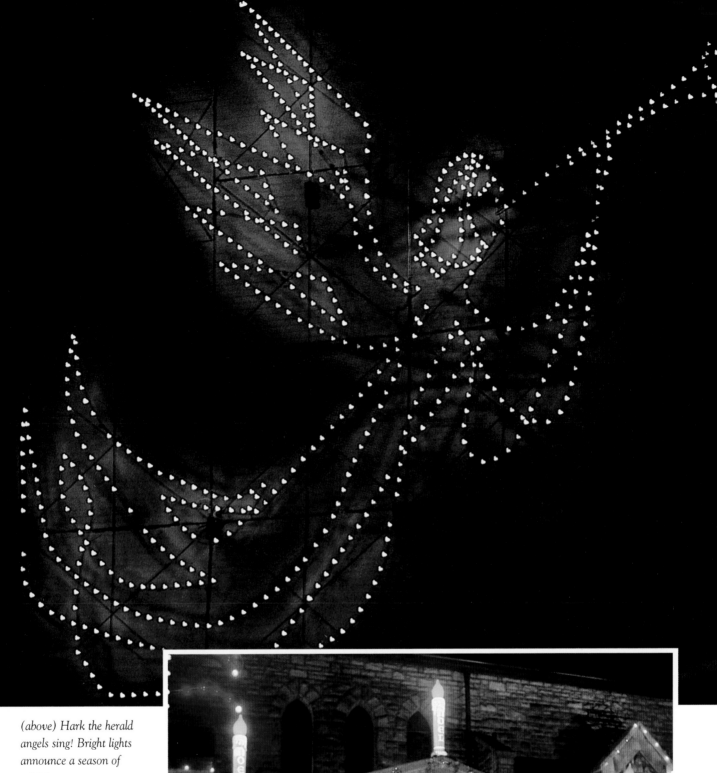

(above) Hark the herald angels sing! Bright lights announce a season of rejoicing.

(at right) Outside a church, a life-size crèche tells the story of the first Christmas.

Réveillon Tourtière

In Québec, Canada, there is a name for the joyous Christmas Eve of feasting, gifts, dancing, storytelling and games that follow midnight mass. It's Réveillon, the time for families to gather together and rekindle warm traditions around a table laden with holiday dishes. Tourtière, a lightly spiced and herbed pork filling in a flaky pastry, is at the heart of Réveillon festivities.

1 tbsp	vegetable oil	15 mL
2 lb	ground pork	1 kg
1-1/2 cups	beef stock	375 mL
3	onions, finely chopped	3
3	cloves garlic, minced	3
2 cups	sliced mushrooms	500 mL
1 cup	finely chopped celery	250 mL
3/4 tsp	salt	4 mL
1/2 tsp	each cinnamon, pepper and dried savory	2 mL
1/4 tsp	ground cloves	1 mL
1 cup	fresh bread crumbs	250 mL
1/2 cup	chopped fresh parsley	125 mL
	Pastry for 9-inch (23 cm) double-crust pie	
1	egg, beaten	1
1 tsp	water	5 mL

In large skillet, heat oil over medium-high heat; cook pork, breaking up with wooden spoon, for 7 to 10 minutes or until no longer pink. Drain off fat.

❧ Stir in stock, onions, garlic, mushrooms, celery, salt, cinnamon, pepper, savory and cloves; bring to boil. Reduce heat to medium-low and simmer, stirring occasionally, for 35 to 45 minutes or until 2 tbsp (25 mL) liquid remains.

❧ Stir in fresh bread crumbs and parsley. Taste and adjust seasoning if necessary. Cover and refrigerate until cold or for up to 1 day.

❧ On lightly floured surface, roll out bottom pastry to 1/8-inch (3 mm) thickness; fit into 9-inch (23 cm) pie plate.

❧ Spoon filling into pie shell, smoothing top. Roll out top pastry. Moisten rim of pie shell with water. Cover with top pastry, pressing edges together to seal. Trim and flute pastry edge.

❧ Combine egg with water; brush some over pastry. Cut decorative shapes from remaining pastry and arrange on top; brush with some of the remaining egg mixture.

❧ Cut steam vents in top; bake in 375°F (190°C) oven for 40 to 45 minutes or until golden brown. Let cool for 10 minutes. Makes 8 to 10 servings.

> *Tip*: To make tourtière ahead of time, omit pastry cutouts. Wrap and freeze unbaked pie for up to 2 months. Partially thaw in refrigerator for 6 hours or until pastry gives slightly when pressed. Cut steam vents and brush with glaze. Bake in 375°F (190°C) oven for 1-1/4 hours or until heated through and pastry is golden, shielding edge with foil if necessary during last 30 minutes.

In background photo:
A wintry landscape in rural Québec

Homemade Doughnuts

*Melt-in-your-mouth doughnuts, or beignes,
are just one of many delectable sweets
served during Réveillon.*

4-1/2 cups	(approx) all-purpose flour	1.125 L
2 tsp	baking soda	10 mL
2 tsp	salt	10 mL
2 tsp	nutmeg	10 mL
1 tsp	cream of tartar	5 mL
2	eggs	2
1-1/2 cups	granulated sugar	375 mL
1-1/4 cups	soured milk or buttermilk	300 mL
1 tbsp	butter, melted	15 mL
	Vegetable oil for deep-frying	
	Cinnamon sugar or icing sugar	

In bowl, sift together flour, baking soda, salt, nutmeg and cream of tartar.

❧ In large bowl, beat eggs until thickened and pale; gradually beat in sugar. Stir in milk and butter. Gradually stir in flour mixture, blending until almost smooth and adding up to 1 cup (250 mL) more flour if necessary to make soft ball that is not as stiff as pie dough. Refrigerate for 1 to 2 hours or until firm enough to roll.

❧ On lightly floured surface, roll out dough to 1/4-inch (5 mm) thickness. Using 3-inch (8 cm) round floured doughnut or cookie cutter for ring and 1/2-inch (1 cm) cutter for center, cut into rounds. Save centers.

❧ In deep-fryer, heat vegetable oil until thermometer reaches 365°F (185°C) or when 1-inch (2.5 cm) cube of white bread turns golden in 50 seconds. Deep-fry doughnuts, a few at a time to avoid crowding, for 3 minutes or until golden. Remove to rack; dunk in cinnamon sugar to coat. Serve warm. Makes about 24 doughnuts.

A Christmas Feast

SAVORY PHYLLO TARTLETS
(RECIPE, P. 74)

❧

SWEET POTATO AND
CARROT CRISP

❧

CHEESY BRUSSELS SPROUTS

❧

MAKE-AHEAD MASHED
POTATO CASSEROLE

❧

ROAST TURKEY WITH
NUTTY STUFFING

❧

DINNER ROLLS

❧

CRANBERRY ORANGE RELISH

❧

CHRISTMAS PLUM PUDDING
WITH
ORANGE HARD SAUCE
(RECIPE, P. 19)

A CHRISTMAS FEAST

❦

OF ALL THE HOLIDAY GATHERINGS, CHRISTMAS DINNER IS THE MOST
ANTICIPATED — AND THE MOST SPLENDID! WITH OUR WONDERFUL (MOSTLY MAKE-AHEAD!)
MENU, THIS CHRISTMAS FEAST IS SURE TO BE YOUR BEST EVER.

Roast Turkey with Nutty Stuffing

❦

*The crowning glory of Christmas dinner is a glorious
bird. This roast turkey, big enough to feed eight to ten
people with leftovers, more than fills the bill with
its crisp golden skin, rich brown gravy and
crunchy stuffing. If you prefer, you may substitute
any of the delicious stuffings on pages 128 and 129.*

15 lb	turkey	6.75 kg
1/4 cup	butter, softened	50 mL
1/2 tsp	each dried crumbled sage and rosemary	2 mL
	Salt and pepper	

Nutty Stuffing

3/4 cup	butter	175 mL
2-1/2 cups	chopped celery	625 mL
2 cups	chopped onions	500 mL
2	cloves garlic, minced	2
1	apple (unpeeled), diced	1
4 tsp	dried sage	20 mL
1-1/4 tsp	pepper	6 mL
1 tsp	each dried rosemary and salt	5 mL
1/4 lb	sliced smoked ham or prosciutto, diced	125 g
14 cups	cubed multigrain or whole wheat bread	3.5 L
1 cup	chopped fresh parsley	250 mL
3/4 cup	pecans, toasted and chopped (see p. 30)	175 mL

Stock

4-1/2 cups	chicken stock or water	1.125 L
1-1/2 cups	(approx) water	375 mL
1	onion, chopped	1
1/2 cup	each sliced carrot and celery	125 mL

Gravy

1/4 cup	all-purpose flour	50 mL
1/4 cup	sherry (optional)	50 mL
	Salt and pepper	

*N*UTTY STUFFING: In large skillet, melt butter over medium heat; cook celery, onions, garlic, apple, sage, pepper, rosemary, salt and ham for 10 to 15 minutes or until vegetables are tender. Place bread, parsley and nuts in large bowl; add celery mixture and toss well. Set aside. (*Stuffing can be covered and refrigerated for up to 1 day or frozen for up to 1 week; thaw in refrigerator for 24 hours before continuing.*)

❦ Remove giblets and neck from turkey and place in large saucepan, reserving liver for another use; set aside.

❦ Rinse turkey inside and out; dry skin and cavity well. Fill neck cavity with stuffing; fold neck skin over stuffing and skewer to back. Stuff body cavity. Tuck legs under band of skin or tie together with string.

❦ Place turkey, breast side up, on greased rack in roasting pan. Combine butter, sage and rosemary; spread over turkey. Sprinkle with salt and pepper.

❦ Tent turkey with foil, dull side out, tucking in ends and leaving sides open. Roast in 325°F (160°C) oven for 4 hours, basting every 30 minutes. Remove foil and roast for 45 to 60 minutes longer or until juices run clear and thermometer inserted into thigh registers 185°F (85°C) and stuffing 165°F (75°C). Transfer to platter; let stand, loosely covered, for about 20 minutes.

❦ STOCK: Meanwhile, to saucepan with turkey parts, add stock, water, onion, carrot and celery; bring to boil. Reduce heat to low and skim off foam; simmer for 3 hours. Strain into measuring cup and skim off fat; add enough water to make 3 cups (750 mL) stock and set aside.

❦ GRAVY: Skim off fat in roasting pan. Stir flour into pan and cook, stirring, over medium heat for 1 minute. Gradually whisk in reserved stock and bring to boil, stirring to scrape up brown bits from bottom of pan. Reduce heat and add sherry (if using); simmer, stirring, for 5 minutes. Season with salt and pepper to taste; strain into warmed gravy boat. Serve with turkey. Makes 8 to 10 servings.

TURKEY TIPS

❧ Count on a 15-pound (6.75 kilogram) turkey to serve 8 to 10 people. That's generous enough to allow for leftovers.

❧ If using frozen turkey, thaw it in its original plastic wrapper in the refrigerator or in cold water.

Refrigerator: Place on tray in refrigerator and allow 5 hours per pound (10 hours per kilogram).

Cold water: Cover turkey with cold water, changing water occasionally; allow 1 hour per pound (2 hours per kilogram).

STUFFING

❧ The turkey should never be stuffed ahead of time, but the stuffing can be made ahead and frozen for up to one week. Remember to transfer the stuffing from the freezer to thaw in the refrigerator for 24 hours before stuffing the bird.

❧ A 12- to 16-pound (5.5 to 7 kilogram) turkey will hold about 5 cups (1.25 L) stuffing in the body cavity and 2 cups (500 mL) in the neck. Bake any extra stuffing in a covered casserole dish along with the turkey for the last 40 minutes of cooking. Drizzle with turkey drippings for extra flavor and moisture.

❧ To make bread cubes, trim crusts from day-old bread slices. Stack several slices together and cut lengthwise into fingers, then cut crosswise into cubes. Spread on baking sheets to dry for up to 8 hours, if desired.

TURKEY ROASTING

❧ Roast in 325°F (160°C) oven.

❧ Roast turkey all at once; don't partially cook at one time and complete at a later date.

❧ Many factors, such as initial temperature of the bird, whether it's fresh or thawed, and its size relative to the oven, can affect cooking time, so check for doneness about three-quarters of an hour earlier than calculated cooking time to avoid overcooking.

❧ For a perfectly roasted turkey every time, use a meat thermometer. Roast for about 20 minutes per pound (500 g) or until juices run clear when turkey is pierced and thermometer inserted into thickest part of thigh registers 185°F (85°C) and when inserted into stuffing, 165°F (75°C).

❧ Smaller birds require a few minutes more cooking per pound and larger birds a few minutes less. Frozen prebasted turkeys roast slightly faster than fresh turkeys. Here are some examples for stuffed turkeys: 10 lb (4.5 kg) — 3 hours and 20 minutes; 12 lb (5.5 kg) — 4 hours; 16 lb (7 kg) — 5 hours and 20 minutes; 18 lb (8 kg) — 5 hours and 45 minutes.

❧ When turkey is done, transfer to warm platter. Tent with foil and let stand for about 20 minutes. This tenting allows time for juices at the surface of the bird to distribute evenly throughout the meat.

CARVING

❧ To carve, cut legs from turkey with carving knife and fork, twisting loose if necessary. Cut thigh from drumstick at joint; carve dark meat from each piece. With tip of knife toward body cavity, carve breast thinly, gradually angling knife to slice thick part of breast. Cut off wings. Scoop stuffing into bowl.

❧ Remove stuffing and meat from carcass within 2 hours of cooking. Immediately wrap and refrigerate stuffing, meat and carcass separately for leftovers and stock.

GIBLET STOCK

❧ In saucepan, cover giblets and neck with about 6 cups (1.5 L) water. Add a chopped onion, bay leaf, sprig of thyme and a few celery tops; simmer ahead of time for about 3 hours, skimming off foam. Strain and use as stock for gravy or with turkey leftovers (see Chapter 10).

GARNISHES

❧ Create orange or lemon baskets by slicing about one-third off the top of the fruit. With sharp knife, make zigzag pattern around edge. Remove most of the pulp with grapefruit knife or spoon. Fill with cranberry sauce, chutney, parsley sprigs or a green vegetable such as peas.

HOW TO PLAN AHEAD AND MAKE THIS
THE BEST CHRISTMAS DINNER EVER!

APPETIZERS

❧ Give the cooks more space by serving a cold appetizer in the living room. Choose something that won't dampen enthusiasm for the Christmas feast — a dip, like the tasty Caesar one on p. 83, served with fresh vegetables and thin slices of baguette or crackers, is always a winner.

VEGETABLES

❧ Avoid last-minute vegetable side dishes that need to be cooked on top of the stove. Instead, choose from delicious freeze-ahead vegetables like Sweet Potato and Carrot Crisp (p. 133) or Bronze Roasted Onions (p. 132) — or serve puréed vegetables, such as turnip, sweet potatoes, parsnips or mashed potatoes, and make them an hour or so before the turkey comes out of the oven. Keep them warm in heatproof serving dishes or saucepans, nestled in a shallow pan of simmering water on the stove top.

❧ Instead of a green vegetable, offer the fresh crunch and flavor of a crisp salad. Dress it with an orange vinaigrette and a sprinkle of red

pomegranate seeds or chopped cranberries, and serve it after the main course.

BEFORE CARVING TURKEY

❧ During the time the turkey stands before carving, make the gravy and pop any other side dishes into the microwave or oven to reheat.

SERVING DISHES

❧ Piping-hot serving dishes ensure piping-hot food. Warm dishes in oven once turkey has been removed and oven turned off. Or, pour boiling water into serving dishes a few minutes before using, then drain, dry and fill the dishes and whisk them to the table.

DESSERT

❧ Choose a make-ahead dessert that doesn't need last-minute tending (see Chapter 6 for a delicious selection).

❧ Don't forget the Christmas cakes and puddings that have been ripening deliciously since late November!

Pacific Northwest Stuffing

❧

The fresh hazelnuts from the Pacific Northwest enhance this aromatic mix of celery, shallots and herbs.

1 lb	sweet Italian sausage	500 g
1 cup	chopped shallots (or 2 cups/500 mL chopped onions)	250 mL
1 tbsp	dried sage	15 mL
1 tsp	dried thyme	5 mL
1 tsp	each salt and pepper	5 mL
12 cups	cubed day-old bread	3 L
2 cups	toasted hazelnuts, chopped (see p. 30)	500 mL
1-1/2 cups	dried currants	375 mL
1/4 cup	chicken stock	50 mL
1/4 cup	Madeira	50 mL
1-1/2 tsp	grated orange rind	7 mL

Remove sausage meat from casing; crumble into large skillet. Cook over medium heat, breaking up with fork, for 10 minutes or until no longer pink.

❧ Drain off all but 1 tsp (5 mL) fat; add shallots, sage, thyme, salt and pepper. Cook for 5 to 7 minutes or until very tender.

❧ In large bowl, combine sausage mixture, bread cubes, hazelnuts, currants, stock, Madeira and orange rind until well mixed. Taste and adjust seasoning. (*Stuffing can be cooled, covered and refrigerated for up to 2 days or frozen for up to 1 week; thaw in refrigerator for 24 hours.*) Makes 16 cups (4 L).

Apricot Orange Wild Rice Stuffing

❧

*Moist, fruity and colorful, this wild rice
and brown rice blend is a delicious
alternative to the traditional bread stuffing.*

2 tbsp	butter	25 mL
2	onions, finely chopped	2
2	stalks celery, finely chopped	2
1	clove garlic, minced	1
2-1/2 cups	chicken stock	625 mL
3/4 cup	orange juice	175 mL
2 cups	long grain brown rice	500 mL
3/4 cup	wild rice	175 mL
1 tsp	each crumbled dried sage and thyme	5 mL
Pinch	ground cloves	Pinch
1 cup	chopped dried apricots	250 mL
1/4 cup	currants	50 mL
3/4 cup	pine nuts or slivered almonds, toasted (see p. 30)	175 mL
1/4 cup	chopped fresh parsley	50 mL
1 tsp	each salt and pepper	5 mL

*I*n large heavy saucepan, melt butter over medium-high heat;
cook onions, celery and garlic, stirring often, for 3 to 5 minutes
or until softened.

❧ Pour in stock and orange juice; bring to boil. Stir in brown
and wild rice, sage, thyme and cloves; return to boil. Reduce
heat to low; cover and simmer for 35 minutes.

❧ Stir in apricots and currants; simmer, covered, for 10 to
15 minutes or until rice is tender. Add pine nuts, parsley, salt
and pepper; fluff with fork to mix. Let cool completely before
stuffing bird. (*Stuffing can be covered and refrigerated for up to
2 days.*) Makes 11 cups (2.75 L).

---

*Tip: If there's too much stuffing for the size of your turkey,
combine the extra with enough chicken stock to moisten, and
then bake in a covered casserole in a 350°F (180°C) oven
for about 20 minutes or until heated through.*

Cornbread and Cashew Stuffing

❧

*It's worth the few minutes it takes to make the
cornbread for this sage and sausage-rich stuffing.*

1 lb	sausage meat	500 g
2	stalks celery, finely chopped	2
1	onion, finely chopped	1
12 cups	cubed Herbed Cornmeal Bread (recipe follows)	3 L
2 cups	giblet stock (see p. 127)	500 mL
1 cup	chopped cashews	250 mL
1/3 cup	finely chopped fresh sage (or 2 tbsp/25 mL dried)	75 mL
1 tsp	dried savory	5 mL

*C*rumble sausage meat into large skillet; cook over medium
heat, breaking up with fork, for 10 minutes or until no longer
pink. Drain off fat.

❧ Add celery and onion; cook, stirring occasionally, for 8 to
10 minutes or until vegetables are tender.

❧ Stir in bread cubes; cook, stirring occasionally, for 5 minutes. Add stock, cashews, sage and savory; mix well. Makes
about 11 cups (2.75 L).

Herbed Cornmeal Bread

2 cups	cornmeal	500 mL
1 cup	whole wheat flour	250 mL
1 cup	all-purpose flour	250 mL
2 tbsp	baking powder	25 mL
1 tsp	each dried thyme, dried tarragon and salt	5 mL
2 cups	milk	500 mL
1/2 cup	butter, melted	125 mL
2	eggs, lightly beaten	2

In bowl, combine cornmeal, whole wheat and all-purpose flours,
baking powder, thyme, tarragon and salt; mix well. Blend
together milk, butter and eggs; add to dry ingredients, stirring
just until moistened.

❧ Pour into greased 8-inch (2 L) square cake pan. Bake in
400°F (200°C) oven for 25 minutes or until golden; let cool.
(*Bread can be wrapped in foil or plastic wrap and frozen for up to
2 weeks.*) Cut into cubes. Makes 12 cups (3 L).

Citrus-Glazed Roast Goose

*A gorgeously burnished roast goose
is an old-fashioned alternative to turkey.*

1	goose (10 to 11 lb/4.5 to 5 kg)	1
Half	lemon	Half
	Salt and pepper	
1	orange, sliced	1
4 cups	boiling water	1 L
3/4 cup	Seville orange marmalade	175 mL
2 tbsp	orange liqueur	25 mL
1 tsp	soy sauce	5 mL
1/2 tsp	ginger	2 mL
1 cup	orange juice	250 mL
1 tbsp	cornstarch	15 mL
1/4 cup	cold water	50 mL

Remove all loose fat from goose. Remove and reserve giblets, neck and wing tips for making stock, if desired. Wipe goose inside and out with damp cloth and dry thoroughly. If desired, remove wishbone for easier carving.

❧ Rub goose inside and out with lemon half, squeezing juice over bird as you work. Sprinkle cavities lightly with salt and pepper; place orange slices in cavities. Fasten neck skin to body with skewer; skewer or sew body cavity closed. With kitchen string, tie legs together; tie wings and legs close to body. With needle, prick skin all over to allow fat to escape during roasting.

❧ Place goose, breast side down, on rack in large shallow roasting pan. Pour 2 cups (500 mL) of the boiling water over goose; roast, uncovered, in 400°F (200°C) oven for 30 minutes.

❧ Reduce heat to 325°F (160°C); roast for 1 hour longer. Pour off and discard liquid in pan. Turn goose over; prick again with needle and pour remaining boiling water over top. Roast for 1 hour longer. Prick goose again. Pour off and discard drippings in pan. Roast for 1 hour longer.

❧ Mix together marmalade, liqueur, soy sauce and ginger; brush over goose. Return to oven and roast for 30 to 60 minutes longer or until juices run clear when thigh is pierced and meat thermometer registers 190°F (90°C). Transfer goose to cutting board; cover loosely with foil and let stand for 15 minutes.

❧ Meanwhile, skim all fat from pan; pour in orange juice and bring to boil, scraping up and mashing any brown bits from bottom of pan. Dissolve cornstarch in water; stir into pan. Cook, whisking constantly, until slightly thickened. Season with salt and pepper to taste. Serve in warmed gravy boat.

❧ Remove skewers and strings from goose. Serve with sauce. Makes 8 servings.

FOR A PERFECT CHRISTMAS GOOSE

CHOOSING A GOOSE
If buying a fresh goose, make sure it is plump and well formed, with smooth skin free of blemishes and pinfeathers.

❧ A 10- to 11-pound (4.5 to 5 kilogram) goose is the largest you should consider (bigger ones might be tough). Since geese have large carcasses and relatively little meat, a goose this size will serve no more than eight people. If you want to serve a larger group, buy two geese.

PREPARATION AND COOKING
Because goose contains a great deal of fat just below its thick skin, it should not be roasted in the same way as leaner birds such as turkey. Although you need to baste a turkey with fat while it roasts, the opposite is true with goose: you must remove grease. Care and a few tricks are needed for roasting a goose, but the succulent meat and crisp skin are worth every ounce of effort.

❧ Pull out any loose pads of fat.

❧ Using a needle, pierce skin and fatty layer without penetrating the lean meat.

❧ Pour boiling water over bird just before placing in oven and again partway through roasting time to melt out fat and crisp the skin.

❧ Discard drippings as they accumulate during the first 2-1/2 hours of cooking. To remove drippings, place foil over oven mitts and lift goose right out of the pan and place on work surface. Pour off drippings into large juice can to discard.

CARVING
Carving a goose demands a different technique than carving a turkey. A more rigid knife is needed because of the narrow body and close-set legs and wings. Removing the wishbone before stuffing the bird will also make carving easier.

❧ Gently move wing bone to locate shoulder joint. With large stiff-bladed chef's knife, cut down firmly through joint, severing tendons to free wing.

❧ Cut through skin in an arc around leg. Press knife down between thigh and body. Cut through joint to free leg. Cut leg in two between thigh and drumstick.

❧ Using long slender carving knife, carve breast into lengthwise slices slightly diagonal to breastbone.

Cranberry Orange Relish

A relish that's tart and chunky is perfect with turkey — whether the bird's hot on the big day or cold in sandwiches.

1-1/2 cups	cranberries	375 mL
1	tart apple, peeled and cored	1
2/3 cup	granulated sugar	150 mL
1/2 cup	chopped pecans, toasted (see p. 30)	125 mL
1/4 cup	raisins	50 mL
1/4 cup	orange marmalade	50 mL
1 tbsp	coarsely grated lemon rind	15 mL
1 tbsp	lemon juice	15 mL
Pinch	cinnamon (optional)	Pinch

*I*n food processor or grinder, chop cranberries and apple.

❧ In bowl, combine cranberry mixture, sugar, pecans, raisins, marmalade, lemon rind, lemon juice, and cinnamon (if using). Cover and refrigerate for at least 8 hours or up to 1 week. Makes about 2 cups (500 mL).

WHAT A GREAT IDEA!

MICROWAVE TEN-MINUTE CRANBERRY SAUCE

A hint of lemon adds to the flavor of this delicious quick-cooking sauce.

❧ *In 8-cup (2 L) microwaveable measure, combine 3 cups (750 mL) cranberries, 1-1/2 cups (375 mL) granulated sugar and 2 tsp (10 mL) grated lemon rind; cover and microwave at High for 7 to 9 minutes or until cranberries pop, stirring once. Let cool. (Sauce can be refrigerated in airtight container for up to 1 week.) Makes about 2 cups (500 mL).*

Jellied Cranberry Beet Relish

Chock-full of ruby-red beets, celery and onions, this tangy-sweet relish is a delicious complement to roast turkey or goose.

2 cups	cranberries	500 mL
1 cup	water	250 mL
1/2 cup	orange juice	125 mL
1/4 oz	unflavored gelatin	1/4 oz
3/4 cup	granulated sugar	175 mL
1 cup	diced cooked beets	250 mL
1 cup	diced celery	250 mL
1/2 cup	chopped onions	125 mL
1 tbsp	horseradish	15 mL
2 tsp	grated orange rind	10 mL

*I*n saucepan, combine cranberries, water and 1/4 cup (50 mL) of the orange juice; bring to boil. Reduce heat to medium and cook for about 4 minutes or until cranberries pop and soften.

❧ Meanwhile, sprinkle gelatin over remaining orange juice; let stand for 1 minute to soften. Add to cranberry mixture along with sugar, stirring until gelatin dissolves. Remove from heat; stir in beets, celery, onions, horseradish and orange rind.

❧ Pour into rinsed but not dried 4-cup (1 L) mold or deep bowl. Cover and refrigerate for at least 2 hours or until set. *(Relish can be refrigerated for up to 24 hours.)*

❧ To unmold, dip into hot water for about 20 seconds, then invert onto serving plate. Makes about 8 servings.

Jellied Cranberry Beet Relish

Bronze Roasted Onions

❧

Long roasting brings out the natural sweetness in onions. Serve with turkey, chicken, lamb or pork.

8	onions	8
1 tbsp	butter	15 mL
1 tsp	granulated sugar	5 mL
1 tbsp	balsamic vinegar	15 mL
1 tsp	olive oil	5 mL
1/4 cup	water	50 mL
1 tsp	dried marjoram	5 mL
3/4 tsp	salt	4 mL
1/2 tsp	pepper	2 mL
1/4 cup	slivered sweet red pepper	50 mL

Peel onions, keeping stem end intact; cut in half through stem.

❧ In large skillet, melt butter over medium heat; sprinkle with sugar. Add onions, cut sides down; cook for 8 to 10 minutes or until beginning to brown. Arrange in 11- x 7-inch (2 L) baking dish; sprinkle with vinegar and oil.

❧ Pour water into skillet and bring to boil, stirring to scrape up brown bits; add marjoram, salt and pepper. Pour over onions.

❧ Cover with foil and bake in 350°F (180°C) oven for 30 minutes; turn onions over and bake for 45 minutes longer, turning once more. *(Onions can be prepared to this point, cooled, covered and refrigerated for up to 2 days or frozen for up to 2 weeks. Let thaw in refrigerator for 24 hours. Let stand at room temperature for 30 minutes before continuing.)*

❧ Sprinkle onions with red pepper; cover and bake for 15 minutes longer, basting occasionally. Makes 8 servings.

Sweet Potato and Carrot Crisp

❧

A nutty crumb topping crisps up a deliciously smooth purée that can be made ahead and frozen.

5	large sweet potatoes (about 2-1/2 lb/1.25 kg)	5
12	carrots (about 2 lb/1 kg)	12
3/4 cup	orange juice	175 mL
2 tbsp	liquid honey	25 mL
2 tbsp	butter	25 mL
2 tsp	cinnamon	10 mL
2	cloves garlic, minced	2
1 tsp	salt	5 mL

Topping

1-1/2 cups	fresh bread crumbs	375 mL
1/2 cup	chopped pecans	125 mL
1/3 cup	butter, melted	75 mL
1 tbsp	chopped fresh parsley	15 mL

Peel and cut sweet potatoes and carrots into large chunks. In large pot of boiling water, cook potatoes and carrots for about 20 minutes or until very tender; drain. Purée in food processor or blender, in batches if necessary.

❧ Add orange juice, honey, butter, cinnamon, garlic and salt; blend well. Spoon into greased 13- x 9-inch (3 L) baking dish. (*Recipe can be prepared to this point, covered and refrigerated for up to 2 days or frozen for up to 2 weeks. Let thaw in refrigerator for 24 hours. Let stand at room temperature for 30 minutes before continuing.*)

❧ TOPPING: Combine bread crumbs, pecans, butter and parsley. Sprinkle over potato mixture. Cover with foil and bake in 350°F (180°C) oven for 20 minutes; uncover and bake for 30 minutes or until heated through. Makes 8 to 10 servings.

In photo:
(left) Sweet Potato and Carrot Crisp (this page);
Bronze Roasted Onions (p. 132)

Make-Ahead Mashed Potato Casserole

❧

Cutting down on last-minute stove-top clutter on the big day is easy when the mashed potatoes are made weeks ahead.

10	potatoes (about 3-1/2 lb/1.75 kg)	10
1/2 lb	cream cheese	250 g
1/4 cup	butter	50 mL
1 cup	chopped green onions	250 mL
1 cup	sour cream	250 mL
1/2 cup	minced fresh parsley	125 mL
Pinch	dried marjoram	Pinch
	Salt and pepper	
1/2 cup	coarse fresh bread crumbs	125 mL

In large pot of boiling water, cook potatoes for 20 minutes or until tender but not mushy. Drain and let cool slightly; peel.

❧ With potato masher, mash until smooth; blend in cream cheese and butter until melted. Mix in onions, sour cream, parsley, marjoram, and salt and pepper to taste.

❧ Transfer to 8-inch (2 L) baking dish; smooth top. Sprinkle with crumbs. (*Casserole can be prepared to this point, covered and refrigerated for up to 2 days or frozen for up to 1 week. Let thaw in refrigerator for 24 hours. Add 10 minutes to baking time.*)

❧ Bake in 400°F (200°C) oven for about 20 minutes or until heated through and top is lightly golden. Makes about 10 servings.

WHAT A GREAT IDEA!

GREEN BEANS — FAST!

This make-ahead trick lets you serve a crunchy green vegetable even when there's no time and space to boil vegetables from scratch.

❧ *In large saucepan of boiling water, cook 1-1/2 lb (750 g) green beans for 3 to 4 minutes or until just tender-crisp. Drain and refresh under cold water. (Beans can be prepared to this point and arranged in single layer on tea towel, then rolled loosely and refrigerated in plastic bag for up to 8 hours.)*

❧ *In large skillet, melt 2 tbsp (25 mL) butter or olive oil with 1/2 tsp (2 mL) dried thyme over medium-high heat; add beans and toss to coat. Cook for 2 minutes or until heated through. Toss with 2 tsp (10 mL) balsamic or wine vinegar; season with salt and pepper to taste. Makes 6 to 8 servings.*

Pearl Onion and Orange Braise

❧

*Pearl onions take devotion to peel but they
are definitely worth the time, especially when sweet
with currants and zesty with orange. Serve as a relish
with turkey, goose, duck, ham or pork.*

4 cups	pearl onions	1 L
1 tsp	grated orange rind	5 mL
3/4 cup	orange juice	175 mL
1 tbsp	olive oil	15 mL
1/2 tsp	salt	2 mL
1/4 cup	currants	50 mL
	Pepper	
2 tbsp	chopped fresh parsley	25 mL
	Orange slices	

*I*n large pot of boiling water, boil onions for 3 minutes; drain
and refresh under cold water. Peel onions; trim root ends, leaving intact so onions don't fall apart.

❧ In saucepan, simmer onions, orange rind and juice, oil and
salt, covered, over medium-low heat for 15 minutes.

❧ Add currants; simmer, uncovered, for 20 minutes or until
onions are tender and glazed. *(Onions can be cooled, covered and
refrigerated for up to 2 days; reheat gently over medium-low heat or
in 325°F/160°C oven for 20 minutes or until heated through.)*

❧ Season with pepper to taste. Sprinkle with parsley. Garnish
with orange slices. Makes 6 servings.

Creamy Onions and Carrots

❧

*Cream cheese adds a smooth holiday-best touch to an
old-favorite onion and carrot combo.*

1-1/4 lb	small white onions	625 g
1/2 lb	baby carrots, peeled	250 g
1/4 cup	butter	50 mL
1/2 cup	finely chopped pecans	125 mL
1/2 cup	fresh bread crumbs	125 mL
2	onions, chopped	2
1/4 cup	all-purpose flour	50 mL
1 cup	milk	250 mL
4 oz	light cream cheese	125 g
	Nutmeg, salt and pepper	

*I*n saucepan of boiling water, cook small onions for 1 minute.
Drain and rinse under cold water; peel.

❧ In saucepan of boiling water, cook onions and carrots for
5 to 7 minutes or until tender-crisp. Drain and place in 6-cup
(1.5 L) baking dish, reserving 1 cup (250 mL) liquid.

❧ In same pan, melt butter; pour half into bowl. Stir pecans
and bread crumbs into bowl until well mixed.

❧ Add chopped onions to remaining butter in pan; cook over
low heat, stirring occasionally, for 5 minutes. Sprinkle with
flour; cook, stirring, for 1 minute. Increase heat to medium;
gradually whisk in reserved liquid and milk. Cook, whisking, for
5 minutes or until smooth and thickened.

❧ Reduce heat to low; stir in cream cheese until melted.
Season with nutmeg, salt and pepper to taste. Pour over onions
and carrots; sprinkle with crumb mixture. *(Recipe can be prepared
to this point, cooled, covered and refrigerated for up to 24 hours. Let
stand at room temperature for 30 minutes before baking.)*

❧ Bake, uncovered, in 350°F (180°C) oven for
20 to 25 minutes or until heated
through. Makes 8 servings.

*Pearl
Onion and
Orange Braise*

Cheesy Brussels Sprouts

Our cheesy cream sauce will make even the most ardent brussels sprouts naysayer a brussels sprouts fan!

2 lb	brussels sprouts	1 kg
3 tbsp	butter	50 mL
3 tbsp	all-purpose flour	50 mL
2 cups	milk	500 mL
1 tsp	Dijon mustard	5 mL
3/4 tsp	salt	4 mL
1/2 tsp	pepper	2 mL
1/4 tsp	nutmeg	1 mL
1 cup	shredded Cheddar cheese	250 mL

Cut X in base of each brussels sprout; cook in large saucepan of boiling water for 7 to 9 minutes or until tender-crisp. Drain and refresh under cold water; press out excess water with towel. Let cool; halve and set aside.

In saucepan, melt butter over medium heat; stir in flour and cook, stirring, for 1 minute. Add milk; cook, stirring, for 3 to 5 minutes or until smooth and thickened. Stir in mustard, salt, pepper and nutmeg. Remove from heat; stir in half of the cheese until melted. Gently stir in brussels sprouts.

Spoon into greased 11- x 7-inch (2 L) baking dish. (*Brussels sprouts can be prepared to this point, covered and refrigerated for up to 1 day.*) Sprinkle with remaining cheese; bake in 375°F (190°C) oven for 30 minutes or until bubbly. Brown under broiler for 2 minutes. Makes 8 servings.

Beet and Pear Purée

Here's a new vegetable for the feast.
Beets meet pears in a delicious tangy-sweet
purée that's brilliantly colored.

8	beets (about 3 lb/1.5 kg)	8
1	can (14 oz/398 mL) unsweetened pears	1
1/3 cup	butter	75 mL
1-1/2 cups	chopped onions	375 mL
1/4 cup	red wine vinegar	50 mL
1/2 tsp	salt	2 mL
Pinch	pepper	Pinch

Place beets in large saucepan and cover with cold water; bring to boil. Reduce heat and simmer, covered, for 40 minutes or until very tender. Drain and let cool; peel and set aside.

❧ Drain and coarsely chop pears, reserving liquid for another use. In large skillet, melt butter over medium heat; cook onions and pears, stirring often, for 10 to 15 minutes or until golden. Add vinegar, salt and pepper; cook for 30 seconds.

❧ In food processor or blender, purée beets and pear mixture until smooth. (*Purée can be prepared to this point, cooled and frozen in airtight container for up to 2 weeks. Let thaw in refrigerator for 24 hours before continuing.*)

❧ Transfer purée to 8-cup (2 L) baking dish. Cover and bake in 350°F (180°C) oven for 25 to 35 minutes or until heated through. Makes 8 servings.

Pear and Rutabaga Casserole

Rutabaga is fancied up for Christmas with
naturally sweet pears and colorful carrots.

1	can (19 oz/540 mL) pear halves	1
1	rutabaga	1
6	carrots	6
2 tbsp	butter	25 mL
1/4 tsp	ginger	1 mL
	Salt and pepper	
	Sprig fresh mint or parsley	

Drain pears, reserving one pear half for garnish and the juice for another use. Peel and cut rutabaga and carrots into large chunks. In saucepan of boiling water, cook rutabaga and carrots for 20 minutes or until tender. Drain.

❧ Transfer vegetables and pears to food processor or blender; purée until smooth. Blend in butter, ginger, and salt and pepper to taste.

❧ Transfer to 6-cup (1.5 L) baking dish. (*Casserole can be prepared to this point, cooled, covered and refrigerated for up to 1 day; reheat in microwave at Medium-High/70% for 12 to 15 minutes, rotating once, or in 350°F/180°C oven for 30 to 40 minutes or until steaming hot.*)

❧ Slice reserved pear lengthwise 4 times without cutting through stem end; fan out slices and place on purée. Garnish with mint sprig to resemble leaves. Makes 8 servings.

Golden Dome of Cauliflower

An easy mustardy cheese sauce gilds a whole cauliflower — a spectacular presentation at the
Christmas table. The sauce is equally delicious over broccoli.

1	cauliflower (about 2-1/2 lb/1.25 kg)	1
2 cups	shredded Cheddar cheese	500 mL
1/4 cup	mayonnaise	50 mL
2 tbsp	Dijon mustard	25 mL
2 tbsp	freshly grated Parmesan cheese	25 mL

Core cauliflower and remove outer leaves, leaving head intact. In large pot, steam cauliflower on rack over boiling water for 20 minutes or until tender-crisp. Transfer to heatproof serving dish.

❧ Combine Cheddar cheese, mayonnaise and mustard; spread over cauliflower. Sprinkle with Parmesan cheese.

❧ Bake in 425°F (220°C) oven for 10 minutes or until topping is bubbling and lightly browned. Makes 6 to 8 servings.

> *Tip*: To microwave cauliflower instead of steaming, place whole head and 2 tbsp (25 mL) water in 12-cup (3 L) casserole; cover and microwave at High for 8 minutes or until almost tender-crisp, rotating twice. Let stand, covered, for 5 minutes. Drain and bake as above.

Sprouts and Chestnuts

Sweet imported chestnuts make their appearance just before Christmas. Add a few to brussels sprouts to give this traditional vegetable holiday pizzazz.

1-1/2 lb	brussels sprouts	750 g
1	strip lemon rind	1
1/4 cup	unsalted butter	50 mL
16	chestnuts, peeled and cooked	16
	Nutmeg, salt and pepper	

Cut X in base of each brussels sprout. In large saucepan of boiling water, cook brussels sprouts and lemon rind over medium heat, partially covered, for 5 to 7 minutes or until tender-crisp. Drain and transfer to plate, discarding lemon rind; keep warm.

❧ In same saucepan, melt butter over medium-low heat; cook chestnuts for 5 minutes or until golden. Return brussels sprouts to pan; season with nutmeg, salt and pepper to taste. Cover and cook for 3 minutes or until brussels sprouts are heated through, shaking pan occasionally to prevent browning. Makes 6 to 8 servings.

EDIBLE CHESTNUTS

Buy glossy dark brown chestnuts at the produce market or supermarket. Choose undamaged ones that feel heavy. Do not gather horse chestnuts for human consumption.

TO ENJOY ROASTED ON OPEN FIRE OR STOVE TOP: Using sharp knife, score a cross on flat side of each chestnut. Place in heavy skillet or in chestnut pan (long-handled skillet with perforated bottom) with a few drops of vegetable oil. Cook over medium heat on stove top or over open fire, shaking pan frequently to prevent burning, until shells and inner brown skins can be easily removed.

TO USE IN RECIPES: Using sharp knife, score a cross on flat side of each raw chestnut. Blanch, 4 or 5 at a time, in boiling water for 2 minutes. Using slotted spoon, remove chestnuts and peel away shells and inner brown skins. Return any hard-to-peel chestnuts to boiling water for a few seconds and try again.

❧ In large saucepan, pour enough boiling water over peeled chestnuts to cover; bring to boil. Reduce heat and simmer, covered, for 30 to 45 minutes or until tender. Drain.

THE RELAXING SIDE OF CHRISTMAS

❧

EVEN THOUGH THE PRESSURE'S OFF, THE FESTIVE SPIRIT
LINGERS ON. RELAX AND ENJOY IT WITH DELICIOUS EASY-TO-FIX DISHES
THAT WILL TEMPT EVEN THE MOST JADED APPETITES.

Cranberry Pistachio Muffins

❧

*Cranberries provide the seasonal red and pistachios the
contrasting green in delicious streusel-topped muffins.*

1 cup	all-purpose flour	250 mL
1 cup	whole wheat flour	250 mL
1/2 cup	granulated sugar	125 mL
1 tbsp	baking powder	15 mL
1/2 tsp	ground coriander (or pinch nutmeg)	2 mL
1/2 tsp	salt	2 mL
1	egg	1
1 cup	milk	250 mL
1/4 cup	butter, melted	50 mL
1 cup	cranberries	250 mL
1/2 cup	pistachio nuts or pecans, coarsely chopped	125 mL

Topping

2 tbsp	packed brown sugar	25 mL
2 tbsp	all-purpose flour	25 mL
1 tbsp	butter	15 mL
1/4 cup	pistachio nuts or pecans, finely chopped	50 mL

TOPPING: In bowl, combine sugar and flour; cut in butter until crumbly. Stir in nuts. Set aside.

❧ In bowl, combine all-purpose and whole wheat flours, sugar, baking powder, coriander and salt; make well in center.

❧ Beat together egg, milk and butter; add all at once to dry ingredients and quickly stir until just moistened. Do not overmix or beat. Fold in cranberries and nuts.

❧ Spoon into large well-greased or paper-lined muffin cups, filling to top. Sprinkle with topping. Bake in 400°F (200°C) oven for 20 to 25 minutes or until tops feel firm when touched. Remove from pan to rack; let cool. (*Muffins can be frozen for up to 1 month.*) Makes 12 muffins.

Cherry Banana Bread

❧

*For round slices of this banana bread, bake the
cherry-studded batter in vegetable or fruit cans
instead of the usual loaf pans. The small loaves
are extra-easy to wrap and freeze for later.*

1/2 cup	butter, softened	125 mL
3/4 cup	granulated sugar	175 mL
1	egg	1
1 tsp	vanilla	5 mL
1 cup	mashed ripe bananas (2 to 3)	250 mL
1/2 cup	plain yogurt	125 mL
1-3/4 cups	all-purpose flour	425 mL
1 tsp	baking powder	5 mL
1 tsp	baking soda	5 mL
1/2 tsp	salt	2 mL
3/4 cup	coarsely chopped red and green candied cherries	175 mL
1/2 cup	toasted slivered almonds (see p. 30)	125 mL

Cut waxed paper strips to line sides of four 14-oz (398 mL) cans; set aside.

❧ In bowl, beat butter with sugar until light and fluffy. Beat in egg and vanilla. Stir in bananas and yogurt until well blended.

❧ Combine flour, baking powder, baking soda and salt; stir into banana mixture until just combined. Stir in cherries and almonds. Divide among prepared cans; place on baking sheet.

❧ Bake in 350°F (180°C) oven for 45 minutes or until cake tester inserted into center comes out clean. Let cool for 10 minutes in cans; turn out upright onto racks. Let cool; remove paper. (*Loaves can be frozen for up to 1 month.*) Makes 4 loaves.

*(clockwise from right) Cranberry Pistachio Muffins;
Cherry Banana Bread; Festive Fruit Wreath (p. 140);
Creamy Ginger Orange Spread (p. 140)*

Creamy Ginger Orange Spread

Candied ginger adds sophisticated flavor to a fluffy cream cheese spread.
Enjoy it with Cranberry Pistachio Muffins or Cherry Banana Bread (recipes, p. 138).

1 cup	light cream cheese	250 mL
2 tbsp	orange juice	25 mL
2 tbsp	ginger marmalade or chopped preserved ginger	25 mL
2 tsp	liquid honey	10 mL
1 tsp	grated orange rind	5 mL

*I*n food processor or with mixer, blend cream cheese, orange juice, marmalade and honey until smooth and fluffy. Mix in orange rind. *(Spread can be refrigerated in covered container for up to 3 days.)* Makes about 1-1/4 cups (300 mL).

Festive Fruit Wreath

This make-ahead wreath is pretty enough
to be the centerpiece of the breakfast buffet table (see photo, p. 139).

1 tsp	granulated sugar	5 mL
1/2 cup	warm water	125 mL
1	pkg active dry yeast (or 1 tbsp/15 mL)	1
1/2 cup	butter, softened	125 mL
2	eggs	2
3/4 cup	milk	175 mL
1 tsp	vanilla	5 mL
4-1/3 cups	(approx) all-purpose flour	1.075 L
1/4 cup	granulated sugar	50 mL
1 tsp	salt	5 mL
1/2 tsp	cinnamon	2 mL
Filling		
1	egg white	1
1/2 cup	icing sugar	125 mL
2 tbsp	rum or orange juice	25 mL
1-1/2 cups	chopped candied fruit	375 mL
1/2 cup	currants	125 mL
Glaze		
1/4 cup	icing sugar	50 mL
2 tbsp	rum or orange juice	25 mL

*D*issolve 1 tsp (5 mL) sugar in warm water; sprinkle with yeast and let stand for 10 minutes or until frothy.

In large bowl, beat together butter, eggs, milk, vanilla and yeast mixture to make lumpy mixture. Combine flour, 1/4 cup (50 mL) sugar, salt and cinnamon; gradually stir into butter mixture until too stiff to handle. Turn out dough onto lightly floured surface; knead for about 10 minutes or until smooth and elastic, kneading in up to 3 tbsp (50 mL) more flour if necessary.

Place in lightly greased bowl, turning to grease all over. Cover with plastic wrap and let rise in warm spot for 1 hour or until doubled in bulk. Punch down dough. On lightly floured surface, roll out dough into 20- x 13-inch (50 x 33 cm) rectangle.

FILLING: In bowl, beat together egg white, icing sugar and rum; stir in fruit and currants. Spread over dough, leaving 1-inch (2.5 cm) border on one long side. Starting at other long side, tightly roll up jelly roll-style, pinching seam to seal; cut into 18 slices.

On greased pizza pan or baking sheet, overlap slices to form wreath with 12-inch (30 cm) outside diameter. Cover with cloth; let rise for 45 minutes or until doubled in bulk.

Bake in 375°F (190°C) oven for 30 to 35 minutes or until sides sound hollow when tapped. Let cool slightly. *(Wreath can be wrapped and frozen for up to 1 month. Let thaw at room temperature for 2 hours. Reheat, covered, in 325°F/160°C oven for 10 to 15 minutes.)*

GLAZE: Mix icing sugar with rum; brush over wreath. Serve warm. Makes 12 servings.

Cranberry Cinnamon Christmas Tree Rolls

🎄

This quick-to-make yeast dough, rolled up with a tangy-sweet cranberry and cinnamon filling and shaped like a Christmas tree, is especially festive and delicious!

1/4 cup	granulated sugar	50 mL
1	pkg active dry yeast (or 1 tbsp/15 mL)	1
1/2 cup	sour cream	125 mL
1/4 cup	butter	50 mL
1 tsp	salt	5 mL
2	eggs	2
1-1/2 cups	whole wheat flour	375 mL
2 cups	all-purpose flour	500 mL

Filling

2 cups	cranberries	500 mL
1-1/4 cups	packed brown sugar	300 mL
1 cup	chopped pecans	250 mL
1 tbsp	cinnamon	15 mL
1/4 cup	butter, melted	50 mL
1/4 cup	corn syrup	50 mL
3/4 cup	icing sugar	175 mL
1 tbsp	milk	15 mL
	Cranberries	
	Candied green cherries, slivered	

Dissolve 1 tsp (5 mL) of the sugar in 1/2 cup (125 mL) luke-warm water. Sprinkle in yeast; let stand for 10 minutes or until frothy.

🎄 In saucepan, heat sour cream, remaining sugar, butter and salt over low heat until sugar dissolves; let cool.

🎄 In bowl, beat eggs with sour cream and yeast mixtures; gradually beat in whole wheat flour. Beat for 2 minutes or until smooth.

🎄 With wooden spoon, gradually beat in enough of the all-purpose flour to make soft, slightly sticky dough. On lightly floured surface, knead for 8 to 10 minutes or until smooth and elastic. Place in greased bowl, turning to grease all over. Cover with plastic wrap and let rise in warm draft-free area for 1-1/2 hours or until doubled in bulk (or in refrigerator overnight).

🎄 FILLING: Meanwhile, in saucepan, bring cranberries and 1/2 cup (125 mL) water to boil; cover and boil gently for 5 minutes. Stir in 1/4 cup (50 mL) of the brown sugar; reduce heat and simmer, uncovered and stirring occasionally, for 5 minutes or until thickened. Let cool. Combine remaining brown sugar, pecans and cinnamon.

🎄 Punch down dough; divide in half. On lightly floured surface, roll out one half to 14- x 12-inch (35 x 30 cm) rectangle. Brush with 1 tbsp (15 mL) of the butter; spread with half of the filling, leaving 1/2-inch (1 cm) border. Sprinkle with half of the pecan mixture. Starting at long side, roll up tightly, pinching seam to seal; brush with 1 tbsp (15 mL) of the butter.

🎄 Using serrated knife, cut 2-inch (5 cm) thick slice from end; reserve. Cut roll into 15 slices. Center smallest slice near top of well-greased foil on large baking sheet. Snugly arrange slices in four more rows, adding one more slice for each row. Center reserved slice lengthwise under tree. Repeat with remaining dough. Cover and let rise for 45 to 50 minutes or until doubled in bulk. Bake in 350°F (180°C) oven for 25 to 30 minutes or until golden.

🎄 In saucepan, heat corn syrup over low heat. Slide buns and foil onto rack; brush with corn syrup. Let cool for 20 minutes. Whisk icing sugar with milk; pipe decoratively over buns. Garnish with cranberries and cherries. Serve warm. Makes 32 buns.

Christmas Frittata

❧

Decorate this crustless holiday quiche with sweet red pepper cutouts and a red onion garland.

9	eggs	9
1 cup	milk	250 mL
1/2 tsp	each nutmeg and oregano	2 mL
1/4 tsp	each salt and pepper	1 mL
1-3/4 cups	shredded Cheddar or Monterey Jack cheese	425 mL
1/4 lb	cream cheese	125 g
2 tsp	vegetable oil	10 mL
1	onion, chopped	1
1/2 cup	diced sweet red pepper (optional)	125 mL
4	cloves garlic, minced	4
1	pkg (10 oz/284 g) spinach, cooked, drained and chopped	1
6	cherry tomatoes, halved	6
	Sweet red and yellow pepper	
	Red onion slices	

*I*n large bowl, whisk together eggs, milk, nutmeg, oregano, salt and pepper; stir in Cheddar and cream cheese.

❧ In small skillet, heat oil over medium-high heat; cook onion, diced red pepper (if using) and garlic for 3 minutes or until softened. Stir into egg mixture along with spinach. *(Recipe can be prepared to this point, covered and refrigerated overnight.)*

❧ Pour into greased 6-cup (1.5 L) tree mold or 8-inch (2 L) square baking dish or 11- x 7-inch (2 L) baking dish. Bake in 350°F (180°C) oven for 40 to 50 minutes or until puffy, golden brown around edges and set in center. Decorate with cherry tomatoes, sweet pepper cutouts and red onion garland. Makes 4 to 6 servings.

Tip: *When fresh spinach is not available, use one 300 g package of frozen spinach, thawed and drained. Discard the coarsest stems before chopping.*

Cointreau Cranberry Crêpes

❧

Creamy custard and a Cointreau-laced cranberry filling transform everyday crêpes into festive breakfast or brunch fare. Make crêpes ahead and freeze them by the stack, each one layered with waxed paper for easy use. Add filling just before serving.

16	Crêpes (recipe follows)	16

Cranberry Filling

2 cups	cranberries	500 mL
1-1/2 cups	granulated sugar	375 mL
1/2 cup	water	125 mL
2 tbsp	orange liqueur	25 mL
1 tbsp	grated orange rind	15 mL

Custard

1 cup	light cream	250 mL
1/4 cup	granulated sugar	50 mL
4	egg yolks, well beaten	4
1 tsp	vanilla or orange liqueur	5 mL
	Whipped cream (optional)	

*C*RANBERRY FILLING: In saucepan, bring cranberries, sugar and water to boil: reduce heat and boil gently, stirring often, for 5 minutes or until skins pop. Stir in liqueur and orange rind; let cool.

❧ CUSTARD: In top of double boiler or in heavy saucepan, stir together cream, sugar and egg yolks; cook over medium-low heat, stirring constantly, for 10 minutes or until smooth and thickened enough to coat back of spoon. Stir in vanilla; let cool.

❧ Spoon about 1 tbsp (15 mL) filling onto each crêpe; top with heaping tablespoon (15 mL) custard. Roll up loosely, tucking in ends; place on serving plate. Top each crêpe with whipped cream (if using) and drizzle with a little more filling. Makes 6 to 8 servings, 2 to 3 crêpes each.

Crêpes

2/3 cup	all-purpose flour	150 mL
Pinch	salt	Pinch
2	eggs	2
1 cup	milk	250 mL
2 tbsp	(approx) butter, melted	25 mL

In bowl, combine flour and salt; make well in center. Whisk together eggs, milk and 1 tbsp (15 mL) of the butter; gradually pour into well, whisking to draw in flour until smooth. Cover and refrigerate for 1 hour. Strain to give smooth, whipping-cream consistency.

❧ Heat 8-inch (20 cm) crêpe pan over medium heat until drop of water sprinkled on pan spatters briskly. Brush with some of the remaining butter.

❧ Stir batter to reblend; pour 2 tbsp (25 mL) into center of pan. Quickly tilt and rotate pan to form thin crêpe. Cook for 40 seconds or until bottom is golden and top no longer shiny.

❧ With spatula, loosen and turn crêpe over, using fingers to assist. Cook for 30 seconds or until golden. Transfer to plate.

❧ Repeat with remaining batter, brushing pan with butter as necessary and stacking crêpes on plate. Makes 16 crêpes.

Christmas Morning Buffet Breakfast

Welcome Christmas morning with this extra-easy festive menu. Because all the dishes are both make-ahead and self-serve, everyone — including the cook! — will be able to relax and enjoy the big day.

MENU

Raspberry Razzmatazz

Tropical Fruit Bowls

Overnight Strata Sandwiches

Chili Sauce or Chutney

Cranberry Pecan Coffee Cake

Tropical Fruit Bowls

Grapefruit stars in this juicy holiday fruit salad. To create zigzag edge on grapefruit, insert sharp knife into whole fruit and make small cut; make second cut at an angle. Continue all the way around grapefruit, then separate halves.

3	grapefruit	3
	Granulated sugar	
2	kiwifruit	2
1 cup	chopped peeled mango or pear	250 mL
1 cup	red grapes	250 mL

Cut grapefruit in half. Using grapefruit knife, remove segments and place in bowl. Squeeze juice from shells onto grapefruit; sweeten with sugar to taste.

❧ Discard pith and membranes. Wrap shells in damp towel. Refrigerate shells and grapefruit for up to 12 hours.

❧ Just before serving, peel, halve and slice kiwifruit; add to grapefruit along with mango and grapes. Spoon into grapefruit shells. Drizzle any juices over fruit. Makes 6 servings.

(clockwise from top) Raspberry Razzmatazz; Overnight Strata Sandwiches; Tropical Fruit Bowls; Cranberry Pecan Coffee Cake

Overnight Strata Sandwiches

Stashed in the refrigerator the night before, this cheese and smoked chicken sandwich strata is ready to bake for Christmas morning breakfast. To serve, just lift off each sandwich. If desired, you can substitute your favorite bread for the egg bread.

3 tbsp	butter, softened	50 mL
12	slices egg bread	12
3 tbsp	Dijon mustard	50 mL
6 oz	sliced smoked chicken, turkey or ham	175 g
6 oz	Cheddar cheese, thinly sliced	175 g
1	tomato, thinly sliced	1
3	eggs	3
1/4 cup	milk	50 mL
1/4 tsp	pepper	1 mL
	Chopped fresh parsley	

Butter one side of each slice of bread; spread other side with mustard. On mustard side of six slices, evenly divide chicken, cheese and tomato. Cover with slice of bread, buttered side out; cut sandwiches in half diagonally.

Arrange sandwiches, cut side down and overlapping, in greased 11- x 7-inch (2 L) baking dish. Whisk together eggs, milk and pepper; pour over sandwiches. Cover and refrigerate for up to 12 hours. Bake in 375°F (190°C) oven for about 30 minutes or until crisp and golden. Garnish with parsley. Makes 6 servings.

Cranberry Pecan Coffee Cake

Feathery light, with the sweet crunch of caramel and pecans and the tang of cranberries, this coffee cake is a delicious ending to breakfast.

1/2 cup	butter, softened	125 mL
3/4 cup	granulated sugar	175 mL
2	eggs	2
1 tsp	vanilla	5 mL
1-1/2 cups	all-purpose flour	375 mL
1-1/2 tsp	baking powder	7 mL
1 tsp	baking soda	5 mL
1/2 tsp	cinnamon	2 mL
1/4 tsp	salt	1 mL
1 cup	sour cream	250 mL

Topping

2/3 cup	packed brown sugar	150 mL
1/3 cup	butter	75 mL
1/4 tsp	cinnamon	1 mL
1-1/4 cups	cranberries	300 mL
1/2 cup	chopped pecans	125 mL

TOPPING: In saucepan, bring sugar, butter and cinnamon to boil over medium heat, stirring. Pour into greased 9-inch (2.5 L) springform pan. Sprinkle with cranberries and pecans; set aside.

In large bowl, beat butter with sugar until fluffy. Beat in eggs, one at a time, and vanilla. Stir together flour, baking powder, baking soda, cinnamon and salt. Using wooden spoon, stir half into creamed mixture; stir in sour cream and remaining flour mixture.

Spread batter over cranberry layer, pushing batter higher around edges. Wrap foil around bottom of pan and set on baking sheet. Bake in 350°F (180°C) oven for 1 hour or until cake tester inserted into center comes out clean.

Let cool in pan for 10 minutes. Invert onto serving platter and serve warm. *(Cake can be cooled completely, wrapped and frozen for up to 1 week. Thaw at room temperature; unwrap and reheat on baking sheet covered with foil in 350°F/180°C oven for 15 to 20 minutes or until heated through.)* Makes 10 servings.

WHAT A GREAT IDEA!

RASPBERRY RAZZMATAZZ

Get Christmas morning off to a refreshing start with a fruity ruby-red drink. For a festive garnish, float raspberries and orange and lime slices in the chilled pitcher.

In large pitcher, dilute 1 can (280 mL) frozen raspberry concentrate according to directions; mix with 3 cups (750 mL) cranberry, white grape or apple juice. Refrigerate until chilled or overnight. Makes 8 cups (2 L).

Post-Christmas Brunch

Invite family and friends over for this hearty brunch featuring an impressive old favorite — Toad-in-the-Hole — updated with herbs and sauces. The simple-to-prepare menu features great make-ahead side dishes. Best of all, the food is guaranteed to please children and grown-ups alike.

Spiced Chunky Applesauce

Sometimes the simplest foods are the most pleasing. Applesauce with a touch of lemon and spice is a case in point. This makes enough to enjoy throughout the week.

5 lb	Golden Delicious apples	2.2 kg
1-1/2 cups	granulated sugar	375 mL
1 cup	apple cider	250 mL
1 tbsp	finely grated lemon rind	15 mL
2 tbsp	lemon juice	25 mL
1/2 tsp	each cinnamon, allspice and ginger	2 mL
Pinch	nutmeg	Pinch
1/4 cup	minced crystallized ginger (optional)	50 mL

Peel, core and cut apples into 1-inch (2.5 cm) chunks. In nonaluminum saucepan, combine sugar and cider; cook, stirring constantly, over medium-high heat until boiling and sugar has dissolved.

❧ Add apples and return to simmer; partially cover and cook over medium-low heat, stirring often, for 1 hour or until apples are softened.

❧ Stir in lemon rind and juice, cinnamon, allspice, ground ginger, nutmeg, and crystallized ginger (if using); cook for 15 minutes or until thickened and chunky. Let cool. (Applesauce can be refrigerated in glass jars for up to 1 week.) Makes 8 cups (2 L).

Savory Sausage Toad-in-the-Hole

Roast the sausages and let the batter rest while enjoying appetizers. Then pour on the batter, pop the "toad" in the oven and watch this dish puff and soar to impressive heights. Enjoy it with Spiced Chunky Applesauce, maple syrup or cranberry sauce.

2 cups	all-purpose flour	500 mL
1/2 tsp	dried savory	2 mL
1/4 tsp	salt	1 mL
2 cups	milk	500 mL
6	eggs	6
2 lb	pork sausage links	1 kg

In bowl, stir together flour, savory and salt. Whisk milk with eggs; gradually whisk into flour mixture until smooth. Let stand for 30 minutes.

❧ Meanwhile, prick sausages; place in greased 13- x 9-inch (3 L) baking dish. Roast in 375°F (190°C) oven, turning sausages once, for 25 to 30 minutes or until golden. Drain off all but 2 tbsp (30 mL) fat.

❧ Remove from oven; increase temperature to 425°F (220°C). Whisk batter; pour over sausages. Bake for 25 to 30 minutes or until puffed and golden. Serve immediately. Makes 8 servings.

(clockwise from top right) Christmas Coleslaw; cranberry sauce; Savory Sausage Toad-in-the-Hole; Spiced Chunky Applesauce; chilled apple cider

Christmas Coleslaw

This colorful salad is just the thing for a holiday menu. Make it the night before to allow the flavors to blend.

6 cups	shredded green cabbage (1 lb/500 g)	1.5 L
6 cups	shredded red cabbage (1 lb/500 g)	1.5 L
3	green onions, thinly sliced	3
1	sweet red pepper, julienned	1
1/4 cups	dried currants or raisins	50 mL

Dressing

3 tbsp	cider vinegar	50 mL
2 tbsp	sweet mustard	25 mL
1 tbsp	packed brown sugar	15 mL
1 tsp	caraway seeds	5 mL
1/2 tsp	salt	2 mL
1/4 tsp	pepper	1 mL
Pinch	allspice	Pinch
1/3 cup	vegetable oil	75 mL
Dash	hot pepper sauce	Dash

In large bowl, toss together green and red cabbage, onions, red pepper and currants until well mixed.

DRESSING: In bowl, whisk together vinegar, mustard, sugar, caraway seeds, salt, pepper and allspice; gradually whisk in oil and hot pepper sauce until smooth. Pour over coleslaw; toss to coat. Cover and refrigerate overnight or for up to 24 hours. Makes 8 servings.

A Holiday Lunch

A lunch is often the best get-together meal for families with children
— especially one that features crowd-pleasing lasagna and colorful make-ahead salads.

Clam Lasagna Roll-Ups

It takes time to make lasagna, but it's so popular and easy to serve that the effort is more than worth it.

6	lasagna noodles	6
1-3/4 cups	Cream Sauce (recipe follows)	425 mL
2 cups	shredded mozzarella cheese	500 mL
1/4 cup	freshly grated Parmesan cheese	50 mL
2 tbsp	fresh bread crumbs	25 mL

Clam Sauce

1 tbsp	olive oil	15 mL
1 cup	chopped onion	250 mL
2	cloves garlic, minced	2
1	can (28 oz/796 mL) tomatoes (undrained)	1
2 tbsp	tomato paste	25 mL
2	cans (each 5 oz/142 g) baby clams (undrained)	2
1 tsp	dried oregano	5 mL
1/4 tsp	hot pepper flakes	1 mL
2 tbsp	minced fresh parsley	25 mL
	Salt and pepper	

Ricotta and Spinach Filling

2 cups	packed fresh spinach	500 mL
2	eggs	2
1/2 lb	ricotta cheese	250 g
1 cup	shredded mozzarella cheese	250 mL
1/2 cup	freshly grated Parmesan cheese	125 mL
2 tbsp	each chopped green onions and fresh parsley	25 mL
2 tbsp	chopped fresh basil (or 1 tsp/5 mL dried)	25 mL

CLAM SAUCE: In heavy saucepan, heat oil over medium heat; cook onion and garlic, stirring, for 5 minutes or until softened. Add tomatoes, crushing with fork; add tomato paste.

❧ Drain clams, reserving 3/4 cup (175 mL) juice; set clams aside. Add juice to saucepan and stir in oregano and hot pepper flakes; bring to boil. Reduce heat and simmer for 25 minutes or until thick enough that space remains after drawing spoon across bottom of pan; let cool.

❧ Add clams, parsley, and salt and pepper to taste. (*Sauce can be covered and refrigerated for up to 1 day or frozen for up to 1 month.*)

❧ RICOTTA AND SPINACH FILLING: Rinse spinach but do not dry. In saucepan, cook spinach with just the water clinging to leaves over medium-high heat for 4 minutes or until wilted. Press out as much moisture as possible; chop finely and place in bowl. Mix in eggs, ricotta, mozzarella, Parmesan, onions, parsley and basil. (*Filling can be covered and refrigerated for up to 1 day.*)

❧ In large pot of boiling salted water, cook noodles for 8 minutes or until tender. Rinse in cold water.

❧ Spread about 3/4 cup (175 mL) of the clam sauce in 13- x 9-inch (3.5 L) baking dish. Drain and pat noodles dry; cut in half. Working with one half at a time, spread with about 3 tbsp (50 mL) filling, leaving 1 inch (2.5 cm) uncovered at one end. Spread about 2 tbsp (25 mL) clam sauce over filling. Starting at covered end, roll up and place, seam side down, in two rows on clam sauce in dish. Spread any remaining clam sauce around rolls.

❧ Pour cream sauce over rolls; sprinkle with mozzarella, Parmesan and bread crumbs. (*Lasagna can be covered and refrigerated for up to 4 hours.*) Bake in 350°F (180°C) oven for 45 minutes or until sauce bubbles and top is crusty and golden. Let stand for 10 minutes. Makes 8 servings.

Cream Sauce

3 tbsp	butter	50 mL
3 tbsp	all-purpose flour	50 mL
1/2 tsp	salt	2 mL
	Pepper	
1-1/2 cups	milk	375 mL

In small saucepan, melt butter over medium heat. Blend in flour, salt, and pepper to taste; cook, whisking, for 1 minute. Gradually whisk in milk; cook for 3 minutes, whisking constantly, or until boiling and thickened. Makes 1-3/4 cups (425 mL).

(clockwise from top) Creamy Cauliflower and Broccoli Crunch (p. 150); Clam Lasagna Roll-Ups; (on plate) slices of Garlic Herb Bruschetta; Avocado and Bibb Lettuce Toss (p. 150)

MENU

❧

Winter Fruit Salad

❧

Clam Lasagna Roll-Ups*

❧

Garlic Herb Bruschetta*

❧

Avocado and
Bibb Lettuce Toss*

❧

Creamy Cauliflower and
Broccoli Crunch*

❧

Christmas Cake,
Truffles and Cookies

❧

Sherbet and Ice Cream

*Recipes included

Creamy Cauliflower and Broccoli Crunch

When you want some crunch in your salad, consider this creamy and delicious one that's great any time of the year.

5 cups	sliced broccoli florets (1 bunch)	1.25 L
4 cups	sliced cauliflower florets (1 small head)	1 L
1	small red onion, thinly sliced	1
1 cup	each light mayonnaise and sour cream	250 mL
1 tbsp	granulated sugar	15 mL
1 tbsp	white vinegar	15 mL
1/2 tsp	salt	2 mL
1/4 tsp	pepper	1 mL
Dash	Worcestershire sauce	Dash

*I*n large bowl, combine broccoli, cauliflower and onion.

In bowl, stir together mayonnaise, sour cream, sugar, vinegar, salt, pepper and Worcestershire sauce; pour over vegetables and toss. *(Salad can be covered and refrigerated for up to 2 hours.)* Makes 8 servings.

Garlic Herb Bruschetta

Add gusto to the lunch with a flavorful bruschetta you can bake after removing the lasagna from the oven.

1	baguette	1
1/3 cup	olive oil	75 mL
2	large cloves garlic, minced	2
2 tsp	dried marjoram	10 mL
2 tsp	dried rosemary, crumbled	10 mL
Dash	hot pepper sauce	Dash
Pinch	salt	Pinch

*S*lice bread into 1/2-inch (1 cm) thick diagonal slices; spread on baking sheets. Stir together oil, garlic, marjoram, rosemary, hot pepper sauce and salt; brush over bread.

Toast in 375°F (190°C) oven for 10 to 15 minutes or until lightly browned. Serve hot. Makes about 8 servings.

> **Tip**: *The best, most flavorful olive oil for enjoying on bruschetta or in salad dressings is extra virgin olive oil.*

Avocado and Bibb Lettuce Toss

Be sure to buy avocados about five days ahead and let them ripen at room temperature out of the sun.

1	head Bibb lettuce, separated	1
2	Belgian endives, separated	2
1	small head radicchio, separated (or 1 more endive)	1
Half	sweet red or green pepper	Half
Half	small Spanish onion	Half
2	avocados	2

Citrus Dressing

1/4 cup	orange juice	50 mL
1 tbsp	red wine vinegar	15 mL
1 tsp	Dijon mustard	5 mL
1/2 tsp	salt	2 mL
1	clove garlic, minced	1
Dash	hot pepper sauce	Dash
1/2 cup	olive oil	125 mL

*C*ITRUS DRESSING: In bowl, stir together orange juice, vinegar, mustard, salt, garlic and hot pepper sauce; whisk in oil. *(Dressing can be covered and refrigerated for up to 2 days; whisk before using.)*

In large salad bowl, arrange Bibb lettuce, endive and radicchio. Cut red pepper into thin strips and onion into thin rings; add to bowl. Peel and pit avocados; cut into bite-size cubes and sprinkle over salad. Drizzle with enough dressing to moisten; toss well. Makes 8 servings.

Warming Drinks

Warm up a frosty afternoon with these relaxing drinks — or choose from our fireside selection on p. 117.

Citrus Mulled Wine

*For a nonalcoholic version,
substitute apple cider for the wine.*

1 cup	water	250 mL
2/3 cup	granulated sugar	150 mL
1 tsp	whole cloves	5 mL
1/4 tsp	nutmeg	1 mL
8	cinnamon sticks	8
1	each lemon and orange, sliced	1
2	bottles (each 750 mL) dry red wine	2

In small saucepan, combine water, sugar, cloves, nutmeg, one of the cinnamon sticks, lemon and orange; bring to boil over medium heat, stirring.

❧ Reduce heat and simmer for 10 minutes; let cool, then strain. (*Recipe can be prepared to this point, covered and refrigerated for up to 1 week.*)

❧ In large saucepan, combine sugar mixture and wine; heat until steaming. Pour into mugs; serve with remaining cinnamon sticks for stirring. Makes 7 servings, each 1 cup (250 mL).

Spirited Tea

*Welcome the gang after skiing or skating with
steaming mugs of this hot tea-based punch.*

8 cups	freshly brewed strong tea	2 L
2 cups	packed brown sugar	500 mL
1	bottle (750 mL) brandy	1
1	bottle (750 mL) dark rum	1
1 cup	lemon juice	250 mL
	Lemon slices	
	Cinnamon sticks	

In large saucepan, combine tea and sugar; bring to boil, stirring. Remove from heat and carefully stir in brandy, rum and lemon juice.

❧ Pour into cups or mugs; garnish with lemon slice. Serve with cinnamon stick for stirring. Makes about 30 servings, each 1/2 cup (125 mL).

Getting Together With The Gang

It all depends on the gang. It might be an afternoon of zooming down the hills on skis or toboggans, or gliding over the rink in new skates. Or maybe everyone is getting together to relax and watch videos. No matter what the activity, here's a crowd-pleaser of a menu to serve when serious hunger takes over. Note: there isn't a scrap of leftover turkey in the soup!

MENU

❧

Corn Chips and Salsa

❧

Crudités and Olives

❧

Two-Pepper Corn Bread*

❧

Mexican Black Bean Soup*

❧

Sliced Honeydew Melon and Cantaloupe

❧

Chocolate Cookie Cheescake (recipe, p.106)

*Recipes included

Two-Pepper Corn Bread

❧

This moist, pepper-studded bread is a wonderfully fragrant addition to any table. You can substitute light cream cheese, if desired.

1/2 lb	cream cheese	250 g
1 tbsp	granulated sugar	15 mL
2	eggs	2
1 cup	cornmeal	250 mL
1 cup	all-purpose flour	250 mL
1 tbsp	baking powder	15 mL
1/2 tsp	salt	2 mL
6	green onions, chopped	6
1	can (4 oz/114 mL) mild green chilies, drained and diced	1
1/2 cup	finely chopped sweet red pepper	125 mL

In bowl, beat cheese with sugar; beat in eggs, one at a time, beating well after each addition.

❧ Combine cornmeal, flour, baking powder and salt; stir into cheese mixture along with green onions, chilies and red pepper just until combined.

❧ Spoon into greased and floured 8- x 4-inch (1.5 L) loaf pan. Bake in 350°F (180°C) oven for 1 hour or until tester inserted into center comes out clean. Let cool in pan for 5 minutes. Let cool completely on rack. Makes 1 loaf.

Mexican Black Bean Soup

❧

*There's nothing like a bowl of warming black bean soup
to take the chill off a winter's day. Garnish with sour
cream, coriander and a slice of green pepper.*

3 cups	black beans	750 mL
1 tbsp	olive oil	15 mL
3	cloves garlic, minced	3
2	onions, chopped	2
2	stalks celery, chopped	2
2 tsp	chili powder	10 mL
2 tsp	chopped fresh or pickled jalapeño pepper	10 mL
1-1/2 tsp	dried oregano	7 mL
1 tsp	ground cumin	5 mL
1/2 tsp	aniseed	2 mL
6 cups	chicken stock	1.5 L
1	can (14 oz/398 mL) stewed tomatoes	1
3/4 tsp	salt	4 mL
1/4 tsp	pepper	1 mL
4 tsp	lime juice	20 mL

Rinse beans, discarding any grit. In large pot, cover beans
with three times their volume of water; bring to boil, cover and
cook for 2 minutes. Remove from heat; let soak for 1 hour.
Drain.

❧ Wipe out pot and heat oil over medium heat; cook garlic,
onions and celery, stirring occasionally, for 5 minutes or until
onions are softened. Add chili powder, jalapeño pepper,
oregano, cumin and aniseed; cook, stirring occasionally, for
1 minute.

❧ Add beans and stock; bring to boil. Reduce heat, cover and
simmer for 75 minutes or until beans are very tender. Add tomatoes, salt and pepper; simmer for 10 minutes.

❧ In food processor or blender, purée 8 cups (2 L) of the soup
in batches. Return to pot; heat through. Stir in lime juice. Taste
and adjust seasoning. *(Soup can be refrigerated for up to 3 days or
frozen for up to 2 months.)* Makes 6 servings.

QUICK VARIATION

❧ Substitute three 19-oz (540 mL) cans of black beans,
drained, for the soaked beans. Reduce stock to 5 cups (1.25 L).
To onion mixture, add beans, stock, tomatoes, salt and pepper;
simmer for only 30 minutes.

Festive Sunday Brunch

❧

Let houseguests wake up to this leisurely Sunday brunch by the fire. A cheesy salmon strata can bake in the oven while everyone relaxes over a bowl of refreshing fruit compote — a peaceful interlude amid the bustle of Christmas festivities.

MENU
❧
Fresh Citrus Compote
with Lime Cream*
❧
Smoked Salmon Strata*
❧
Green Beans with Red Onion
❧
Chocolate Pecan Fruitcake
(*recipe, p. 13*)
❧
Christmas Cookies

*Recipes included

Fresh Citrus Compote with Lime Cream

❧

A tangy compote makes a great eye-opener at a brunch and an equally welcome and refreshing dessert after holiday meals.

4	oranges	4
4	large tangerines	4
2	white grapefruit	2
2	red or pink grapefruit	2
2 tbsp	(approx) orange liqueur	25 mL

Lime Cream

4 oz	cream cheese	125 g
1/2 cup	sour cream	125 mL
2 tbsp	granulated sugar	25 mL
1 tsp	(approx) grated lime rind	5 mL
2 tbsp	lime juice	25 mL

Peel oranges, tangerines and white and red grapefruit; cut away thin outer membrane covering sections. Holding fruit over bowl to catch juice and using sharp knife, slice toward center between sections and membrane walls, removing one segment at a time.

❧ In large bowl, gently stir together fruit, juice and liqueur, adding up to 2 tbsp (25 mL) more liqueur, if desired. Cover and refrigerate overnight.

❧ LIME CREAM: In food processor, blend cream cheese and sour cream until smooth. Add sugar, lime rind and juice; process just until blended. Transfer to small serving bowl. (*Cream can be covered and refrigerated for up to 4 days.*) Sprinkle with more lime rind.

❧ Serve compote in individual dishes and top with lime cream. Makes 8 servings.

Smoked Salmon Strata

꙰

Completely prepared the evening before, this satisfying casserole is ready to pop into the oven a few minutes before everyone assembles.

16	thin slices Italian-style bread	16
2 tbsp	butter	25 mL
1 cup	sliced leeks	250 mL
1 cup	sliced mushrooms	250 mL
1/4 lb	sliced smoked salmon	125 g
2 cups	shredded Swiss cheese (about 1/2 lb/250 g)	500 mL
6	eggs	6
4 cups	light cream	1 L
1 tsp	Dijon mustard	5 mL
	Pepper	

Cut bread slices into cubes to make about 11 cups (2.75 L); set aside.

꙰ In small saucepan, melt butter over medium heat; cook leeks and mushrooms for 3 to 4 minutes or until leeks are softened. Remove from heat. Cut salmon crosswise into 1/2-inch (1 cm) wide strips; stir into leek mixture.

꙰ In two greased 8-inch (2 L) baking dishes, arrange half of the bread cubes. Top with salmon, then half of the cheese; sprinkle with remaining bread cubes.

꙰ Beat together eggs, cream, mustard, and pepper to taste until well blended; pour over layers. Sprinkle with remaining cheese. Cover and refrigerate overnight.

꙰ Bake, uncovered, in 325°F (160°C) oven for 35 to 45 minutes or until tops are golden. Serve hot. Makes 8 servings.

CHRISTMAS WRAP-UP

❧

JUST WHEN YOU THOUGHT NOTHING MORE
COULD BE DONE WITH LEFTOVERS, VOILÀ! — WE'VE COME UP WITH TEMPTING
NEW WAYS TO DRESS UP THE LAST BITS OF THE BIRD.

Microwave Turkey Gumbo Stew

❧

*Turkey goes Cajun in a spicy and satisfying soup
that will have everyone asking for seconds!*

2 tbsp	all-purpose flour	25 mL
1 tbsp	vegetable oil	15 mL
1 cup	chopped onions	250 mL
1	stalk celery, diced	1
1	sweet green pepper, diced	1
1	can (19 oz/540 mL) tomatoes (undrained)	1
1 cup	turkey stock (recipe, p. 158) or chicken stock	250 mL
1/4 cup	long grain rice	50 mL
2	cloves garlic, minced	2
1 tsp	dried oregano	5 mL
1/2 tsp	pepper	2 mL
1 cup	partially thawed okra or peas	250 mL
1-1/2 cups	cubed cooked turkey	375 mL
	Salt	
	Hot pepper sauce	

*I*n 12-cup (3 L) microwaveable casserole, mix flour with oil; microwave, uncovered, at High for 8 to 10 minutes or until golden, stirring 3 times.

❧ Stir in onions, celery and green pepper; microwave at High for 4 to 6 minutes or until softened, stirring once.

❧ Add tomatoes, stock, rice, garlic, oregano and pepper; cover and microwave at High for 15 to 20 minutes or until rice is tender, stirring twice and breaking up tomatoes.

❧ Cut okra into bite-size pieces; add to pot. Stir in turkey; cover and microwave at High for 2 minutes or until heated through. Season with salt and hot pepper sauce to taste. Makes 4 servings.

> **Tip**: *Cajun gumbos are thickened with a dark roux, an oil and flour mixture that is cooked until golden. Microwaving the roux eliminates the constant stirring of stove-top cooking.*

Come Share the Bird!

Christmas dinner! Festive mood,
With roasted turkey, longed-for food.
And ours was huge, a very prize
Of what they label "family size."
A steaming mound, a taste delight
Of dressing and of dark and light,
Of breast and drumstick. What a plate!
The clock ticked on and still we ate.

We nibbled till good nights were said,
And, stomachs filled, we crawled to bed.
We slept like fattened, wint'ring bears;
'Twas noon before we came downstairs.
"So there you are!" exclaimed our host.
"Come have some turkey, creamed on toast."
We ate, perforce, what else to do?
But then came dinner — turkey stew.

Next day my eyes began to glaze
For there at lunch what met my gaze
But sandwiches — huzzah, huzzah —
All filled with turkey, pale and blah.
I bit my lip, tried not to cry
At sight of dinner — turkey pie.
Next day we played at nouveau riche
And, mangling French,
tried *dindon* quiche.

That night into my dreams there came
A turkey calling out my name.
Then out from every nook and cranny
Came gobblers gobbling, oh, so many!
I jumped straight up. I fled outside
And found a trembling Cousin Clyde,
Who said he'd had an awful fright —
Been chased by turkeys half the night.

Lunch came. I looked and tried to run.
Host pulled me back to "join the fun."
"Enjoy!" he urged. "Come on and eat.
Cook's fixed us all a special treat.
She's fried up something really yummy;
Her turkey hash will thrill your tummy."
I tried to answer with a joke.
But all I managed was a croak.

All week, that's how the dishes came;
The names were new, the meat the same.
Ours was one sorry, woeful plight,
When Cook announced, "No fowl tonight."
"What's that?" we cried. "D'you really mean — "
"The bones," she smiled, "are all picked
clean."
Free at last, we let fly a whoop!
But then she served us turkey soup!

— *Florence Weekes*

Turkey Minestrone

If you want to freeze this rustic Italian-inspired soup, don't add the pasta until you're reheating it.

2 tbsp	vegetable oil	25 mL
1	onion, chopped	1
1	clove garlic, minced	1
3/4 cup	diced cooked ham	175 mL
4	carrots, chopped	4
2	stalks celery, chopped	2
1	zucchini, diced	1
4 cups	turkey stock (recipe, this page)	1 L
1	can (28 oz/796 mL) plum tomatoes (undrained), coarsely chopped	1
2 cups	shredded cabbage	500 mL
2 cups	coarsely chopped cooked turkey	500 mL
1	can (14 oz/398 mL) kidney beans, drained	1
1 cup	chopped green beans	250 mL
2/3 cup	macaroni or other small pasta	150 mL
	Salt and pepper	
	Freshly grated Parmesan cheese	

*I*n large saucepan or soup pot, heat oil over medium heat; cook onion and garlic for 3 minutes or until softened.

❧ Add ham, carrots, celery and zucchini; cook, stirring occasionally, for 3 minutes. Add stock and tomatoes; bring to boil. Reduce heat and simmer, uncovered, for 30 minutes.

❧ Add cabbage, turkey, kidney beans and green beans; bring to boil. Reduce heat and simmer for 15 minutes or until vegetables are almost tender.

❧ Add pasta; cook for 10 minutes or until tender but firm. Season with salt and pepper to taste. Ladle into warm soup bowls; sprinkle with Parmesan. Makes 10 servings.

Jambalaya

Choice morsels of turkey, ham and spicy sausage cook with rice for an excellent buffet dish.

1 tbsp	vegetable oil	15 mL
1/4 lb	hot or sweet Italian sausage	125 g
1	large stalk celery, coarsely chopped	1
1	large onion, chopped	1
2	cloves garlic, minced	2
1/2 tsp	hot pepper flakes	2 mL
1-1/2 cups	parboiled rice	375 mL
2-1/4 cups	turkey stock (recipe, this page)	550 mL
1	can (19 oz/540 mL) tomatoes (undrained)	1
1/2 tsp	Cajun spice or chili powder	2 mL
3 cups	chopped cooked turkey	750 mL
1 cup	cubed cooked ham	250 mL
1 cup	frozen peas, thawed	250 mL
1/2 cup	chopped fresh parsley	125 mL
	Salt and pepper	

*I*n Dutch oven, heat oil over medium-low heat; prick sausage and cook, turning often, for 20 minutes or until no longer pink inside. Remove and set aside.

❧ Drain all but 2 tbsp (25 mL) drippings from pan; cook celery, onion, garlic and hot pepper flakes over medium heat for 3 minutes or until onion is softened. Add rice and cook, stirring, for 3 minutes.

❧ Stir in stock and tomatoes, breaking up with spoon; add Cajun spice and bring to boil. Cover and bake in 350°F (180°C) oven for 25 minutes.

❧ Cut sausage into thin slices; stir into rice mixture along with turkey and ham. Cover and bake for 10 to 15 minutes or until rice is tender. Gently stir in peas and parsley; season with salt and pepper to taste. Makes 6 servings.

TURKEY STOCK

*K*eep a supply of this flavorful stock on hand and use whenever turkey or chicken stock is called for.

❧ Break turkey carcass into three or four pieces. In stock pot, bring carcass and 16 cups (4 L) water to boil; skim off any froth. Add 1 each chopped celery stalk, carrot and onion, 1 bay leaf, 1/2 tsp (2 mL) each dried thyme and whole black peppercorns, and 3 sprigs fresh parsley; simmer, partially covered, for 2 hours.

❧ Strain through cheesecloth-lined sieve set over bowl; let cool. Cover and refrigerate until fat solidifies; discard fat. *(Stock can be refrigerated in airtight container for up to 3 days or frozen for up to 4 months.)* Makes about 12 cups (3 L).

Mexican Turkey Hot Pot

※

Sprinkle bowls of this chunky soup with Cheddar or Monterey Jack cheese.

2 tbsp	vegetable oil	25 mL
1	large onion, coarsely chopped	1
1	large clove garlic, minced	1
1/2 tsp	hot pepper flakes	2 mL
3	potatoes, peeled and cubed	3
4 cups	turkey stock (recipe, p. 158) or chicken stock	1 L
1 tsp	dried oregano	5 mL
1	can (19 oz/540 mL) tomatoes (undrained)	1
1	can (14 oz/398 mL) pinto or kidney beans, drained and rinsed	1
2 cups	frozen lima beans	500 mL
2 cups	diced cooked turkey	500 mL
1-1/2 cups	corn kernels	375 mL
3 tbsp	chopped fresh coriander or parsley	50 mL
1 tbsp	lime or lemon juice	15 mL
	Salt and pepper	

*I*n saucepan, heat oil over medium heat; cook onion, garlic and hot pepper flakes, stirring, for 3 to 5 minutes or until softened.

※ Add potatoes, stock and oregano; cover and simmer for 10 to 15 minutes or until potatoes are tender.

※ Add tomatoes, breaking up with spoon; add pinto and lima beans, turkey and corn. Simmer, covered, for 5 minutes or until lima beans are tender. Stir in coriander, lime juice, and salt and pepper to taste. Makes 8 servings.

Holiday Pot Pie

Put leftover turkey to delicious use in this festive-looking pot pie.

5 cups	chicken stock	1.25 L
3 cups	cubed smoked ham	750 mL
2 tbsp	vermouth (optional)	25 mL
3	carrots, sliced	3
3	stalks celery, sliced	3
2	sweet potatoes, peeled and cubed	2
1	bay leaf	1
1/2 tsp	dried savory	2 mL
1 cup	frozen peas	250 mL
1/2 cup	diced sweet red pepper	125 mL
1/3 cup	butter	75 mL
1	onion, chopped	1
3/4 cup	all-purpose flour	175 mL
3/4 tsp	dry mustard	4 mL
3 cups	cubed cooked turkey	750 mL
	Pepper	
	Pastry for 9-inch (23 cm) single-crust pie	
1 tbsp	milk	15 mL

*I*n Dutch oven, combine chicken stock, ham, vermouth (if using), carrots, celery, sweet potatoes, bay leaf and savory; bring to boil. Reduce heat and simmer, covered, for 15 to 20 minutes or until carrots are tender-crisp.

❧ Add peas and red pepper; simmer for 2 minutes. Drain, reserving liquid; discard bay leaf. Set vegetable mixture aside.

❧ In Dutch oven, melt butter over medium heat; cook onion for 3 minutes or until softened. Sprinkle with flour; cook, stirring, for 3 to 4 minutes or until lightly golden. Stir in mustard.

❧ Gradually whisk in reserved liquid until smooth. Increase heat to medium-high; cook, whisking constantly, until boiling and thickened. Add reserved vegetable mixture and turkey; season with pepper to taste. Pour into 12-cup (3 L) casserole dish.

❧ On lightly floured surface, roll out pastry to 1/4-inch (5 mm) thickness. With floured cutters, cut out desired shapes. Overlap cutouts over entire casserole; brush with milk.

❧ Bake on baking sheet in 400°F (200°C) oven for 30 to 35 minutes or until pastry is golden brown and filling is bubbly. Makes 8 servings.

Baked Turkey and Swiss Croque Monsieur

These make-ahead savory sandwiches are ideal for a late-morning holiday breakfast.
Assemble them the night before, then just pop them into the oven until puffed and golden brown.
Serve with chilled cranberry sauce, relish or maple syrup.

1	loaf unsliced white bread	1
1/4 cup	cream cheese, softened	50 mL
6 oz	thinly sliced cooked turkey	175 g
6 oz	sliced Swiss cheese	175 g
1/4 cup	butter, softened	50 mL
6	eggs	6
1/2 tsp	each salt and dried tarragon	2 mL
1/4 tsp	dried savory	1 mL
1-1/2 cups	milk	375 mL
	Chopped fresh parsley	

Slice bread into twelve 3/4-inch (2 cm) thick slices; spread 2 tsp (10 mL) cream cheese over each of six slices. Top each with turkey, then Swiss cheese; top with remaining bread.

❧ Spread butter over bottom of 13- x 9-inch (3 L) glass baking dish; arrange sandwiches in single layer in dish.

❧ Whisk together eggs, salt, tarragon and savory until smooth; whisk in milk. Ladle mixture over each sandwich, covering evenly. Cover with plastic wrap and refrigerate for at least 90 minutes or overnight.

❧ Bake, uncovered, in 375°F (190°C) oven for 40 to 45 minutes or until crisp, puffed and golden brown. Let stand for 3 minutes. Garnish with parsley. Remove each sandwich with spatula to serve. Makes 6 servings.

Tex-Mex Turkey Casserole

The turkey blends so deliciously with the zesty tomato sauce and crisp tortilla-chip topping that family
or friends will never guess it's leftovers!

2 tsp	vegetable oil	10 mL
1	onion, chopped	1
1	clove garlic, minced	1
2 tsp	chili powder	10 mL
1 tsp	ground cumin	5 mL
1/2 tsp	dried oregano	2 mL
1/2 tsp	salt	2 mL
Pinch	each hot pepper flakes and pepper	Pinch
1	can (28 oz/796 mL) tomatoes (undrained)	1
2 cups	corn kernels	500 mL
1	sweet red or green pepper, chopped	1
1/4 cup	chopped fresh parsley	50 mL
40	unsalted tortilla chips	40
2 cups	cubed cooked turkey	500 mL
1-1/2 cups	shredded Monterey Jack or Cheddar cheese	375 mL

In large skillet, heat oil over medium heat; cook onion and garlic for 3 minutes or until softened. Stir in chili powder, cumin, oregano, salt, hot pepper flakes and pepper; cook for 1 minute.

❧ Add tomatoes, crushing with potato masher; bring to boil. Reduce heat and simmer for 20 to 30 minutes or until most of the liquid has evaporated.

❧ In bowl, combine corn, red pepper and parsley. Arrange one-third of the tortilla chips in greased 8-inch (2 L) square baking dish. Top with half of the turkey, half of the corn mixture, half of the tomato sauce and 1/2 cup (125 mL) of the cheese. Repeat layers, ending with all of the remaining cheese. Crush remaining tortilla chips; set aside.

❧ Bake, covered, in 350°F (180°C) oven for 20 minutes. Uncover and sprinkle with reserved tortilla chips; bake for 10 minutes longer or until heated through. Makes 4 servings.

Turkey Cannelloni

Pasta makes a nice change of menu during the holidays — and offers another delicious way to disguise turkey leftovers.

1	pkg (300 g) fresh lasagna noodles	1

Filling

1 tbsp	vegetable oil	15 mL
1/2 cup	finely chopped onions	125 mL
1	pkg (10 oz/284 g) fresh spinach, trimmed	1
3/4 lb	ricotta cheese	375 g
1/4 cup	freshly grated Parmesan cheese	50 mL
2	eggs, beaten	2
1 tsp	dried basil	5 mL
3/4 tsp	salt	4 mL
	Pepper	
3 cups	finely chopped cooked turkey	750 mL

Tomato Sauce

1 tbsp	vegetable oil	15 mL
1	onion, finely chopped	1
1	clove garlic, minced	1
1	can (14 oz/398 mL) tomato sauce	1
1 tsp	dried oregano	5 mL
1/2 tsp	each granulated sugar, salt and fennel seeds	2 mL
	Pepper	

Cream Sauce

1/4 cup	butter	50 mL
1/4 cup	all-purpose flour	50 mL
1 cup	turkey stock (recipe, p. 158) or chicken stock	250 mL
1 cup	milk	250 mL
1/3 cup	freshly grated Parmesan cheese	75 mL
	Salt and pepper	

FILLING: In small skillet, heat oil over medium heat; cook onions until softened, stirring occasionally. Set aside.

❧ Rinse spinach; shake off excess water. Cook spinach with just the water clinging to leaves for 3 to 5 minutes or until wilted. Drain and let cool slightly; squeeze dry and chop to make about 1/2 cup (125 mL).

❧ In large bowl, beat together ricotta, Parmesan, eggs, basil, salt, and pepper to taste; stir in turkey, onions and spinach. Set aside.

❧ TOMATO SAUCE: In saucepan, heat oil over medium heat; cook onion and garlic until tender. Stir in tomato sauce, oregano, sugar, salt, fennel seeds, and pepper to taste; simmer for 15 to 20 minutes or until thickened slightly. Set aside.

❧ CREAM SAUCE: In saucepan, melt butter over medium heat; whisk in flour and cook, stirring, for 2 minutes. Pour in stock and milk; bring to boil and cook, stirring constantly, for 3 minutes or until thickened. Remove from heat and stir in Parmesan. Season with salt and pepper to taste.

❧ Cut lasagna noodles into 5-inch (12 cm) lengths. Cook in large pot of boiling water for 8 minutes or until tender but firm. Drain well and rinse under cold running water; drain again and arrange on damp towels.

❧ ASSEMBLY: In well-greased 13- x 9-inch (3.5 L) baking dish, spread all but 1/2 cup (125 mL) of the tomato sauce. Along one short end of each pasta rectangle, spread about 1/4 cup (50 mL) of the filling. Roll up jelly roll-style and place, seam side down, in tomato sauce in casserole. Repeat with remaining filling to make 12 to 14 cannelloni.

❧ Pour cream sauce over cannelloni; drizzle with reserved tomato sauce. (*Cannelloni can be prepared to this point, covered and refrigerated for up to 1 day.*) Bake, uncovered, in 350°F (180°C) oven for 40 to 50 minutes or until sauce is bubbly. Makes about 6 servings.

Turkey Cranberry Pancakes

🎄

Brighten up your post-Christmas brunch with
these flavorful pancakes. Serve warm
with extra cranberry sauce or jelly.

1	egg	1
1/2 cup	milk	125 mL
1/4 cup	sour cream	50 mL
1/4 cup	butter, melted	50 mL
1 cup	all-purpose flour	250 mL
1-1/2 tsp	baking powder	7 mL
1/2 tsp	salt	2 mL
1-1/2 cups	chopped cooked turkey	375 mL
1/2 cup	cranberry sauce	125 mL
2 tbsp	chopped green onion	25 mL

*I*n large bowl, beat together egg, milk, sour cream and butter. Stir in flour, baking powder and salt just until blended. Fold in turkey, cranberry sauce and onion.

🎄 Heat nonstick pan or lightly greased griddle until a few drops of water bounce and sizzle when sprinkled on pan. Drop 1/4 cup (50 mL) batter for each pancake onto hot pan, spreading into circle 1/2 inch (1 cm) thick.

🎄 Cook over medium-high heat for 4 minutes or until bubbles appear on top; turn and cook for 4 minutes or until bottom is golden brown. Remove to warm serving platter. Makes 8 to 10 pancakes.

WHAT A GREAT IDEA!

TURKEY PÂTÉ

*S*erve this pâté with crackers or spread it on sliced bread to make a sandwich. If taking it along for lunch, store almonds separately to keep them crisp.

🎄 *In bowl or food processor, combine 1/2 lb (250 g) cream cheese, 1/3 cup (75 mL) mayonnaise, 1/4 cup (50 mL) mango chutney and 1 tsp (5 mL) curry powder. Stir in 2 cups (500 mL) finely chopped cooked turkey. Spoon into serving dish; cover and refrigerate until chilled. To serve, sprinkle with 1/2 cup (125 mL) toasted slivered almonds. Makes 3 cups (750 mL).*

Winter Waldorf Salad

This colorful make-ahead salad is a perfect partner with any of the "leftover" dishes in this chapter.

2	Granny Smith apples	2
2	Red Delicious apples	2
2	Golden Delicious apples	2
1 cup	diced celery	250 mL
1 cup	seedless red grapes	250 mL
1/3 cup	raisins	75 mL
3/4 cup	chopped walnuts, toasted (see p. 30)	175 mL
	Lettuce leaves	
1/2 cup	pomegranate seeds	125 mL

Waldorf Dressing

1/2 cup	mayonnaise	125 mL
1/2 cup	sour cream	125 mL
3 tbsp	liquid honey	50 mL
2 tsp	grated lemon rind	10 mL
1 tbsp	lemon juice	15 mL
1/2 tsp	ginger	2 mL
Pinch	salt	Pinch

Dice unpeeled apples; place in bowl and add celery, grapes and raisins.

❧ WALDORF DRESSING: Whisk together mayonnaise, sour cream, honey, lemon rind, lemon juice, ginger and salt; pour over salad and toss gently to coat.

❧ Cover salad with plastic wrap; refrigerate until chilled. *(Salad can be refrigerated for up to 2 days.)*

❧ To serve, add nuts to salad and toss gently to mix. Mound salad on lettuce-lined plates. Garnish with pomegranate seeds. Makes 8 servings.

Mincemeat Muffins

Use a bit of leftover mincemeat to turn ordinary muffins into holiday breakfast treats.

1 cup	all-purpose flour	250 mL
3/4 cup	whole wheat flour	175 mL
1/4 cup	granulated sugar	50 mL
2 tsp	baking powder	10 mL
1/4 tsp	salt	1 mL
1/4 tsp	nutmeg	1 mL
1	egg	1
1 cup	mincemeat	250 mL
1 cup	milk	250 mL
1/4 cup	butter, melted	50 mL
1/2 cup	chopped walnuts	125 mL

Topping

2 tbsp	packed brown sugar	25 mL
1 tbsp	all-purpose flour	15 mL
1/2 tsp	cinnamon	2 mL
1/4 tsp	nutmeg	1 mL
1 tbsp	butter	15 mL

TOPPING: In small bowl, combine sugar, flour, cinnamon and nutmeg; cut in butter until crumbly. Set aside.

❧ In large bowl, stir together all-purpose and whole wheat flours, sugar, baking powder, salt and nutmeg. Stir together egg, mincemeat, milk and butter. Add to flour mixture along with nuts; stir just until combined.

❧ Spoon into well-greased muffin cups; sprinkle with topping. Bake in 400°F (200°C) oven for 20 minutes or until tops are firm to the touch. Makes 12 muffins.

WHAT A GREAT IDEA!

FRUITCAKE TRUFFLES

Here's a delicious new way to use up leftover fruitcake.

❧ In saucepan, melt 6 oz (175 g) chopped semisweet chocolate, 3 tbsp (50 mL) whipping cream and 3 tbsp (50 mL) butter over very low heat until smooth.

❧ Stir in 2 tbsp (25 mL) orange liqueur or orange juice and 1 cup (250 mL) fruitcake crumbs. Chill for 2 hours or until firm.

❧ Shape into 1-inch (2.5 cm) balls. Chill for at least 20 minutes. (Truffles can be prepared to this point, wrapped well and refrigerated or frozen for up to 3 weeks.)

❧ Roll in icing sugar and chill for at least 20 minutes. Makes about 30 truffles.

Starting a New After-Christmas Tradition

Once the Christmas tree has lost its brightly ribboned packages, spirits dampen and the festive mood fades quickly. But for many Italian families, the anticipation lingers. Soon there will be an event that happens only once a year — sausage making, a time-honored tradition from a rural heritage. It occurs around Epiphany, on January 6.

❧ Today, the year-round availability of foods has affected the old style of eating, and preserving meats for leaner times is no longer necessary. But the ritual of involving the family in a commonly shared, food-centered activity has survived in many Italian homes in North America, extending the festive atmosphere.

❧ During the cooking, an incredibly sweet smell of fried pork fills the air. Appetites that seemed lost forever (destroyed by the indulgences of the holidays) are miraculously restored. The sausage meat is a perfect accompaniment to polenta, another convivial group endeavor. Our long-cooking polenta (recipe, this page) needs lots of strong biceps to take turns stirring. Invite close friends for a post-Christmas carol sing, so there will be plenty of arms.

❧ Whether it's stuffing sausages, stirring polenta or making pastries, looking to old traditions or starting new ones with family and friends can extend the joys of Christmas beyond the 25th.

Polenta with Sausage

❧

If you like, eat this the fun peasant-style way. Spread the polenta on a large wooden platter, dimple the top and cover with the cooked meat mixture. Sprinkle with cheese, then let everyone dig in.

10 cups	water	2.5 L
1	small potato, peeled and thinly sliced	1
1 tbsp	salt	15 mL
2 cups	cornmeal	500 mL
1/4 tsp	pepper	1 mL
1 lb	hot Italian sausage, casings removed	500 g
1/4 tsp	dried sage	1 mL
1/3 cup	olive oil	75 mL
2	large cloves garlic, sliced	2
2 cups	freshly grated Parmesan cheese	500 mL

In large saucepan, bring water, potato and salt to boil; cook for 3 minutes or until tender.

❧ While water is still boiling, gradually stir in 1-3/4 cups (425 mL) of the cornmeal, 1/4 cup (50 mL) at a time. Reduce heat to medium; cook, stirring constantly and keeping polenta boiling, for 20 minutes.

❧ Add remaining cornmeal; cook, stirring constantly, for 20 minutes or until polenta is smooth and mounds softly on spoon. Stir in pepper. Let stand for 5 minutes.

❧ In large skillet, cook sausage meat with sage over medium-high heat for 5 minutes or until meat is no longer pink. With slotted spoon, remove meat to bowl; drain off fat.

❧ Add oil and garlic to skillet; cook over low heat for 3 to 4 minutes or until garlic is just golden. Combine with sausage.

❧ Using greased serving spoon, spread thin layer of polenta in large shallow pasta bowl. Spread with half of the sausage mixture; sprinkle with half of the cheese. Repeat with remaining polenta, sausage mixture and cheese. Makes 6 to 8 servings.

VARIATION

❧ POLENTA WITH PORK: Instead of using sausage mixture, use pork. In heavy skillet, combine 1 lb (500 g) ground pork, 1 sliced clove garlic, 1 tsp (5 mL) chili powder, 1/2 tsp (2 mL) each dried oregano, fennel seeds and salt, 1/4 tsp (1 mL) each dried sage, pepper and hot pepper flakes. Cook over medium-high heat for 5 minutes or until pork is no longer pink; drain of fat.

RING OUT THE OLD, RING IN THE NEW!

WHETHER YOU PARTY IN THE NEW YEAR
WITH A CROWD OR WITH YOUR CLOSEST FRIENDS, HERE'S EVERYTHING YOU NEED
TO MAKE IT A MEMORABLE OCCASION. HAPPY NEW YEAR!

Crêpe Cones

*Welcome in the New Year with appetizer crêpes
shaped into cones and deliciously stuffed with either
salmon and cream cheese or Brie and chutney.
For a festive sweet ending, fill crêpes with
ice cream and top with warmed Pear
Mincemeat (p. 36) or chocolate sauce. With
crêpes, anything goes — and goes splendidly.*

1 cup	all-purpose flour	250 mL
1/4 tsp	salt	1 mL
3	eggs	3
1-1/4 cups	milk	300 mL
3 tbsp	(approx) butter, melted	50 mL

Filling

1/4 lb	cream cheese, softened	250 g
1/2 cup	sour cream	125 mL
1/4 cup	chopped fresh dill	50 mL
1	clove garlic, minced	1
1	green onion, finely chopped	1
1/2 tsp	grated lemon rind	2 mL
	Salt and pepper	
1 cup	watercress leaves (or 2 cups/500 mL coarsely chopped spinach)	250 mL
1/2 lb	thinly sliced smoked salmon, cut in strips	250 g
48	watercress or parsley sprigs	48

In bowl, combine flour and salt; make well in center. Whisk together eggs, milk and 2 tbsp (25 mL) of the butter; gradually pour into well, whisking to draw in flour until smooth. Cover and refrigerate for 1 hour. Strain to give smooth whipping cream consistency.

❧ Heat 8-inch (20 cm) crêpe pan over medium heat until drop of water sprinkled on pan spatters briskly. Brush with some of the remaining butter.

❧ Stir batter to reblend; pour 2 tbsp (25 mL) into center of pan. Quickly tilt and rotate pan to form thin crêpe. Cook for 40 seconds or until bottom is golden and top no longer shiny.

❧ With spatula, loosen and turn crêpe over, using fingers to assist. Cook for 30 seconds or until golden. Transfer to plate. Repeat with remaining batter, brushing pan with butter as necessary and stacking crêpes on plate. (*Cooked crêpes can be stacked between sheets of waxed paper, wrapped and refrigerated for up to 3 days or frozen for up to 2 months.*)

❧ FILLING: Combine cheese, sour cream, dill, garlic, onion, lemon rind, and salt and pepper to taste. Working in batches, spread paler sides of crêpes with 1 tbsp (15 mL) filling, leaving 1/2-inch (1 cm) border. Cut in half; top with watercress leaves and salmon.

❧ Forming point at center of straight edge of crêpe, roll into cone. (*Cones can be covered and refrigerated for up to 4 hours; remove from refrigerator 30 minutes before serving.*) Garnish each cone with watercress sprig. Makes 48 hors d'oeuvres.

VARIATION

❧ BRIE PECAN FILLING: Remove rind from 1-1/4 lb (625 g) Brie cheese; let soften. Beat with 1/2 cup (125 mL) chutney. Add 1 cup (250 mL) each chopped green onion and chopped toasted pecans (see p. 30). Spread each crêpe with 2 tbsp (25 mL) filling; sprinkle with watercress leaves. Omit salmon. Cut in half; roll up. Serve warm. Garnish with watercress sprig.

---

*Tip: To serve cones warm, cover filled crêpes
and bake, seam side down, in two 13- x 9-inch
(3 L) baking dishes in 350°F (180°C) oven
for 5 to 10 minutes or until heated through.*

Come to an Open House!

When the guest list outnumbers the chairs, an open house is a practical yet enjoyable way to entertain. Our Open House menu is hearty, with flavors that are sure to please friends, family and neighbors alike. For guests who prefer not to indulge, it's always thoughtful to offer nonalcoholic drinks and bowls of crudité.

MENU

Herb and Cheese Crostini*

Shrimp Satay*

Peanut Dipping Sauce*

Southwestern Wings with Coriander Dip*

Roast Beef and Olive Rolls*

Pita Crisps in a Basket

Holiday Cookies

White Wine or White Grape Juice Spritzers

*Recipes included

(clockwise from top) Herb and Cheese Crostini; Southwestern Wings with Coriander Dip; Roast Beef and Olive Rolls; Shrimp Satay

Herb and Cheese Crostini

*Guests will reach for seconds of these delicious cheesy-topped appetizers.
You can toast the bread slices and spread them with the herbed cheese mixture hours ahead,
then bake them just before serving. Serve hot, warm or at room temperature.*

2	baguettes	2
2 tbsp	olive oil	25 mL
1 lb	cream cheese	500 g
1/4 cup	each chopped fresh parsley and dill	50 mL
1/4 cup	chopped green onions	50 mL
1/4 cup	chopped sun-dried tomatoes (optional)	50 mL
2 tbsp	lemon juice	25 mL
2	cloves garlic, minced	2
1/2 tsp	pepper	2 mL
1/4 tsp	hot pepper sauce	1 mL
	Salt	

*C*ut bread into 1/2-inch (1 cm) thick slices to make about 40 pieces. Broil on baking sheets for 2 minutes or until just beginning to turn golden. Turn slices over and broil for 2 minutes longer. Brush one side with oil.

❧ In bowl, blend together cream cheese, parsley, dill, green onions, tomatoes (if using), lemon juice, garlic, pepper, hot pepper sauce, and salt to taste; spread over bread slices. (*Crostini can be prepared to this point, covered and refrigerated for up to 8 hours.*)

❧ Just before serving, bake crostini in 400°F (200°C) oven for 5 to 7 minutes or until hot. Makes 40 hors d'oeuvres.

Shrimp Satay

*Nothing says celebration with more pizzazz than shrimp — especially when sassy ginger, hoisin and
chili flavors make them irresistible. Serve with Peanut Dipping Sauce (below), if desired.*

1/3 cup	canned sweetened coconut cream	75 mL
2 tbsp	hoisin sauce	25 mL
2 tbsp	peanut butter	25 mL
2 tbsp	soy sauce	25 mL
1 tbsp	chopped gingerroot	15 mL
1 tsp	hot oriental chili paste or hot pepper sauce	5 mL
1 tsp	sesame oil	5 mL
2	cloves garlic, minced	2
2 lb	raw shrimp, peeled and deveined (about 4 dozen)	1 kg
1/4 cup	chopped fresh coriander or green onions	50 mL

*I*n bowl, combine coconut cream, hoisin sauce, peanut butter, soy sauce, gingerroot, hot chili paste, sesame oil and garlic; mix until smooth.

❧ Add shrimp and stir to coat well. Marinate for 30 minutes at room temperature or for up to 2 hours in refrigerator.

❧ Thread 2 shrimp onto each of 24 soaked 6-inch (15 cm) wooden skewers. On greased broiler pan or grill, broil shrimp for 2 to 3 minutes on each side or until opaque inside. Arrange on serving plate and sprinkle with coriander. Serve hot or at room temperature. Makes 24 hors d'oeuvres.

W H A T   A   G R E A T   I D E A !

PEANUT DIPPING SAUCE

*I*n blender or food processor, blend 1/2 cup (125 mL) smooth peanut butter, 1/4 cup (50 mL) each soy sauce and lemon juice, 2 tsp (10 mL) sesame oil and 1 tsp (5 mL) hot oriental chili paste or hot pepper sauce until smooth. Add 1 cup (250 mL) mayonnaise; blend well. Add 1/2 cup (125 mL) chopped fresh coriander or parsley and 1/4 cup (50 mL) chopped green onions. (*Sauce can be covered and refrigerated for up to 2 days.*) Makes 2 cups (500 mL).

Roast Beef and Olive Rolls

❧

Sliced roast beef has never had it this good! Rolled in flour tortillas and garnished with olives, this popular sandwich filling is transformed into special-occasion party fare.

8	flour tortillas (10 inches/25 cm)	8
3/4 cup	black olive paste* or finely chopped pitted black olives	175 mL
1/2 cup	mayonnaise	125 mL
1 lb	thinly sliced rare roast beef	500 g
4 cups	shredded romaine lettuce	1 L

Arrange tortillas in single layer on work surface. Combine olive paste with mayonnaise; spread over tortillas. Cover with slices of meat, leaving 1-inch (2.5 cm) border at one end. Top with lettuce.

❧ Starting at end with meat, roll up tightly, sealing border with mayonnaise mixture. Wrap tightly and refrigerate for up to 4 hours.

❧ Cut each roll into 6 to 8 slices; arrange, cut sides up, on platter. Makes 60 hors d'oeuvres.

*Available in Italian or specialty food stores.

WHAT A GREAT IDEA!

VERSATILE TORTILLAS

Look for tortillas in the cooler or freezer section of your supermarket. They're handy for quick pizza bases or as accompaniments for Mexican Black Bean Soup (p. 153) and casseroles. For a quick snack, fill with beans, shredded Cheddar and salsa and heat in the oven for a few minutes.

Southwestern Wings with Coriander Dip

❧

These succulent wings can be prepared ahead and either baked at the last minute or simply reheated.

4 lb	chicken wings	2 kg
1-1/4 cups	all-purpose flour	300 mL
1-1/4 cups	cornmeal	300 mL
2 tbsp	ground cumin	25 mL
2 tsp	salt	10 mL
2 tsp	black pepper	10 mL
1 tsp	cayenne pepper	5 mL
4	eggs	4
1/4 cup	olive or vegetable oil	80 mL

Coriander Dip

1-1/2 cups	sour cream	375 mL
1/2 cup	mayonnaise	125 mL
1 cup	chopped fresh coriander or parsley	250 mL
1/2 cup	chopped fresh chives or green onions	125 mL
1	can (4 oz/125 g) chopped mild green chilies	1
2	jalapeño peppers, seeded and minced	2
1 tsp	salt	5 mL

Remove tips from chicken wings; separate wings at joints. Set aside.

❧ In shallow dish, combine flour, cornmeal, cumin, salt, and black and cayenne peppers.

❧ In another shallow dish, beat eggs. Dip wings into flour mixture, shaking off excess; dip into eggs, allowing excess to drain off. Dip again into flour mixture and press mixture in firmly. (*Wings can be prepared to this point, covered and refrigerated for up to 8 hours.*)

❧ Brush baking sheets with oil; arrange wings on sheets and drizzle with remaining oil. Bake in 375°F (190°C) oven for 20 minutes; turn wings over and bake for 20 to 25 minutes longer or until brown, crisp and no longer pink inside.

❧ CORIANDER DIP: In bowl, combine sour cream with mayonnaise; stir in coriander, chives, green chilies, jalapeño peppers and salt.

❧ Serve wings with dip on large platter. Makes 40 hors d'oeuvres.

A Relaxing New Year's Eve

Relax and enjoy the last evening of the year with friends and this fuss-free potluck menu. Let the cooks in the crowd show off with the make-ahead main dishes — while the rest of the gang rounds up the dips and spreads, salad greens, crusty bread and, of course, the potables.

MENU

Pâtés, Dips and Spreads
(*see Chapter 5 for a delicious selection*)

Carbonnade of Beef*

Barley Casserole*

Oriental Coleslaw*

Salad of Mixed Greens

Baguettes or other Crusty Bread

Chocolate Cookie Cheesecake
(*recipe, p. 106*)

Fresh Clementines

Recipes included

Carbonnade of Beef

This Belgian-inspired stew gets its unique flavor from beef simmered with sweet onions and bitter beer into mellow richness. A barley casserole (next page) and crusty bread are musts for sopping up every last bit of the tasty sauce.

3 lb	chuck or round steak	1.5 kg
2 tbsp	all-purpose flour	25 mL
2 tsp	each paprika and salt	10 mL
1 tsp	pepper	5 mL
1/4 cup	butter or oil	50 mL
6	large onions, sliced	6
3	cloves garlic, minced	3
4	carrots, cut into large chunks	4
1/2 cup	each chopped celery leaves and fresh parsley	125 mL
1/2 tsp	dried thyme	2 mL
1	bay leaf	1
1/3 cup	all-purpose flour	75 mL
2-1/2 cups	beer	625 mL
3 tbsp	packed brown sugar	50 mL
2 tbsp	cider vinegar	25 mL
1/3 cup	finely chopped fresh parsley	75 mL

Trim excess fat from meat; cut into 1-inch (2.5 cm) cubes. In large bowl, combine 2 tbsp (25 mL) flour, paprika, salt and pepper; add meat and toss to coat.

In large heavy saucepan or Dutch oven, melt half of the butter over medium-high heat; brown beef, in batches and adding more butter if necessary. Remove meat and set aside.

Add remaining butter to pan; cook onions and garlic, stirring and adding 1 tbsp (15 mL) water if pan is browning too much, for 5 minutes or until softened. Stir in carrots, celery leaves, parsley, thyme and bay leaf; stir in 1/3 cup (75 ml) flour.

Return meat to pan; pour in beer. Add sugar; bring to boil. Reduce heat to low; cover and simmer for 1-1/2 hours. Uncover and simmer for 1-1/2 hours longer or until meat is tender and sauce slightly thickened.

Stir in vinegar; simmer, uncovered, for 10 minutes. Remove bay leaf. (*Stew can be cooled, covered and refrigerated for up to 3 days; reheat over medium-low heat for about 45 minutes.*) Garnish with finely chopped parsley. Makes 8 servings.

Barley Casserole

Barley is a grain that bakes up like a
dream and is a perfect partner to any stew.
Here, accented with vegetables and pine nuts, it's
a particularly nice change from the usual rice.

1 tbsp	butter	15 mL
10	green onions, chopped	10
4	large cloves garlic, minced	4
2	each celery stalks and carrots, finely chopped	2
1-1/2 cups	pearl or pot barley	375 mL
1/2 tsp	each salt and pepper	2 mL
4-1/2 cups	chicken stock	1.125 L
2 tbsp	chopped fresh parsley	25 mL
3/4 cup	pine nuts or slivered almonds	175 mL

In large heavy ovenproof skillet, melt butter over medium heat; cook onions, garlic, celery and carrots for 3 minutes or until just softened.

❧ Stir in barley, salt and pepper until well coated. Pour in 2-1/2 cups (625 mL) of the chicken stock; cover and bake in 350°F (180°C) oven for 30 minutes.

❧ Stir in parsley and remaining stock; sprinkle with pine nuts. Bake, uncovered, for 45 minutes or until liquid is absorbed and barley is tender. Makes 8 servings.

Barley Casserole

Oriental Coleslaw

Anticipate rave reviews for this tangy salad
with the surprise crunch of chow mein noodles and
the refreshing crispness of bean sprouts.

1/2 cup	sliced almonds	125 mL
1/2 cup	sunflower seeds	125 mL
1/4 cup	sesame seeds	50 mL
2 cups	each shredded red and green cabbage	500 mL
2 cups	bean sprouts	500 mL
6	green onions, chopped	6
1 cup	fried chow mein noodles	250 mL

Dressing

3 tbsp	rice vinegar or cider vinegar	50 mL
1 tbsp	granulated sugar	15 mL
1 tbsp	soy sauce	15 mL
1 tsp	sesame oil	5 mL
1	clove garlic, minced	1
1/4 tsp	each salt and pepper	1 mL
3 tbsp	vegetable oil	50 mL

Spread almonds, sunflower and sesame seeds on baking sheet; bake in 350°F (180°C) oven for 5 to 8 minutes or until golden and fragrant. Let cool.

❧ In large bowl, combine red and green cabbage, bean sprouts and onions.

❧ DRESSING: In small bowl, whisk together vinegar, sugar, soy sauce, sesame oil, garlic, salt and pepper; whisk in oil.

❧ Just before serving, toss almond mixture with cabbage mixture; gently toss with dressing until well mixed. Stir in noodles. Makes 8 servings.

> **Tip**: If you make the coleslaw one day ahead, refrigerate the salad and dressing separately.

A Celebration Dinner Party

Spinach Pasta
with Scallops and Herbs*

Sirloin with Balsamic Vinegar*

Festive Green Beans
(*see p. 133*)

Honey-Glazed Carrots
with Rosemary

Lemon Semifreddo
(*recipe, p. 97*)

*Recipes included

Spinach Pasta with Scallops and Herbs

❧

Delight your guests with this impressive appetizer dish — ribbons of green spinach pasta topped with creamy scallops and fragrant herbs. What a feast for the eyes and the palate!

3/4 cup	fresh bread crumbs	175 mL
1/2 cup	chopped fresh parsley	125 mL
1/4 cup	chopped fresh basil or dill	50 mL
1/4 cup	chopped fresh chives or green onions	50 mL
1/4 cup	olive oil	50 mL
1/4 tsp	pepper	1 mL
Pinch	hot pepper flakes	Pinch
1-1/2 lb	scallops	750 g
3	cloves garlic, minced	3
1 cup	dry white wine	250 mL
1/2 cup	whipping cream	125 mL
	Salt	
1 lb	green linguine noodles	500 g

Spread bread crumbs on baking sheet; bake in 350°F (180°C) oven for 3 to 5 minutes or until toasted and golden.

❧ In large bowl, combine parsley, basil, chives, 2 tbsp (25 mL) of the oil, black pepper and hot pepper flakes; stir in bread crumbs. Add scallops and toss to coat well.

❧ In large skillet, heat remaining oil over medium heat; cook garlic, without browning, for 1 minute or until very fragrant.

❧ Add coated scallops and cook for 2 minutes, stirring constantly. Pour in wine and bring to boil; cook, stirring constantly, for 2 to 3 minutes or just until scallops are opaque.

❧ Stir in cream and bring to boil. Taste and season with salt if necessary; remove from heat. (*Recipe can be prepared to this point, covered with waxed paper and set aside at room temperature for up to 30 minutes. Reheat briefly just before tossing with pasta.*)

❧ Meanwhile, in large pot of boiling salted water, cook fresh pasta for 3 to 5 minutes, dried pasta for 8 to 10 minutes, or until tender but firm. Drain well and toss with hot sauce. Taste and adjust seasoning if necessary. Makes 8 appetizer servings.

Tip: If you can't find fresh dill and chives, simply increase the parsley to 3/4 cup (175 mL) and use a pinch of dried basil or dillweed.

Sirloin with Balsamic Vinegar

❧

A thick sirloin steak is never inexpensive. But sirloin is all lean, fine-flavored meat with no waste and it doesn't require elaborate preparation to be impressive company fare. Bite for bite, it's worth every penny.

3 lb	sirloin steak (2 inches/5 cm thick)	1.5 kg
2 tbsp	olive oil	25 mL
	Salt	

Marinade

1 cup	dry Italian red wine	250 mL
3 tbsp	extra virgin olive oil	50 mL
3 tbsp	balsamic or red wine vinegar	50 mL
2 tbsp	lemon juice	25 mL
1 tbsp	Dijon mustard	15 mL
2	cloves garlic, minced	2
1 tsp	each dried rosemary and thyme	5 mL
1 tsp	pepper	5 mL
1/2 tsp	dried oregano	2 mL

Marinade: In large shallow dish, combine wine, oil, vinegar, lemon juice, mustard, garlic, rosemary, thyme, pepper and oregano.

❧ Pat steak dry and add to dish, turning to coat. Cover and marinate for 1 to 2 hours in refrigerator.

❧ Remove steak and pat dry; pour marinade into saucepan and set aside. Brush steak with oil. Broil or grill about 5 inches (12 cm) from heat for 7 to 10 minutes per side for rare or until desired doneness. Let rest for 5 minutes before carving diagonally across the grain into thin slices.

❧ Meanwhile, bring marinade to boil; boil, uncovered, for 8 minutes or until thickened and reduced to about 1/2 cup (125 mL). Taste and season with salt if necessary. Serve a little sauce with each portion of meat. Makes 8 servings.

Putting on the Ritz

*Toast the New Year with a glitter-and-dazzle dinner starring
oysters, succulent lamb loins and a raspberry tiramisu finale. Share it with
friends who enjoy fine food — and love champagne!*

Oysters on the Half Shell

*To start the celebrations, there's no classier way to serve oysters than the classic — freshly
shucked (see below), with a squirt of lemon and a sprinkle of freshly ground pepper.*

24 to 36	oysters	24 to 36
6	lemon wedges	6
6	large sprigs parsley	6
	Pepper	

*M*ake bed of crushed ice on six deep plates and place in freezer.

❦ Shuck oysters, retaining as much liquor as possible in cupped bottom shell. Discard flat upper shell. Balance oysters in bottom shell on bed of ice.

❦ Garnish each plate with lemon wedge and parsley. Season with pepper to taste. Makes 6 servings, 4 to 6 oysters each.

OYSTERS

BUYING TIPS
❦ Oysters are sold fresh in the shell, freshly shucked in their liquor, shucked and frozen, smoked and canned in oil, and canned in soups.

❦ Because fresh oysters deteriorate rapidly after they die and go through a chemical reaction, it is very important that the ones you buy in the shell are alive. A gaping shell is a definite indication of a dead oyster. You can also tell if the oysters are alive by tapping the shell: a sharp cracking

sound indicates a live oyster, while a dull hollow sound is evidence of a dead one.

❦ If you prefer to buy already-shucked oysters, look for those with clear, not milky, liquid and very little odor.

HOW TO SHUCK
❦ With a stiff brush, scrub the oyster shells under cool running water. Do not allow oysters to stand in water because they will start pumping it through their bodies, pumping out their flavorful saline liquor at the same time.

❦ Shuck oysters over a sieve that's set over a bowl to strain the liquor and catch pieces of shell. Use an oyster knife with a short strong blade, pointed tip and heavy hand guard. Protect your holding hand with a thick glove or cloth.

❦ With the curved shell down, insert the tip of the blade into the hinge and twist. Once the seal is broken, wipe the blade clean, reinsert it and slide it along the inside of the upper flat shell to cut the oyster from the top shell. Discard upper shell.

❦ Slide knife under the oyster to sever it from the lower shell. Hold the shell level to keep as much liquor as possible with the oyster. Top up with liquor from bowl. Serve or cook immediately.

MENU

❧

Oysters on the Half Shell

❧

Garlic Roasted
Lamb Loins

❧

Couscous Pilaf Timbales

❧

Pepper, Mushroom and
Snow Pea Sauté

❧

Raspberry Tiramisu
(recipe, p. 99)

❧

Champagne

Garlic Roasted Lamb Loins

Garlic, simmered in stock and wine, mellows into a flavorful sauce
that makes succulent lamb loins simply superb.

2-1/2 lb	boneless lamb loins	1.25 kg
1 tsp	pepper	5 mL
3/4 tsp	dried thyme	4 mL
2 tsp	butter	10 mL
2 tsp	olive oil	10 mL

Garlic Sauce

2	large heads garlic	2
1-1/2 cups	chicken stock	375 mL
3/4 cup	dry white wine	175 mL
3 tbsp	butter	50 mL
	Salt and pepper	

Trim lamb and pat dry; sprinkle with pepper and thyme. Cover and refrigerate for at least 1 hour or up to 5 hours.

❧ GARLIC SAUCE: Meanwhile, separate garlic into cloves but do not peel. Rinse cloves and place in saucepan with enough boiling water to cover; bring to boil. Reduce heat and simmer for 20 to 30 minutes or until softened. Drain and let cool. Squeeze out pulp into sieve or food mill and press through; set aside. *(Purée can be covered and refrigerated for up to 1 day.)*

❧ Divide butter and oil between two large ovenproof skillets; melt over high heat. Cook lamb for 45 to 60 seconds per side or just until browned. Transfer skillets to 400°F (200°C) oven and roast lamb for 6 to 10 minutes or until desired doneness. Transfer to cutting board; tent with foil to keep warm.

❧ Divide stock and wine evenly between same two skillets. Bring to boil over high heat, scraping up all brown bits from bottoms of skillets; pour contents of both skillets through sieve into saucepan. Boil hard, stirring often, for 5 minutes or until liquid is reduced by about one-third. Whisk in garlic purée; boil for 1 minute. Chop butter into 6 pieces and swirl 1 piece at a time into sauce. Season with salt and pepper to taste.

❧ Slice lamb diagonally across the grain into thin slices; arrange on warmed plates. Spoon sauce over. Makes 10 serv-

Pepper, Mushroom and Snow Pea Sauté

This easy sauté makes a colorful accompaniment to the lamb and couscous. To save time, partially cook vegetables,
then chill and refrigerate them until the last minute before tossing them together over high heat.

2	large sweet red peppers	2
1	large sweet yellow pepper	1
1/2 lb	snow peas	250 g
2 tbsp	butter	25 mL
2 cups	sliced mushrooms	500 mL
2 tbsp	chicken stock	25 mL
	Salt and pepper	

Halve, core and seed red and yellow peppers. In large saucepan of boiling water, cook peppers for 4 to 5 minutes or until skins are loosened. Drain and let cool slightly; peel and slice peppers into 1-inch (2.5 cm) wide strips.

❧ Trim snow peas. In large saucepan of boiling water, blanch for 30 seconds. Drain and refresh under cold water; drain again. *(Vegetables can be covered and refrigerated in separate containers for up to 4 hours.)*

❧ In large wok or skillet, melt butter over medium-high heat; stir in peppers, snow peas and mushrooms just until coated. Sprinkle with stock; cover and cook for 1 to 2 minutes or just until vegetables are tender-crisp. Season with salt and pepper to taste. Makes 10 servings.

Couscous Pilaf Timbales

This attractive side dish can be made ahead and reheated just before serving.
If desired, mound in a bowl to serve instead of packing it into molds.

1/4 cup	butter	50 mL
1 cup	finely chopped shallots, leeks or onions	250 mL
1 cup	finely diced carrots	250 mL
2-1/2 cups	chicken stock	625 mL
2 cups	couscous	500 mL
1/4 cup	pine nuts or slivered almonds, toasted (see p. 30)	50 mL
	Salt and pepper	

*I*n saucepan, melt butter over medium heat; cook shallots and carrots for 5 minutes or until softened. Stir in stock and bring to simmer; cook, covered, for 5 to 8 minutes or just until carrots are tender.

❧ Stir in couscous, nuts, and salt and pepper to taste. Remove from heat; cover and let stand for 5 minutes. Fluff with fork.

❧ Grease ten 1/2-cup (125 mL) timbale molds or custard cups. Line bottoms with rounds of waxed paper; grease paper. Pack couscous mixture into molds. Turn out onto individual plates; peel off paper. Makes 10 servings.

> **Tip**: Timbales can be prepared ahead and kept warm for up to 40 minutes by setting them in roasting pan with enough boiling water to come halfway up sides and covering.

A TOAST TO THE NEW YEAR!

*N*othing says "celebration" quite like a glass of sparkling champagne. To get full enjoyment from this festive bubbly, brush up on champagne know-how.

❧ Count on six generous glasses from each bottle. Serve in chilled flutes — slim tulip-shaped glasses. Always hold a glass of champagne firmly by its base and stem, never with your hands warming the glass.

❧ Although France may have been the originator of champagne, versions of this festive drink now come from many parts of the world, with producers in Canada, Spain, Germany and Italy providing excellent value in celebratory bubblies.

❧ When opening champagne, direct the cork away from everyone, including yourself! Holding the bottle at a 45 degree angle, remove the foil and wire muzzle. Grip the cork firmly with a napkin and gently twist the bottle from the base. Ease the cork out slowly, allowing just a smoky hiss as it emerges. Have the glasses ready and slowly pour a little wine into each, then slowly top up to two-thirds full.

❧ Champagne labelled brut is very dry; extra dry is a bit sweeter, and sec and demi sec are successively more sweet.

The Contributors

Photography Credits

OTTMAR BIERWAGEN:
pages 2, 60, 67 (inset).

FRED BIRD: pages 1, 6 (top
right and middle), 7 (top
and bottom), 11, 16 and
17, 21, 23, 24, 27, 29, 30, 33,
35, 36, 38, 41, 62, 63, 64, 66,
75, 76, 79, 81, 82, 84, 85, 86,
88, 90, 92, 95, 96, 99, 100,
102, 103, 105, 106, 109, 113,
119, 122 (inset), 124 and 125,
127, 128, 131, 132, 134, 135,
137, 139, 141, 142, 143, 144,
147, 149, 151, 152, 153, 155,
156, 159, 160, 162, 163, 167,
169, 173, 174, 176, 177, 192.

CHRISTOPHER CAMPBELL:
pages 9, 49, 56, 57, 67 (border),
68 (top), 116, 164.

MICHAEL CREAGEN:
page 114.

BOB DION: pages 3, 42, 44
(top).

JIM EAGER: pages 7 (middle),
44 (bottom), 45, 47, 111.

FRANK GRANT: pages 6 (top
left), 43, 51 (top), 52 (left), 54,
58, 59, 61, 121 (top).

SHERMAN HINES: pages 4
and 5, 6 (bottom), 50, 55, 123.

JOHN STEPHENS PHOTOG-
RAPHY: pages 46, 52 (right),
53, 68 (bottom), 69 (bottom),
70 (bottom), 72 (bottom left),
73 (bottom).

PETER H. STRANKS: pages
51 (bottom), 67 (bottom),
69 (top), 70 (top), 72 (top and
bottom right), 73 (top),
121 (bottom).

RON TANAKA: page 71.

MIKE VISSER: page 179.

CLIVE WEBSTER: page 14.

TED YARWOOD: page 48.

INDEX

EDITORIAL DIRECTOR: Hugh Brewster
PROJECT EDITOR: Wanda Nowakowska
EDITORIAL ASSISTANCE: Beverley Renahan
PRODUCTION DIRECTOR: Susan Barrable
PRODUCTION ASSISTANCE: Donna Chong
BOOK DESIGN AND LAYOUT: Gordon Sibley Design Inc.
COLOR SEPARATION: Colour Technologies
PRINTING AND BINDING: Lotus Printing Inc.

CHRISTMAS
was produced by
Madison Press Books